A BELL CURVE

The Rise and Decline of Traditional Religion

ANDREW FRIEND

authorHOUSE®

AuthorHouse™
1663 Liberty Drive
Bloomington, IN 47403
www.authorhouse.com
Phone: 1-800-839-8640

First published by AuthorHouse 6/2/2011

ISBN: 978-1-4567-5804-2 (e)
ISBN: 978-1-4567-5803-5 (sc)

Library of Congress Control Number: 2011907395

Printed in the United States of America

TABLE OF CONTENTS

PREFACE

Even though it seems that religion has always been part of human life, it was not always a definable, conscious activity. A radical change in the human mind took place in the comparatively short period of a thousand years, overlapping the second and first millennia BCE. It prepared the way for the emergence of various religions and philosophies that became part of the identity of people everywhere. Religion has never been static and fixed. Even a perfunctory examination will force one to conclude that change has not only taken place but that it continues so to do.

At the outset the use of the word "man" needs to be addressed. Jacques Barzun, in his book *From Dawn to Decadence,* points out that the frequent repeating of "man and woman," followed by the compulsory "his and her," is clumsy. It creates emphasis where it is not wanted and destroys sentence smoothness. *Man, He,* and *Him* will most often be used as the quick neutral words referring to human beings as such.

The abbreviations that indicate which side of the great calendar divide an event took place will be BCE and CE. The former stands for Before Common Era and the latter--Common Era. Not only Christianity but all religions and religion in general will be considered; thus something more neutral than BC and AD is more fitting.

1

THE EMERGENCE OF A MEANING-SEEKING CREATURE

In what seems to be a paradox, the further that we have become removed in time from our early human history the more we have learned about it. In the past century, in particular, there has been an exponential growth in our understanding of not only early history, but pre-history as well (that which happened prior to the advent of writing).

The French paleontologist Teilhard de Chardin provided his understanding of the evolving universe in *The Phenomenon of Man*. He described two great thresholds of change: first came the transition on this planet from non-life to life, resulting in the emergence of the biosphere that made possible the sustenance of living organisms. Over a timespan of millions of years, through a process that Charles Darwin called "natural selection" and Alfred Russel Wallace, a contemporary, described as the "struggle for existence," anatomically modern humans emerged in Africa about 200,000 years ago.

By studying mitochondrial DNA, scientists have calculated that a woman existed in that period who was the source of the mitochondrial DNA in every person alive today. She is neither our only ancestor nor our oldest, but simply our "most recent common ancestor."[1] Scientists have blended DNA analysis with archaeological and fossil evidence to create a coherent whole. "They believe that from the beginnings in Africa, the modern humans went first to Asia between 80,000 and 60,000 years ago. By 45,000 years ago, or possibly earlier, they had settled Indonesia, Papua-New Guinea and Australia. The moderns entered Europe around 40,000 years ago. . . . By 35,000 years ago, they were firmly established in most of the Old World. . . . Finally around 15,000 years ago, humans crossed from Asia to North America and from there to South America.[2]

The second great threshold of change occurred only in the human species, and that was from life to reflective thought. This resulted in the emergence of the noosphere - a term coined in 1925, which refers to human intellectual activities. Thinking became part of the life of Homo sapiens.

David Suzuki draws attention to the fact that

> Human beings are not distinguished by an armory of weapons such as quills, fangs or talons, nor are we possessed of exceptional speed, strength or agility. Our sensory acuity cannot compare with that of the other animals. Yet not only have we survived, we have flourished within a remarkably brief time on the evolutionary scale. The key to our success is the possession of the most complex structure on Earth: the human brain.[3]

Lee Berger, a South African paleoanthropologist (the study of ancient humans) has theorized that the larger brain size of early humans was attributable to the protein-rich diet available in Africa. Seafood may have fueled early humans' brains. Mollusks were eaten as early as 160,000 years ago. Seafood provided the fatty acids that modern humans needed to fuel their outsized brains.[4]

A major reason for the human capacity to flourish has been mutual support. Berger says that the pervasive existence of human fossils in parts of South Africa is proof of the incredible binding power among humans. He was one of four strangers seated together when he said,

> Look at us. You couldn't take four of any other mammalian species and sit down as we are doing here. This is the proof that we are the cooperative species. . . . We are undoubtedly a peaceful species. We developed a pedo-morphic face - childlike, nonthreatening. . . . When we make a threatening pose we don't show our teeth like other animals do. (We lost our canines). . . . All evidence in first contact proves we are a peaceful species. The aggression comes later. . . . Warfare, until the twentieth century was largely symbolic. It is only in recent times that human technology has led to the idea of mass slaughter.[5]

Early humans learned to make sense of patterns such as the migration of animals and the seasonal succession of plants; they could "read" the landscape around them and find the things they needed. A widespread example of this was found amongst native Americans. These skills are still being employed by some of the San people in southern Africa as well as indigenous tribes in South America and Papua-New Guinea.

Such skills and knowledge were, and are, profoundly local, embedded in the flora, climate and geology of a region. This information was woven together into a worldview, tied to a unique locale, and peopled with spirits and gods. The narrative of the people at the center of such stories provided answers to those age-old questions: Who are we? How did we get here? What does it all mean?[6]

Dean H. Hamer, a behavioral geneticist, believes that faith is hardwired into our genes, that we are compelled to seek the meaning of life. From a very early date it appears that human beings have been distinguished by their ability to have ideas that went beyond everyday experience. We have always experienced our world as being profoundly mysterious. Karen Armstrong believes that "one of the essential yearnings of humanity is the desire to get above the human state. As soon as human beings had completed the evolutionary process they found that a longing for transcendence was built into their condition."[7] Hamer's research showed that spirituality, the seeking after transcendence, is part of our nature.

"Transcendence" as it is used here does not refer to its use in Christian theology, that of God being beyond the field of nature, but rather to that which is beyond all concepts. As Joseph Campbell explains it, "Our senses are enclosed in the field of time and space, and our minds are enclosed in a frame of the categories of thought. But the ultimate thing (which is no thing) that we (try) to get in touch with is not so enclosed."[8]

The capacity for spirituality and the desire to reach out beyond oneself is an essential part of being human.[9] One challenge that existed from the beginning is that even though certain concepts such as faith, the meaning of life, and an animate and ensouled nature, are not part of the visible world, they are indisputably part of reality. How have we come to grips with the invisible, intangible world? By means of symbols. Human beings are symbol-creating creatures. "Man's ultimate concern must be expressed symbolically, because symbolic language alone is able to express the ultimate."[10]

The Greek word for symbol is *symallein* - to throw together. A symbol points beyond itself to something else and is essentially separate from the unseen reality to which it directs one's attention. Two hitherto disparate entities become inseparable, and this linkage causes that invisible, intangible reality to be present. A symbol opens up levels of reality that otherwise are closed to us. It unlocks dimensions and elements of one's soul which correspond to the dimensions and elements of reality.[11]

Symbols cannot be replaced, nor can they be taken literally. To do so is at best to make the symbol meaningless, and far worse, to distort and destroy the reality that is symbolized. This came to be a widespread practice among monotheists in the Common Era. It was especially done with regard to extended symbols, otherwise known as myths, with tragic consequences.

It has not yet been established as to when early humans first developed creative and symbolic thinking. Ludwig von Bertalanffy, the father of General Systems Theory, linked the origin of civilization with symbolism, seeing the creation and use of symbols as being unique to Homo sapiens. All specifically human behavior can be traced to our invention of a symbolic world.

Bertalanffy divided symbols into two groups - discursive symbolism, such as language and mathematics, and nondiscursive as expressed in the various art forms. The former is consciously created while the latter rises out of the unconscious.[12]

Lloyd Geering sees language as resulting from the natural human ability to create symbols, the basis of language being the symbolization of sounds.[13] Man takes possession of the world in symbolic images by naming things. In one of the creation myths at the beginning of the book of Genesis (2: 19, 20), one finds Adam giving names to the various creatures.

The evolution of language was without doubt linked with the ever increasing need for early humans to not only survive but to solve social problems. Our ancestors had to move "from an egocentric, individual struggle to necessary concern with the welfare of others, including the welfare of the entire group."[14] The development of language would have resulted in the transfer of exponentially increasing information, such that its impact is to be seen archaeologically. In the late Mesolithic era (about 10,000 to 8,000 BCE) for example, ceremonial graves become commonplace.[15] Geering has drawn attention to the link between human language and culture:

> Slowly, over time, we humans have collectively created language and culture. This has the effect of turning our previous assumptions upside down. Human culture is the man-made environment of thought and meaning in which we live and move and have our being. We become human as we are shaped by the culture into which we are born. But we in turn help to shape the culture we pass on to the next generation. . . . As the human species spread around the globe, it created thousands of languages, cultures and subcultures . . . an invisible, ever changing stream.[16]

Nondiscursive symbols would have developed before the evolution of language. The oldest known indications so far of an early human capacity for symbolic thought are 100,000-year-old shell ornaments. Two were found in a cave in Skhul, in present-day Israel, along with the remains of at least 11 modern humans. (These are the oldest remains ever found outside Africa. This excursion appears to have ended there.)

Another bead was discovered at Qued Djebbana in Algeria and is estimated to be 90,000 years old. These three shells were found many miles from the sea, indicating that they were brought to those locations deliberately. Shells being adapted to be beads were found elsewhere.

Some 75,000 years ago a craftsman sat in a cave overlooking what is now known as the Indian Ocean near the southern tip of the African continent. He (or she) held an ochre mudstone, about three inches long, which had been polished. With a stone point the worker etched a geometric design on the flat surface - simple crosshatchings framed by two parallel lines with a third line down the middle. This stone now offers no clue to its original purpose, but to see it is to immediately recognize it as something only a person could have made. Carving the stone was a very human thing to do. This is the oldest known example of an intricate design made by a human being. Christopher Henshilwood, an archaeologist at the University of the Witwatersrand in South Africa says that "the ability to create and communicate using such symbols is 'an unambiguous marker' of modern humans, one of the characteristics that separate us from any other species, living or extinct."[17]

Forty-one shells were unearthed in this same cave. All of them are of the same genus, and all were pierced at the same end - they had clearly been adapted to serve as beads. These shells appear to have been selected for size - and all bore distinctive wear marks. They also retained traces of red ochre, suggesting that the beads had been painted or sewn onto fabric that had been coated with this ochre.

The etched geometric design and the shells are not only proof of the advent of symbolic thought, but of individual identity, of selfhood, of aesthetics, as well as indicating a means of social communication.

Artifacts that have been discovered in Europe reveal that the people who arrived there 40,000 years ago brought with them a capacity for art and other forms of spiritual activity. Three sets of caves of inestimable value, because of their works of art, have been discovered. Altamira in northern Spain has works that were created in the Paleolithic era (20,000 to 8,000 BCE). The other two locations were found in France.

The Lascaux caves were discovered in the 1930s, and about 180 miles east of them, deep within the limestone hills of the Ardeche region, lies Chauvet, the 34,000-year-old grotto called the Sistine Chapel of prehistoric art, discovered by speleologists in 1994. Even though the Lascaux paintings are a few thousand years younger than those found at Chauvet, the latter are more sophisticated. The Lascaux drawings are more like symbols of the animals they represent, whereas the faces of the animals at Chauvet are more alive. One feels the presence of the animal.

Carbon dating conducted on campfire remnants, torch marks, and the paintings themselves placed the work in two intervals between 32,000 and 23,000 BCE. To give a better perspective of the antiquity of this work, it needs to be compared with Stonehenge. Its structures on the Salisbury Plain in England, which address the cycles of the moon, were built between 1800 and 1400 BCE. The Chauvet cave works were preserved by accident when something caused the rocks above the natural chamber to tumble down about 22,000 BCE, concealing its entrance.

The paintings are of 14 types of beasts, including lions, mammoths, horses, rhinoceroses, and panthers - often portrayed in groups and usually in motion. The animals are not symbols - they live and breathe and display emotions. Art historian Valerie Feruglio says of the artwork that it is so emotional, it is like seeing a Leonardo drawing and feeling him do it.

Prehistorian Bernard Gilly believes the cave is testimony to a surprisingly advanced culture. "The work in the cave is so complex, it's obviously the work of a developed society, an impressive civilization that could organize a sanctuary of this amplitude."

A major function of the cultures created by local clusters of people was to provide a way to deal with the unseen world. Things in the environment that moved were seen as having intentions. This attributing of a soul (anima) to the mover is known as animism and has not been limited to primal cultures. It infused the classical civilizations of Greece and Rome as well as extending into the Middle Ages.[18] It is not unusual, even now, for some Western subcultures to fall back on animistic concepts to explain certain phenomena and/or to seek for certain benefits.

Panpsychism (soul through all) was sensed as being an immediate and compelling reality, pregnant with power, that could be either beneficial or hostile. The human proclivity for using symbols to come to grips with the unseen world led to the creation of gods to explain these mysterious forces of nature. The word "god" was a generic term referring to a class of spiritual beings. These were gods of nature, and they controlled human destiny by operating behind and through all visible phenomena.

The attention paid these gods sprang from the basic needs of food supply, birth and death, growth and decay. One example is that of carved figures representing fertility gods. They have been a widespread relic of the primal world. Furthermore, "trees, stones, and heavenly bodies were never objects of worship in themselves but were revered because they were epiphanies of a hidden force that could be seen powerfully at work in all natural phenomena, giving people intimations of another more potent reality."[19]

These hidden forces were seen to respond when attention was paid to them: prayers and sacrifices, for example, could change the weather and were thought to keep the world in existence. The cause and effect were pragmatic in character and not at all theoretical. People performed their rituals because they appeared to work. An example of this is the Levitical laws followed by the Hebrews: these gave the "how" but not the "why." They were followed in order to assure the regular working of the universe.

Ancestor worship was also of crucial importance. It was believed that the dead exerted a powerful impact on the living. It therefore behooved the latter to venerate and preserve them. The kings and other leaders were heard as continuing to speak after they died. Their remains, therefore, received special attention. They were seen to have become gods. Even into the early part of the Common Era the Roman emperors and certain other dignitaries were treated as gods after their death.

Ancestor worship also pointed to a world that had preceded the world of human beings. In China, for example, "Rituals to departed kinfolk provided a model for an idealized order, which was conceived as a family. . . . Rivers, stars, winds and crops all had indwelling spirits which lived harmoniously together in obedience to the Sky God."[20]

The evidence that human beings are meaning-seeking, spiritual creatures is undeniable. During the last two millennia people have been able to change or abandon their religious affiliations, but they cannot rid themselves of the genetic propensity to be spiritual.

If any further proof was required, it was surely provided by the effects of an ideology that was enforced for the greater part of the twentieth century on a major portion of the planet's population. The precipitating event was the Russian Revolution, but during the second half of this period it was also inflicted upon Eastern Europe and China.

The motivation and inspiration came from the writings of Karl Marx (1818-1883) who had concluded that historical religion, among other factors, was stunting human potential. He promoted a society that was free of religious inhibitions by formulating a new symbolic framework. Communist-inspired revolutionary activity started in Russia in 1905, and by 1918 it had gained the upper hand.

In order to stem the passing of religious beliefs and traditions from one generation to the next, the Soviet Union classified the religious education of children a political crime. A person convinced that he possessed spiritual truth was required to conceal it from his or her own children. Those parents imprisoned for sharing religious beliefs with their offspring were prohibited from ever returning to their children and their home areas.

A major weapon of the Soviet Union was that of propaganda. Not only were college courses offered in this "discipline," it was studied at graduate and post-graduate levels as well. The full force of propaganda was brought to bear on stamping out religious and spiritual beliefs and practices.

Aleksandr Solzhenitsyn was a political prisoner for many years, starting towards the end of World War II. He wrote in *The Gulag Archipelago* of his encounter with a young Jewish prisoner who had been born five years after the establishment of the revolution. They had just read a prayer of the late President Roosevelt that had been published in Soviet newspapers as an act of ridicule. Solzhenitsyn's reaction was to say, "Well, that's hypocrisy of course." The youth's response was to ask, "Why? Why do you not admit the possibility that a political leader might sincerely believe in God?" Solzhenitsyn was speechless. He thought, "But what a direction the attack had come from! To hear such words from someone born in 1923? . . . The principal thing was that some kind of clean, pure feeling does live within us, existing apart from all our convictions, and right then it dawned upon me that I had not spoken out of conviction but because the idea had been planted in me from outside." He could only ask, "Do you believe in God?" "Of course," the youth tranquilly replied.[21]

The power of Soviet propaganda was such that America, especially, was fearfully influenced by it. It was so good that the Soviet Union came to believe its own lies. They put so much energy into polishing the veneer that hid the real Russia that when the veneer wore through, there was found to be nothing of substance underneath. The joke told about China really applied to the Soviet Union: China's plan to obliterate their enemies was to put small atomic bombs into suitcases and leave them at strategic places. The plan, however, had to be abandoned as they had no suitcases. When the true picture of the Soviet Union emerged, it was as if an illusionist had performed the ultimate trick and made a superpower disappear. There was no there, there - in terms of a superior way of life.

The anti-religious propaganda was first aimed at peasants and senior citizens. But the posters displayed 50 years later showed young people as the ones being foolishly deluded by religion. A government-conducted survey in the 1970s revealed that 30 percent of the USSR population believed in God.

Malcolm Muggeridge called it "the most extraordinary fact of the twentieth century." He was referring to the amazing renewal of Christianity in, of all places, the countries that had been most drastically subjected to the oppression, brainwashing, and influence of the first overtly atheistic and materialistic regime to exist on earth.

A similar process has taken place in Cuba. People who grew up without God in what was once an officially atheistic country were never enrolled in catechism classes. But now Cuba's young people are flocking to the Catholic Church and other faiths, searching for lost traditions and a spirituality they realize is lacking in their lives.

The French playwright Jean Anouilh wrote, "Propaganda is a soft weapon: hold it in your hands too long, and it will move about like a snake and strike the other way."

Such is the vitality of human spirituality that it is nurtured and stirred in countless different ways. A Soviet writer, Anatoli Kusnetsov, came to have a spiritual orientation. When asked how it happened, he said that Stalin made one fatal error: he neglected to suppress the works of Tolstoy.

Solzhenitsyn came to have a profound spiritual experience while in prison. So much so that he was grateful for his incarceration. "I was happy! There on the asphalt floor, under the bunks (due to lack of same), in a dog's den, with the dust and crumbs from the bunks falling in your eyes. I was absolutely happy, without any qualifications." Such was his influence upon people when set free that the Kremlin finally banished him from the Soviet Union in a desperate attempt to silence him. Solshenitsyn was lionized when he first came to America. But when he began to comment on the shallowness and materialism that characterized life in the USA, he found himself banished again, this time to a farm in Vermont.

China, too, in spite of, or perhaps because of, its booming economy is also undergoing spiritual revival. For more than 2,500 years the Confucian doctrines of filial piety, moral righteousness, and hierarchical relationships were the guiding principles of life and government in China. *The Analects* - the collected teachings of Confucius - was their "Bible."

When the Communists came to power in 1949, Mao declared Confucianism to be counterrevolutionary. He banned *The Analects,* and his Red Guards ransacked temples. Confucian scholars were tortured during the Cultural Revolution of 1966 to 1976.

Yu Dan, a female Chinese Ph.D. scholar, recently wrote *Insights on the Analects.* Up until then the writings of Confucius were only available in classical Chinese, which parallels what Latin is to the average speaker of English. Her book sold three million copies in four months - a record in modern Chinese publishing history. Bootleg copies of Yu Dan's television speeches and lectures are in great demand.

Christianity is flourishing as well. Communist China has always sponsored a state-sanctioned Church - its typical heavy-handed means of control. Despite draconian countermeasures, the underground church that formed in spite of repression, survived. It met in private homes. In recent years this movement has become more open, even to

13

the point of having public meeting places. Opposition and harassment are still taking place, yet China now has more professing Christians than members of the Communist Party.

Possibly the strongest evidence of spiritual vitality in China is the Falun Gong movement, a spiritual practice founded in 1992 by Li Hongzhi. It draws on Oriental mysticism and consists of five sets of meditation exercises that seek to develop the heart and character of practitioners according to the principles of Truthfulness, Compassion, and Forbearance.

"What's not to like?" one may ask. The Chinese government, however, feels exceptionally threatened, one reason doubtless being the exponential growth of Falun Gong. Even though it has no official membership nor rosters, the government published a figure of 70 million practitioners in 1998. It is believed that they comprise at least half of China's labor camp population.

In April 1999, more than 10,000 followers silently protested arrests and beatings at the Chinese Communist Party headquarters. The government response was to "ban" the practice with crackdowns and a massive propaganda campaign. There has been a steady flow of reports of abuse. Two-thirds of all reported torture cases are against the Falun Gong. It is strongly believed that China is harvesting organs from practitioners.

Falun Gong material has been translated into more than 40 languages. Its website claims 100,000,000 practitioners in more than 80 countries.

If Homo sapiens is anything, apart from his physical features, he is a meaning-seeking creature.

2

THE ROLE AND FUNCTION OF MYTH

From earliest times human beings, in their search for understanding and meaning, made much use of symbols. One of the, if not *the*, most important is the narrative symbol known as myth. The role of myth was, and continues to be, that of enabling people to cope with the unknown and the unknowable. It continues to be essential to one's wellbeing.

The anatomically modern human emerged 160,000 years ago with a variety of attributes, chief among them being the development of a bicameral cerebral cortex. This made possible, among other things, reflective and imaginative thinking. Language was the product of symbolism, of the mind's ability to imagine and create sounds. Once verbal communication became possible, man invented stories that enabled him to place his life in a larger setting, giving a sense that, despite all the chaos, life had meaning and value. He began to have ideas and experiences that could not be explained rationally. They were vaguely intuitive. Imagination was at work. Myth was becoming a vital part of life.

Harry Levin has referred to this story-telling faculty as fabulation. Man can think of something that at least at first has no objective existence. The function of myth-making takes place somewhere between the strictly cognitive and the vaguely intuitive.

> It is out of the limbo between rational intelligence and the unconscious that fictions are generated. . . . When we are out of touch with the facts we utilize fiction to explain the unexplainable by some sort of approximation to it.[1]

Such is the dynamic at play in the creation of myths. As Joseph Campbell, the preeminent mythologist has described it, "The myth comes from the imagination and leads back to it."[2]

At its very core myth is about the unknown - that for which one initially has no words. It looks into the heart of a great silence.[3] Myth was the means that emerged for coming to grips with that which was beyond one's observation, understanding, or definition - a vehicle for making contact with the unknown and invisible. From its beginning myth has enabled people to have an understanding of things that otherwise would remain unknown.

Myths have nothing to do with facts, nor were they ever meant to entertain or merely be explanations of natural phenomena. Rather they were "recounting events in which men were involved to the extent of their existence."[4] They were "the narration in story form of the universal facts of life to which man must adjust himself."[5] The word "universal" refers to the fact that myth deals with the totality of a people's existence.

> Myth is a totality first of all because mythological thinking is striving for a total worldview, for an interpretation or meaning of all that is significant. Mythology is not a peripheral manifestation, not a luxury, but a serious attempt at integration of reality and experience, considerably more serious than what we loosely call today one's 'philosophy of life.' Its goal is a totality of what is significant to man's needs, material, intellectual and religious.[6]

In similar vein Karen Armstrong writes, "Mythology is an art form that points beyond history to what is timeless in human existence, helping one get beyond chaotic random events, and glimpse the core of reality."[7] Campbell has put it very simply: "Myths are the stories we tell ourselves about ourselves, about our fundamental nature, and the things that are important to us."[8] They help us to cope with our predicaments and to find our place in the world.

Myth has always been able to reach regions of the human mind that otherwise would have remained inaccessible. It was, as Armstrong points out, an early form of psychology. Myth showed people how to cope with their own interior crises and helped explain their unconscious fears. "The stories of gods or heroes descending into the underworld, threading through labyrinths and fighting with monsters brought to light the mysterious workings of the psyche."[9] Campbell was fascinated by the fact that

> whenever men have looked for something solid on which to found their lives, they have chosen, not the facts in which the world abounds, but the myths of an immemorial imagination - preferring even to make life a hell for themselves and their neighbors, in the name of some violent god, rather than to accept gracefully the bounty the world affords?[10]

Sigmund Freud and Carl Jung explained their insights by making major use of classical myths, giving them in turn a new interpretation.

Rather than being for entertainment, myth "tells us what has to be done to become a fully human person." In earlier times it "forced people to confront the inexorable realities of life and death "and to come through with a degree of acceptance."[11] Myth speaks to and sustains that which is more than concern about physical survival. It wants life to be experienced. It deals with the totality of people's existence. As

Campbell has poetically stated, myths "lead the young from their estate in nature, and bear the aging back to nature and on through the last dark door."[12]

In this regard myth changes with one's age. A fairy tale is a myth for children. As one grows older a sturdier mythology is needed.[13] In similar vein Armstrong says "as our circumstances change, we need to tell our stories differently in order to bring out their timeless truth."[14]

Myth, which preceded the concept and establishment of religion, is about human experience. Myth has a fluidity which puts it in sharp contrast with theology and its unchallengeable explanations of a given religion. In contrast with theology, there is never a single, orthodox version of a myth. Most of the myths are self-contradictory. One may even find four or five myths in a given culture, all giving different versions of the same mystery.

Even though myth, in its sustaining and nourishing role, permeated all aspects of life from earliest times, it has never been a religion as we understand the term in this the Common Era. In the Fertile Crescent of the fourth millennium BCE, worship was a critical human activity. Yet there was no word for the concept or practice of religion in the Mesopotamian, Egyptian, and Hebrew languages of that period. This was due to the fact that "religion" was not a separate category of daily life or worldview. People of that era were not aware of practicing a religion or of being religious.

From our perspective we call their practices "folk religion," and yet it had, and still has, very little in common with the religions of the Common Era. It is true that there are commonalities such as rituals, taboos, and obligations, but these were carried over from pre-religious times as means to practice and sustain the various belief systems. But the rituals and songs of mythology have no composers, and their taboos and moral injunctions have no legislators. There was also a conspicuous absence of written creeds, theologians, and hierarchy officials.

A vital aspect of myth is that it needs to take place in a ritual setting. It is without efficacy, and indeed myth is no longer myth if it occurs in a profane or trivial context. It is like reading the lyrics of an opera or song without the accompanying music and singers. No spiritual or psychological impact can be made. In such circumstances myth is robbed of its original force and power, and is instead reduced to a form of literary art. "The main theme in ritual is the linking of the individual to a larger morphological structure than his own physical body."[15]

In the earliest times, especially, myth and its accompanying ritual reminded the participants of the process of regeneration, of death and rebirth, and of the demands of survival. Initiation rites for boys, for example, were a process of death and rebirth. They were intended to bring about a constructive reorganization of the deeper forces within a person. As Campbell describes it, "the boys became no longer their mothers' sons, but their fathers'."[16] These practices remain crucial in traditional societies to this day. The rituals tended to be particularly drastic and life-changing for boys if they were to become men. For girls the commencement of menstruation indicates that the girl has become a woman. Nature does it to her. Even so, some cultures have initiation rites for girls as well.

Initiation rites are still with us. Most are mild, such as the ceremonial aspects of graduating from an educational institution or turning 21 in British cultures. Hazing makes more challenging demands and can, at times, result in injury and even death. Boot camp is another example. Aspiring soldiers are put through a vigorous program that tests their potential to become effective participants in military activities. Part of the goal is to re-orientate them so that they will unhesitatingly carry out orders.

Campbell informs us that the earliest evidence of anything like mythological thinking and ritual is associated with graves. "Something was there that isn't there anymore. Where is it now?" Burials have always involved the idea of a continued life behind the visible plane that is somehow supportive of the visible one to which we have to relate.[17] In similar fashion Armstrong explains that in the Paleolithic period (20,000-8,000 BCE)

> Mythology and its accompanying rituals helped people
> to move from one stage of life to another, in such a way
> that when death finally came it was seen as the last and
> final initiation to another totally unknown mode of
> being.[18]

The commonplace activities, such as hunting, fishing, birth, and marriage, that combined to sustain survival, were felt to involve forces beyond one's control. Certain rituals were required in order to make preservation possible. Before the development of agriculture, people depended entirely on hunting and gathering. The earliest societies learned that, in order to survive, one was forced to participate in a hideous act, that of killing and eating another living thing. Myth and ritual were created to help people cope with their complicated emotions stemming from such activities. These elements did not tell the hunters how to kill their prey, but rather how to participate without a sense of fear or guilt in this necessary act of life.[19]

The role and function of the shaman emerged in hunting societies. He was the forerunner of the priest. The shaman experienced visions and dreams that captured the ethos of the hunt and gave it spiritual meaning. The basic hunting myth was about a kind of covenant between the animal and human worlds.[20] As Campbell explains it, the animal gave its life willingly, with the understanding that its life transcended its physical entity, and that it would be returned to the soil through some kind of ritual of restoration. The hunt thus became a ritual of sacrifice and the hunters performed, in turn, acts of atonement to the departed spirits of the animals, hoping to coax them into returning in order to be sacrificed again. The hunters thus saw themselves "locked in a 'mystical, timeless' cycle of death, burial, and resurrection" with the hunted. Their relationship was one of reverence. There was a mythological identification. Killing was not simply a slaughter - it was a ritual act, as eating is now when one precedes it by saying grace. The animal was perceived to be a god, or a messenger of a god, and so it was thanked.[21]

Campbell believes that the mythic imagination was in full bloom during the time of the hunter. This in turn gave rise to a burst of magnificent art.[22] The Caves at Lascaux and Chauvet in France and Altamira in Spain were the very first temples and cathedrals. As Armstrong says, "They set the scene for a profound meeting between humans and the god-like archetypal animals adorning the walls and ceilings" of these Caves.[23] This art gave form to their spiritual impulse.

The concept of planting seed as a means of producing food began about 10,000 years ago. This led to the agrarian Neolithic revolution - a landmark development in more ways than one. Corn as we have known it since the discovery of the new world was the product of sophisticated cross-pollination - a process that had started some 9,000 years earlier. The Neolithic Period started about 8,000 BCE and lasted for four millennia. Even though agriculture was a product of knowledge gained from and about the earth, it did not become divorced from the mysteries of life. As people turned from hunting to planting, the stories they told to explain these new mysteries changed too. People gained an entirely new understanding of themselves and their world. Farming became, like hunting, sacramental. Cultivation was seen to be bringing the participants into a sacred realm.

The seed became a magical symbol of the endless cycle of life. The plant died, and upon being buried its seed was born again. Campbell has drawn attention as to how this symbol was later seized upon by the world's great religions as the revelation of eternal truth - that from death came life, "from sacrifice, bliss."[24] New rituals evolved, such as the handling of the first seeds of the harvest, which needed to be "offered up." The Neolithic myths continued to force people to face up to the reality of death. Agriculture was not easy or idyllic - it was a constant, often desperate struggle against drought and the violent forces of nature, which were in turn seen as manifestations of sacred power. In some parts of the world human beings were sacrificed as an ultimate effort to gain favors from the gods.

The sacred was now encountered in the earth and its products, which were themselves sacred. The crop was a revelation of divine energy. Gods, human beings, animals, and plants all shared the same nature and could, therefore, invigorate and replenish one another. A native reportedly once said to a missionary: "Your god keeps himself shut up in a house as if he were old and infirm. Ours is in the forest, and in the fields, and in the mountains when the rain comes."[25]

Goddess religions now emerged. The nurturing, maternal earth became the Mother Goddess. She was called Aphrodite in Greece and later Venus by the Romans. Women played a dominant role in the planting and harvesting done by these Neolithic societies. Since her magic was that of giving birth and nourishment, as does the earth, her magic supported the magic of the earth. The soil was seen to be female, the seeds divine semen, and rain the sexual union of heaven and earth. Ritual sex accompanied the planting of crops. The Hebrew Scriptures reveal that these ritualized orgies were practiced in Israel well into the sixth century BCE. There were ceremonies in honor of Asherah, the fertility goddess of Canaan and Syria, even in the temple in Jerusalem

(II Kings 23: 4-7). Such practices were condemned by the prophet Hosea (4:11-19).

Myth and its vital role has been found to be in play wherever humanity exists. It has shown itself to be an extra-historical record, not of what has happened, but rather of what we are. Myths are "narrative recordings of humanity's most basic beliefs, drives, aspirations, yearnings and fears."[26] The human psyche - the inward experience of the human body - has been found to be essentially the same all over the world.

All mythologists who have made comparative studies of the subject have reached the same conclusion, as have scholars in a variety of related disciplines. "Archaeological researches and in-depth studies in the spheres of philology, ethnology, philosophy, art history, folklore, religion [and] psychological research . . . all have combined to suggest a new image of the fundamental unity of the spiritual history of mankind."[27]

The cultural history of humanity has to be viewed as a unit. Its themes, such as Deluge, Virgin Birth, and Resurrected Hero, have worldwide distribution, appearing everywhere in new combinations of the same few archetypes. They have always been embraced as

> revelations of the verities to which the whole culture
> is a living witness and from which it derives both its
> spiritual authority and its temporal power. No human
> society has yet been found in which such mythological
> motifs have not been rehearsed in liturgies; interpreted
> by seers, poets, theologians, or philosophers; presented
> in art; magnified in song; and ecstatically experienced
> in life-empowering visions.[28]

A brief description follows of some of the archetypes that may register with those who tap into the Judeo-Christian worldview.

Creation Myths:

The myths dealing with foundational essentials - how the world and the gods came to be - began by showing how the gods themselves first came into existence. It was understood to be an evolutionary process in which the first deities emerged from sacred primal matter. The foundation Babylonian myth, *Enumah Elish,* taught that the first deities to emerge from the slime were inseparable from the elements. Other gods later emanated from them in couples, each pair more clearly defined than the one before. An ordered cosmos then came into being as these divine elements separated from each other.[29]

Armstrong points out that a creation story never provided people with facts about the origins of life. The reconciliation of one's mind to the conditions of life was fundamental to this motif. The story was "usually recited in a liturgical setting, especially during a crisis, when people felt that they needed an infusion of divine energy. Therapeutic in purpose, the idea was to tap into the timeless energies that supported human existence."[30]

An analysis of three hundred creation myths of the North American Indians showed that the great majority of them appear likewise in Eurasia and elsewhere. Some examples of recurring themes are that the first parents are the sun and the moon or the earth and the sky; the first impregnation comes from the rays of the sun; the first humans are fashioned from earth by a creator or emerge as vegetables from the earth and cannot at first walk straight.[31] Some such myths expressed a profound identification with a particular place as in ancient Greece.

The bulk of the creation myths were developed in the first half of the second millennium BCE, and most cultures have more than one version. The stories found in the book of Genesis were composed at a later date. The story in the second and third chapters of Genesis was written first about 900 BCE during the reign of Solomon. Three or four centuries later the second story was placed before this version, creating a new lens by which the Garden of Eden may be understood.

The Genesis stories were perhaps a response to the *Enumah Elish,* which are the first words of that epic and mean, "When on high." Its gods Apsu (fresh water) and Tiamat (salt water) were male and female gods of chaos. Genesis depicts the uncreated as impersonal - "without form and void." Marduk, Babylon's supreme deity, assisted by seven wind gods, inflates Tiamat with air, kills her, and creates earth and the sky from her divided carcass. In Genesis, the divine "spirit" or "wind" hovers over the "deep" before dividing the waters. From the blood of a dead god Marduk creates humanity to be slaves of the gods. Genesis gives humankind a divine component, "Let us make the human being in our image. . ."; and enjoins responsible power rather than slavery, "Let them have dominion over. . ." (1.16).[32]

The Genesis 1 story depicts a simultaneous creation ex nihilo (from nothing) of "male and female." In the Genesis 2 version, "the Lord God formed man from the dust from the ground. . . ." A Hebrew pun is reflected here: "man" is ha-adam; adam derives from adamah - arable soil. This chapter 2 version may have been influenced by, or serve as a response to, the Sumerian Dilmun (paradise) myth. The myth recounts how the god Enki is cursed by the goddess Ninhursag, becasue he ate plants that she bore. Ninhursag then creates the goddess Nin-Ti, "lady of the rib" or lady who makes live," to heal his broken body. Adam may be seen as "giving birth" to Eve, as Dionysius is born from the "thigh" of Zeus and Athena from his head.

Adam calls the woman Eve, the "mother of all living." Eve, Chaya in Hebrew, means "life." The term has a common Aramaic root meaning "serpent." "Mother of all living" is, in turn, an epithet for the near-eastern goddess Aruru.[33]

Paradise Myths:

This type of myth is encountered all over the world. There are two major categories: 1) those concerning the primordial close proximity between Heaven and Earth; 2) those referring to actual means of communication between Heaven and Earth. When Heaven was rudely "separated" from Earth, when it became "distant," the paradisial state was over and humanity arrived at its present state.

These myths all show primitive man enjoying blessedness, liberty, and friendship with animals, together with a knowledge of their language. All this was lost as a consequence of the "fall," i.e., that mythical occurrence which has brought about rupture between Heaven and Earth.[34]

All of these characteristics are portrayed in the biblical Garden of Eden.

Sibling Rivalry:

Thirty-two instances of this myth have been discovered. It appears in all six continental regions but appreciably more in the insular Pacific and Sub-Saharan Africa. Rivalry between brothers is most common, usually in the form of fratricide.[35]

There are other biblical antedeluvian characters that appear in Near Eastern myths; Enoch, for example, the seventh antedeluvian hero, who "walked with God; and was not, for God took him" (Genesis 5: 21-24). The Babylonian myths also record that the seventh antedeluvian hero was taken by the gods in order to be in the lowly estate of a servant.[36]

There is also the mythical quality of events described in Genesis 6: 1-4 which tell of the Nephilim ("fallen ones") who "were on the earth in those days . . . when the sons of God came into the daughters of men, and they bore children to them. These were the mighty men of old . . . giants in the earth." This was a common aspect of Near Eastern and especially Greek myths (e.g., Europa, Io, and Semele) as well as some African deities. Kings were sometimes referred to as being "sons of God." David was so-called. This, doubtless, contributed to the concept of "the divine right of kings."

Flight and Ascent:

Enoch was not the only character to be caught up by the gods. Myths with this theme have appeared in all cultures. They expressed a universal desire for transcendence and liberation from the constraints of the human condition. There is, for example, Elijah's ascent to Heaven in a fiery chariot, indicating that he had left the frailty of the human condition behind. Jesus ascending to Heaven is another example, as is Muhammad flying from Mecca to Jerusalem and then climbing a ladder to the divine throne. Armstrong interprets these events as signaling the arrival at a new level of spiritual attainment.[37]

Flood Myths:

"Catastrophe" stories such as earthquakes, famines, and plagues should be grouped with this archetype as a universal or near-universal theme in mythology. The Destruction of an old world and the creation of a new one is likewise a frequently recurring myth.

The flooding of the Tigris and Euphrates rivers in Mesapotamia was unpredictable and destructive, giving rise to the many ancient Near Eastern and Greek deluge myths. Such events were usually, but not always (34 out of 50 studied), treated as punishment. A total of 51 flood myths have been found in Taiwan, South China, Southeast Asia and Malaysia.[38]

Such is the context of Noah's flood, which is itself the blending of two different versions. (See Appendix A.) This story, in turn, has a shared mythic structure with that of Utnapishtim in the Gilgamesh epic.

Both heroes, warned by gods about the floods, build boats. Utnapeshtim's is a cube, but the design is in both cases divinely given. Utnapishtim takes on board craftspeople; Noah brings only his immediate family. Both survive a flood caused by rain descending from the vault of the heavens and the subterranean waters coming up. The Earth is being uncreated and dissolved into watery chaos. Both arrive on a mountain and offer sacrifices. In the Gilgamesh epic, the gods "smelled the savor, smelled the sweet savor; the gods crowded like flies about the sacrificer." Genesis 8: 21 reads, "When YHWH smelled the pleasing odor, he said in his heart: 'I will never again curse the ground'. . . ."[39]

The Hero-Deliverer:

This is the most pervasive of all mythological archetypes. "Myths and folk tales from every corner of the world have parallels that develop a vast and amazingly constant statement of the basic truths by which man has lived throughout the millenniums of his residence on the planet."[40] In his thoroughly documented book - *The Hero with a Thousand Faces* - Joseph Campbell draws on more than 400 myths and mythological characters from every part of the planet, including the most remote and isolated. The *Vedas* says, "Truth is one, the sages speak of it by many names."[41]

As mentioned in the Creation archetype, the very earliest myths from Mesopotamia described the creation of the gods themselves

- "emanations of the Uncreated Creating," which in turn became "the Created Creating Ones," which then led on into human history.[42] In the very earliest myths the gods were visible, but then only their secondary effects were seen as the gods were perceived to withdraw from the visible world. The process would now be carried forward by the heroes - seen as being "more or less human in character" - and through whom the destiny of the world was to be realized. Creation myths would begin to yield to legends and epics. "Metaphysics yields to prehistory, which is dim and vague at first, but becomes gradually precise in detail. The heroes become less and less fabulous, until at last, in the final stages of the various local traditions, legend opens into the common daylight of recorded time."[43] An integral dynamic in all this would be the origin of human consciousness which took place in most of the world in the second and first millenniums BCE. The next four chapters will deal with this development.

The composite hero of mythology is someone who has exceptional gifts. With equal frequency he is either honored by his society, or unrecognized, or disdained. He and/or his world suffer from a symbolic deficiency. The typical path of the hero's mythological adventure is an enlargement of the rites-of-passage formula, viz. separation - initiation - return. The hero-deliverers are the symbolic carriers of the human destiny. They are also more than mere human beings who, because of their faith and courage, have surpassed the limitations of their fellow humans - herohood is predestined, rather than simply achieved.

The hero is endowed with extraordinary powers from birth, or even the moment of conception. In many of the myths there are virgin and other kinds of miraculous birth. In 34 different myths from the Mediterranean basin and western Asia, the hero is invariably a child of most distinguished parents; often the son of a king. His origin is often preceded by difficulties such as prolonged barrenness. During, or preceding, the pregnancy there is a prophecy in the form of a dream or oracle, cautioning against his birth, and usually threatening danger to the father. The child of destiny also has to face a long period of obscurity, or extreme danger, impediment, or disgrace.

As a rule he is surrendered to the water in a pot or basket. He is then saved by animals or lowly people, such as shepherds, and is suckled by a female animal or a humble woman. The miraculous childhood reveals that a special divine manifestation has become incarnate in the world.[44] Great emphasis is placed on the mother of the hero, and often worship of her, along with her divine son, take place. The childhood cycle concludes with the return or recognition of the hero, when, after a long period of obscurity, his true character is revealed.

The hero ventures forth from the everyday world into a region of supernatural wonder: amazing forces are encountered there and a decisive victory is won. He then returns with the power to bestow benefits on one and all. The whole life of the hero is shown to have been a pageant of marvels with the great central adventure as its culmination. The last act of his biography is that of his death or departure. Needless to say, death does not hold any terror for him as he is reconciled with the grave, where he only sleeps and will arise at the destined time, or else he is present in another form.[45]

So engrained is the myth of the Hero-Deliverer that the lives of historical figures are often told in a way that conforms to this archetypal pattern. Abraham and Moses come readily to mind, as does the Buddha and Muhammad. In the Mediterranean basin the Hero is typically represented by the legend of Hercules, many of whose traits were later absorbed into the portrayal of Jesus Christ.[46]

Stories themed on the Hero-Deliverer continue to captivate and enthrall humanity. He has been portrayed in purely fictional characters as in the various super-heroes, who were first introduced to the world in comic books. The Star Wars movies owe their success to portraying various aspects of the Hero in its main characters. Sometimes he is fully human as with Indiana Jones, James Bond, and Western characters such as Shane. Yet others are given mythical qualities as in the *Lord of the Rings* and *Tales of Narnia* series. None have been more in demand than the Harry Potter books. Children have eagerly devoured its volumes, even though some of them are more than 700 pages in length.

A mythological image representing a central concept can be very similar in different cultures and yet interpreted in entirely different ways. The term "god," for example, often serves as a designation of mythic beings. In India a god is an individual's conceptualization of the ground of his own being. A god can also be symbolic, as he is in Greek mythology. The personages and episodes involving the Greek gods are neither regarded nor represented as being historic. They do not refer to actual events that are supposed to have occurred at some time, but rather to metaphysical or psychological mysteries. The Fall is viewed in similar fashion. In the biblical context the god is regarded in some way as an actual being. In similar fashion the Fall is taken to be a prehistoric fact.[47]

The mythological tree has been used and interpreted in a similar way. There is, for example, the Tree of the Knowledge of Good and Evil in Genesis chapters two and three. This figure appears to represent the scene described in chapter 3. It is in fact an old Sumerian scene, sketched a full thousand years before Eden was talked about. The scene

portrays the female power in human form and the male serpent behind her, the Tree of Life before, and beyond that, a male personage wearing the horned headdress of a god who has evidently come to partake of the fruit of the wonderful tree. A number of scholars have recognized in this scene something analogous to the episode in Eden, a full thousand years before Yahweh's day however, and when the figure rendered in the Bible as a mere creature, Eve, would have been recognized as a goddess, the great mother goddess Earth, with the primal self-renewing serpent, symbolic of the informing energy of creation and created things, her spouse.[48] ....
....

The various interpretations of the mythological tree configurate greatly differing theologies, sociologies, and psychologies; and yet, the Bo tree, Holy Rood, and the Tree of Immortal Life in the center of Yahweh's garden, actually are but local inflections of a single mythological archetype, and the image was long known, moreover, before any of these cultic readings. . . . Like life itself, such mythological archetypes simply are. Meanings can be read into them; meanings can be read out of them. But in themselves they are antecedent to meaning. Like ourselves, like trees, like dreams, they are "thus come."[49]

Even though myth has been primarily concerned with the origins of life, of coming to grips with the great unknown, and of the seeking of an understanding of the deepest levels of the human mind, it is also inextricably linked with advances in knowledge. A classic example is that of cosmology. In the earliest times people studied the stars, not because they were primarily concerned with cosmological speculation, but rather because of a preoccupation with origins, including that of the cosmos and the gods. Other benefits came to be gained that helped them cope with life, such as awareness of approaching seasonal changes and glimpses into the future.

Karen Armstrong has defined two terms that go to the heart of myth, viz. *mythos* and *logos*. The original meaning of *mythos*, as used by Homer and other Greek poets, was "word" or "speech." This was in differentiation from *logos,* which referred to a "tale" or "story." The meanings of the two terms in effect came to be exchanged. *Mythos* and its family of related words came to be associated with that part of life that in the Common Era would be referred to as "religion." Mythology, for example, refers to the body of myths that address a people's worldview. *Logos,* in turn, is defined as that which provides rational, pragmatic ideas that enable people to better function in the world. *Logos* is not concerned with answering questions about the ultimate issues and values of life, nor can it mitigate human loss and sorrow. It is instead primarily concerned with trying to discover something new and is essentially pragmatic. The derivatives from *logos* have attached themselves to the sciences or "-ologies."[50]

Logos and *mythos* are inextricably linked; they do not form a "dichotomy" - a division into two opposing parts, such as good and evil, nor does the word "dualism" (two irreconcilable substances such as mind and matter) apply here. *Mythos* has provided the fertile ground and inspiration that gives rise to *logos*. The use of imaginative constructs to fill the gaps in one's knowledge has applied, not only to existential matters, but to scientific endeavors as well. "Religions, philosophies, arts . . . prime discoveries in science and technology, the very dreams that blister sleep, boil up from the basic magic ring of myth."[51]

A reviewer of *Einstein's Mistakes - The Human Failings of Genius* observed that Einstein had "a mystical, intuitive approach to physics" that led him to the right answers. It was this dynamic that led to the formulation of the Theory of Relativity, which in turn has enabled scientists to bring ever more knowledge to light. It is not unusual for science-fiction writers and artists to imagine devices that initially seem to be nothing more than the product of a fertile imagination. Five hundred years ago Leonardo Da Vinci drew up plans for wings with a view to enable human flight. A set was recently made to his specifications, and it enabled brief flight. Not a few of the devices described and used in the writings of Jules Verne and others have come to be a common part of life. In the mid-twentieth century the late Arthur C. Clarke visualized that satellites could be stationed at strategic places above our planet. They became a central part of worldwide communication long before he died.

Down through the Centuries logos has grown, sometimes very slowly, if at all, as in the Middle Ages, and at other times in leaps and bounds as it led to the Enlightenment and beyond. This growth has directly impacted mythos. Some myths have died, others have been adapted, and yet others have arisen in response to awareness of new frontiers to be crossed. Overall mythos has not faired well in the Common Era. The trouble started with the Council of Nicea which was established by the Emperor Constantine with a view to codifying and standardizing Christian beliefs. The Age of Reason further reduced the role of myth. And then the emergence of a scientific view of history tended to absolutize stories. Events were declared to be either factual or fictional.

This resulted in the gradual decline of the role of myth. Its various concepts came to be treated as either being factual, or failing that, as only having value as entertainment. The word "myth" in turn would come to have a negative connotation as it came to mean that which is not based on fact. Mythology no longer had aspects that correspond to science, logic, and faith, but was, instead, a distorted substitute of them. As Campbell explains it, "mythology has been interpreted by the modern intellect as a primitive fumbling effort to explain the world."[52]

Much of the mayhem that marred and marked the twentieth century can be traced to the loss of the influence of myth. Ideologies came to be treated as irrefutable truths that had to be enforced at any cost. Stories of ancestral prowess came to be seen as evidence of a certain people being superior to the rest as Nazism maintained. This in turn justified genocide and enslavement of others.

Thankfully mythos did not disappear altogether. The Age of Romanticism, which developed in Europe in the late eighteenth and early nineteenth centuries as a movement in literature, philosophy and art, was a reaction to and a correction of the focus on facts wrought by the Enlightenment. It came to be appreciated anew that a vital ingredient that makes humanity human is the exercise of "a leap of faith." The observation has been made that the greatest intellectual achievement of the twentieth century was to rediscover the value of myth.

> Mythology is not a peripheral manifestation, not a luxury, but a serious attempt at integration of reality and experience. . . . Its goal is a totality of what is significant to man's needs, material, intellectual, and religious.[53]

We have come to learn that myths are " 'stories of discovery,' by which whole cultures and civilizations both discover and express their basic wisdom."[54]

3

THE SOURCE FOR THE CONCEPT OF
GODS - THE BICAMERAL MIND

Two phenomena that are familiar to one and all, the one widely used as a means of entertainment, the other anything but amusing, are vestiges of what Julian Jaynes referred to as the bicameral mind. These actualities are hypnotism and schizophrenia. His treatise that seeks to explain the dynamics of such a mind, one that was common to all of humanity until the first millennium BCE, is titled *The Origin of Consciousness in the Breakdown of the Bicameral Mind*. The next three chapters draw heavily from this book.

The development of agricultural skills, leading to the transformation from a way of life fully dependent on hunting and gathering to a food-producing economy through the domestication of plants and animals, is the gigantic step that made civilization possible. Jaynes defines civilization as the art of living in towns of such size that everyone does not know everyone else.

A very significant change in human affairs was set in motion. Instead of a nomadic tribe of twenty or so hunters living in the mouths of caves, towns with populations of a couple of hundred were formed. People began burying their dead in clusters in ceremonial graves. By 6000 BCE farming communities had spread over much of the Near

East. A thousand years later they had penetrated much of the Tigris-Euphrates and Nile valleys. Cities with 10,000 inhabitants became not uncommon, and the great dynasties of Ur and Egypt began to make their enormous impact on history. The process spread across the Mediterranean Sea and then went on to invade the Indus River valley and beyond, the Ukraine, Central Asia, and along the Yangtze River in China. Independently, parallel developments took place in Mesoamerica and the plains and highlands spreading from the Andes Mountains in South America.

Students of early civilizations had come to believe that the major motive that brought people together in large concentrations was fear. The ruins of such centers consistently left telltale signs of battle in their art and architecture. The "mother city" that left no trace of preparations for defense and attack was finally found in Caral, Peru. Even though it is twenty miles from the Pacific Ocean and surrounded by desert, water was plentiful due to the rivers that flow from the Andes to the sea. It was easy to develop desert transforming irrigation. Caral became a huge Garden of Eden and a trading center. Traces of goods that came from Ecuador, the Andes, and the rain forests, have been found. The basic diet was fish from the Pacific coast. All this developed about 2600 BCE.

It was the formation of cities that brought the bicameral mind into play. This condition proved to be a form of social control, and it was this dynamic that made possible the movement of people from small hunter-gatherer groups to large agricultural communities. What follows is a summary of Jayne's thesis. To familiarize oneself with the details and better understand how the bicameral mind functioned, it will be necessary to study his book. Suffice to say that other scholars of pre- and early history have made observations that are in harmony with Jaynes's presentation.

The term "bicameral" refers to the left and right hemispheres of the brain. The bicameral mind was all about speech, thus the speech areas of the brain were involved in an important way. It is the left cerebral hemisphere of the brain, controlling the right side of the body, which, in right-handed people, contains the three speech areas. Human language is involved only with this hemisphere. The other half of the brain was the base for the "language of the gods," which consisted of auditory hallucinations. These voices were perceived to be coming from superior beings, called gods, and who had supreme authority over the world in which the recipients of the messages lived.

Jaynes stresses that it is absolutely certain that such voices do exist, and that hearing them is just like hearing actual sound. Furthermore, it is highly probable that the bicameral voices of antiquity were, in quality, very much like the auditory hallucinations of contemporary people. Even those who have been profoundly deaf from birth or very early childhood can somehow experience auditory hallucinations. This is the common experience of deaf schizophrenics. They are also heard by many completely normal people to varying degrees. Roughly one-third of human beings hear hallucinated voices at some time during their lives. There is a genetic source for such hallucinations in all of us, and this was the basis of the bicameral mind.

The bicameral mind was not in any way static. It slowly developed from the ninth through the second millennium BCE, even though it seemed to be static when viewed in the space of a century. This was the preconscious era in human development and experience. Early civilizations had a profoundly different mentality from that of our own. People were in fact not conscious as we are. At that time human nature had two clear compartments, an executive part called a god and a follower part - the person himself. Neither part was conscious. Early humans had no awareness of their awareness of the world - no internal mind-space to introspect upon. The divine part of one's nervous system, by which one was ordered about in a slave-like manner, was a voice, or voices of others known as gods, formed in a clearly established hierarchy. People were not responsible for their actions, and therefore could not be given credit or blame for anything that was done over those many millennia of time. There was no role for ethics, nor place for "sin." The individual obeyed these hallucinated voices because he could not perceive what to do by himself.

It is a much observed fact that whenever more than one of a particular kind of creature share a common space, a hierarchical order becomes established. It is often referred to as a pecking order. This stems from a consistent pattern among newly born chicks who, when positioning themselves to eat from a container of food, establish an accepted order as to their place in the line. Human beings, especially in earlier times, have been subject to this same dynamic. The person at the top became the king. A similar hierarchy applied to the gods and their hallucinated voices. In some societies the human leader was viewed as a god-king; in others he was the mouthpiece of the supreme deity.

From Egypt to Peru, from Ur to the Yucatan, whatever civilization arose - their death practices, idolatry, concepts of a divine government, and hallucinated voices - all bore witness to a different mentality to that of our own. The earliest writings in a language that we today can clearly comprehend, viz. the *Iliad,* reveal the same difference in mentality. The bulk of the poem is consistent in its lack of consciousness and points back to a very different kind of human nature. Perusal of various speeches of gods in other ancient literature such as the Hebrew Bible, confirm this fact.

The gods, which were understood to be the source of these hallucinations, were in no sense "figments of the imagination" of anyone. They were man's volition - the source of the exercise of the will.

The voice occupied his nervous system, probably his right hemisphere, and from stores of admonitory and preceptive experience, transmuted this experience into articulated speech which then "told" the person what to do. These omniscient, omnipotent voices came in the form of neurological commands, and to hear them was to obey them. Bicameral people did not imagine; they experienced. In these preconscious times every kingdom was in essence a theocracy, with every subject the slave of these voices.

The function of the gods was chiefly the guiding and planning of action in novel situations. The gods sized up problems and organized actions according to an ongoing pattern or purpose, resulting in intricate bicameral civilizations coordinating the necessary activities required for survival, such as planting and harvest times and the sorting out of commodities.

The gods were not supernatural or superior beings as found in the hero myths. They were none other than the kings who had died. The king who even while he was alive ruled by hallucination. The king, upon his death, became a living god. This "metamorphosis" has continued into the Common Era. Roman emperors and other prominent citizens were habitually declared to be gods after their deaths. This was undoubtedly a motivating force in the practice of ancestor worship. A variation of the deification of the dead continues to this day. The Roman Catholic Church looms large in this respect. The canonization of certain prominent deceased Catholics is a process that climaxes with their being declared by the current Pope to be saints. They are often beseeched in prayer as fervently as any god may be.

The situation that initiated an hallucination was stress, as it continues to be for schizophrenics. Thus the stress caused by a person's death was more than enough to trigger his hallucinated voice. The dead king became a hallucinated presence. The earliest grave discovered, so far, of a king (± 9000 BCE) is at a place called Eynan in the Middle East. His head was propped up and cradled in stones. Jaynes believes that, in the hallucinations of the people, he was still giving commands. In many of the early cultures the heads of even the ordinary dead were often severed from the body. Food was also placed in the graves. There is even evidence of a double burial of the same corpse, the second being in a common grave after the voices had ceased.

As these early cultures developed into bicameral kingdoms, the graves of their important citizens were more and more filled with weapons, furniture, ornaments, and particularly, vessels of food. This is also true of the very first chamber tombs all over Europe and Asia after 7000 BCE. The kings of Ur, during the first half of the third millennium BCE, were entombed with their entire retinues, sometimes buried alive, in a crouched position around them as for service. A similar pattern is seen in the Indus, Chinese, and later, Inca civilizations.

It is very possible that the Incas were still in the bicameral mode when the Spanish Conquistadores arrived. This is a viable reason for explaining the unsuspicious meekness of their surrender. How could an empire, whose armies had triumphed over the civilizations of half a continent, be captured by a small band of 150 Spaniards in the early evening of November 16, 1532? Were there no bicameral voices coming from the sun or from the golden statues in the dazzling towers of Cuzco?

That the dead were the origin of gods is also found in the writings of those bicameral civilizations that became literate. In a bilingual incantation text from Assyria, the dead are directly called Ilani, or gods. "And on the other side of the world three millennia later, Sahagun, one of the earliest reporters of the Mesoamerican scene, reported that the Aztecs 'called the place Teotihuacan, burial place of the kings; the ancients said: he who had died became a god; or when someone said - he who has become a god, meant to say - he has died."[1]

Thus from Mesopotamia to Peru, the great civilizations have at least gone through a stage characterized by a kind of burial that indicated that the individual was still, in some way, alive. And where writing could record it, the dead were often called gods. At the very least this is consistent with the hypothesis that their voices were still being heard in hallucination.

Another feature of early civilizations that indicated bicamerality is the enormous numbers and kinds of human effigies and their obvious centrality to ancient life. The first effigies in history were the propped up corpses of chiefs and the remodeled skulls. In some cases the skulls had realistic features in clay added to them, and shells or gems inserted to serve as eyes. They were then set in prominent places.

This was followed by the making of figurines. They have been found in almost all the ancient kingdoms, beginning with the first stationary human settlements. During the seventh and sixth millennia BCE, the figurines were very primitive, being carved from small stones or made of clay. As the statues got larger, the size of the eyes were often exaggerated to twice the normal size or more. This is evidence of the social interaction brought about by eye-to-eye contact.

In the Mayan culture there was an enormous profusion of figurines. When a Spanish mayor of a city ordered the abolition of idolatry in 1565, he was stunned to see upwards of a million idols brought out. According to an observer, "the unhappy dupes believed the idols spoke to them."

With time the figurines gave way to life-size statues and larger. An elaborate ritual for the opening of the mouth of new statues developed in Egypt and Mesopotamia - further evidence that people heard hallucinations from them.

Cuneiform literature often refers to god-statues speaking, even as late as the early first millennium BCE. The Hebrew Bible also indicates that one of the types of idol referred to, the Terap, could speak. Ezekiel 21: 21 describes the king of Babylon as consulting with several of them. A similar pattern was found in Mosoamerica and Peru. The conquered Aztecs told the Spanish invaders how their history began when a statue from a ruined temple belonging to a previous culture spoke to their leaders. Similarly the first Spaniards in Peru reported that the devil himself actually spoke to the Incas out of the mouths of their statues. To the bicameral mind the statue was not representing a god - the god himself was a statue. And this god had his own house - a god-house.

Throughout the bicameral era it was not any human being per se who was a ruler, but rather the hallucinated voices of the gods. The ordinary citizen would not have heard directly the voices of the great gods who owned the cities - this would have weakened the political fabric. There were, however, personal gods who served as intermediaries. Each individual - king or serf - had his own personal god, whose voice he heard and obeyed.

In the early millennia of the bicameral age, life had been simpler, confined to a small area, with a straightforward political organization. Few gods were needed at that stage. But as the third millennium BCE approached, and throughout its time span, the tempo and complexity of the social organization called for a far greater number of decisions in an ever increasing number of contexts at any given time. This resulted in an enormous proliferation of deities which could be invoked in whatever situation one might find oneself. From the great god-houses of the Sumerian and Babylonian cities of the major gods, to the personal gods enchapeled in each household, the world must have literally swarmed with sources of hallucination, and hence the increasing need for priests to order them into strict hierarchies.

Initially the king's tomb was the god's house. The king's grave at Eynan was a two-tiered formation - a forerunner of the multitiered ziggurats and gigantic pyramids of the Nile. By the middle of the sixth millennium BCE, god-houses in Mesopotamia were set on mud-brick platforms. In a long central room, the god-idol on a platform at one end looked down on an offering table at the other. In a typical settlement ordinary houses and buildings would be found grouped around one larger and more magnificent dwelling. This building served no practical use such as a granary or barn - instead it contained some sort of human effigy - evidence of a bicameral culture. This city plan wouldn't strike one as unusual because we are familiar with the town plan of a church surrounded by lesser houses and shops - this is partly the residue of our bicameral past.

The rituals practiced in these god-houses paralleled those taking place in churches today. The statues were washed by priests by means of the sprinkling of holy water, the origin, perhaps, of our sprinkling and annointing ceremonies. In front of the god were tables, the origin of church altars, on one of which flowers were placed, and on the other food and drink for the divine hunger. The church, temple, or mosque is still called the House of God. In it we still speak to the god, still bring offerings to be placed on a table or altar before the god or his emblem.

The god-house would get steadily higher, which required that it had to get bigger. Height has always been a mythical symbol of the divine. People have always tended to aspire to the transcendence represented by the sky. That is why mountains are so often holy in mythology. They stand midway between Heaven and Earth - a place where people could meet with their god. To this day people do not just attempt to reach mountain peaks because they are there. There is an undeniable elemental and spiritual basis to the quest. Many of the first British climbers were academics and clergymen.

With cities of many thousands came the building of huge monumental god-houses which came to characterize and dominate population centers from then on, perhaps serving as hallucinogenic aids to all that could see them. In most of the great city sites excavated in Mesopotamia, the house of a chief god was the ziggurat, a great rectangular tower, rising by diminishing stages to a shining summit on which was built a chapel. To stand, even today, under such mountainous ziggurats as that of Ur, still hovering above the excavated ruins of its once bicameral civilization, with its ramps of staircases rising into the sun, is to feel the grip such architecture alone can have upon one's being.

The ziggurat came to replace the mountain as the center of the world. Armstrong says that Mesopotamians saw the city as a place where they could encounter the divine. The gods lived in the cities side by side with the people. Their cities were transcendent, because they went beyond anything known before. They partook of the divine creativity of the gods, who had brought order out of chaos.[2]

In Egypt the god-house took the form of a pyramid. The divine kings were not sorrowfully entombed, but merrily "empalaced." Complexes of festive courts and galleries, merry with holy pictures and writing, often surrounded by acres of the graves of the god's servants, and dominated by the pyramid itself, soaring sunward, a variation of the shining ziggurat.

The earliest bicameral kingdoms of the Americas are also characterized by these huge, otherwise useless, centrally located buildings: the odd-shaped clumsy Olmec pyramid of about 500 BCE at La Venta, with its corridor of lesser mounds containing mysterious jaguar-face mosaics. About 300 years later the gigantic pyramid of the sun at Teotihuacan (literally "Place of the Gods") was built. It has a greater cubic content than any in Egypt, being an eighth of a mile long on each side and higher than a twenty-story building. A room for the god on its summit was reached by a system of steep stairs. And on top of the god-room, tradition states, there was a gigantic statue of the sun. A processional flanked by other pyramids leads towards it, and from miles away on the Mexican plateau one can still see the remains of a great city. Houses for priests, numerous courtyards, and smaller buildings were all of one story in height so that from anywhere in the city one could see the great pyramidal house of the gods.

At about the same time the many Mayan cities in the Yucatan peninsula, showing the same bicameral architecture, appear. Each city was centered with a steeply rising pyramid topped with a god-house, richly decorated with the Olmec-type jaguar masks together with other murals and carvings.

The Incas in South America were preceded by half-a-dozen Andean civilizations, the earliest being the Kotosh, dating before 1800 BCE. The Incas themselves became a power about 1200 BCE. At the beginning their realm was suggestive of a typical god-king bicameral structure. By the time of its conquest by Pizarro in 1532, it was probably in transition to a subjective mindset. The vast empire that they had become by then suggests this. The king was divine, a descendent of the sun - the creator-god of land and people. Upon his death his house became a temple. A life-sized golden statue was made of him sitting on his golden stool. It was served daily with food.

Rather than bringing the construction of ziggurats to an end, the arrival of the historical religions resulted in many more such temples being built. Buddhist, Hindu, and Shinto ziggurats abound. One of the most famous is the stone temple at Angkor Wat in Cambodia. It was once the center of a Hindu-Buddhist kingdom that started in the 800s CE and survived for 600 years. The Muslims have built their many ziggurats with their soaring minarets - some of their most famous being the Alhambra in Spain and the mosques of Isfahan in Iran and Istanbul. Jews, in turn, have built many prominent synagogues, especially in Europe, that abound in the beauty that is common to ziggurats. And then there are the Christian Cathedrals - a hallmark of Europe, but not just there. Approaching any town in South Africa, the one building that cleaves the sky is the Dutch Reformed ziggurat.

When Thomas Huxley, a famous British biologist, visited America in 1876, he asked, as the ship approached the New York harbor, what were the tower and the tall building with a cupola - then the city's most conspicuous structures. When he was told that they were the Tribune newspaper and the Western Union Telegraph buildings, he replied, "Ah, that is interesting; that is American. In the Old World the first thing you see as you approach a great city are [church] steeples; here you see first, centers of intelligence."[3]

The development of steel at the turn of the twentieth century made possible the construction of skyscrapers that have come to dwarf the ziggurats, but the latter continue to be built. Los Angeles dedicated a new Catholic ziggurat - Our Lady of the Angels - at the commencement of the new millennium. It cost $190 million to build and replace St. Vibiana's Cathedral that had been built 125 years earlier. It was but one of two dozen Catholic cathedral renovation or construction projects taking place. The Mormons are building so many cathedrals that the makers of their icons must be kept very busy.

A peculiarly American ziggurat has been the emergence of the mega-church over the last fifty years. These congregations number in their thousands, requiring the building of enormous sanctuaries that still have to house two or more successive services. One has to wonder if this trend has come to negatively impact the centers of intelligence to which Huxley referred. The George W. Bush presidency witnessed the appointment of the equivalent of Soviet-styled political commissars whose task it was to nullify and distort scientific findings that conflicted with the Bush administration's goals and worldview.

A constant of the ziggurat over these last six millennia has been the beauty and ornateness of these structures. They are always the most prominent and costly building, and yet least used, on any sacred campus. In most religious complexes the ziggurat is only used one day a week. The mega-church is the exception with respect to its physical impact - function has received priority, often at the expense of form.

The building of ziggurats is not the only evidence of human creativity and resourcefulness. The development of writing is another. This curious and very remarkable practice began in the fourth millennium BCE in Mesopotamia and Egypt. It started with *pictures* of *visual events,* evolving to become *symbols* of *phonetic events.* Speech became transmitted into little marks on stone, clay, or papyrus so that speech could be seen rather than just heard, and seen by anybody, not just those within earshot at the time.

Phonetic symbols, as on this page, are meant to tell a reader something that he does not know. However, the closer writing was to pictorial symbols, the more it was a memory-aiding device to release information which the reader already had. Examples of this are led by the pictograms of Uruk, the iconography in the early depiction of gods, and more recently the glyphics of the Maya and the picture codices of the Aztecs. Phonetic symbols were initially intended for the ear. Those who had developed the skill would read aloud for the benefit of the others. The King James Bible was translated with the benefit in mind of those who would hear it being read. That is why it is still widely read in Christian worship services to this day.

Two kinds of early writing which fell between the extremes of pictures and phonetic symbols are Egyptian hieroglyphics ("hier" implying that it was the "writing of the gods"), and the more widely used writing which came to be called cuneiform, due to its wedge-shaped characters. Its remains are very extensive, with thousands of tablets waiting to be translated. Cuneiform was used for at least four languages - Sumerian, Akkadian, Hurrian, and later Hittite. Instead of an alphabet of twenty-six letters or of twenty-two, as in the Assyrian language of Aramaic (which replaced cuneiform around 200 BCE), it is a clumsy and ambiguous communication system of over 600 signs.

People are conquered by an army, but a society is run with words. Writing made communication at a distance possible. Mesopotamia put writing to civil use a thousand years before Egypt did. Cuneiform was first used for business, such as debt records. In Ur, by 2100 BCE, the judgments of gods, through their steward mediums, began to be recorded. This is the beginning of the idea of law. Such written judgments could and would be placed in strategic locations, thus allowing the cohesiveness of a larger society.

The words of the gods would be engraved on a stone column, called a stele. (This is probably why the Ten Commandments given to the Israelites by Moses were described as being engraved on stone tablets.) One example would have been a stele set up in a field to tell how that land was to be farmed. These stelae were treated as epiphanies, as well as being sources of auditory hallucinations.

In 1792 BCE the civil use of writing in this way broke open a new kind of government. It was brought about by the commanding figure of Mesopotamian history and greatest of all steward kings - Hammurabi, steward of Marduk, the supreme deity of Babylon, referred to in chapter two. His stewardship lasted for 42 years, and he succeeded in merging most of the city-states of Mesopotamia into a hegemony under Marduk. Writing became a new method of social control which, by hindsight, we know would soon supplant the bicameral mind.

The most famous relic of this period is the Code of Hammurabi.

It was an eight-foot-high black basalt stele erected beside an idol of himself. The rules of the Code should not be thought of in the modern terms of laws which are enforced by officials such as police, something that was unknown at that time. Rather they are the lists of practices in Babylon itself, the statements of Marduk which needed no more enforcement than their authenticity on the stele itself.

The fact that they were written down and more generally the wide use of writing for communication, indicate a reduction in the auditory hallucinatory control of the bicameral mind. Together, they put into motion cultural determinants which, coming together with other forces a few centuries later, resulted in a change in the very structure of the mind itself.

The cuneiform writings tell us that throughout Mesopotamia from the earliest times of Sumer and Akkad, all lands were seen as being owned by gods and that the humans were their slaves. Each city-state had its own principal god (Babylon's was Marduk), and the king was described in the earliest available writings as "the tenant farmer of the god." The king's legitimacy derived from the fact that he alone had access to the Sky God and was thus the earthly counterpart of God. Later, with the development of consciousness and the emergence of the monotheistic religions, priests would come to be viewed in the same light. The priest sees himself, and is seen, as the one who has access to God, and thus is his representative and mouthpiece.

The government was theocratic in structure. There was a divine order which all people obeyed and followed without question. There was no scope for an individual spiritual quest, because sacred knowledge was a given, received from the gods. A retrogression to this mindset would later take place in some of the so-called organized religions, particularly Christianity and Islam. Sacred knowledge, delivered by the priests, has to be, and very often is, unquestionably embraced by the practitioners of these religions.

As societies grew and stratified, priests came to have a powerful role. They did the accounting and recording, in addition to preserving the myths. Sacred lore was the preserve of the priest. The masses were expected to follow their priests, whose power was based on their role of working for the collective economic and spiritual welfare. This dynamic gave people a sense of security.

Two main forms of theocracy had emerged by the third millennium BCE. One was the *steward-king* theocracy in which he was the manager and caretaker of the god's lands. The aforementioned Hammurabi is a prime example. This was the most widespread form of theocracy among bicameral kingdoms. It was found throughout Mesopotamia, in the Mycean part of Greece, as well as India, China, and probably Mesoamerica.

The second was the *god-king* theocracy in which the king himself was a god. The clearest examples of this form existed in Egypt and at least some of the kingdoms of the Andes, and probably the kingdom of Japan until the end of World War II. Such titles as "King of Kings" and "Lord of Lords" were applied to Babylonian and Persian emperors (Ezra 7: 12, Ezekiel 26: 7, Daniel 2: 37). The latter phrase is used to address Yahweh in Psalm 136: 3.

The foundation for and belief in the divine right of kings, de facto gods - free to do as they pleased, stems from this era. It did not dissipate in Europe until the twentieth century. A similar mindset was found in the United States of America as a new nation, which is not surprising when one considers that the bulk of the population had European roots. It was revealed in the concept of "manifest destiny" - the conviction that the annexation of territory was preordained, a part of God's plan to extend "the area of freedom" across the North American continent.

A loose confederation of central European states formed the Holy Roman Empire in 962, ostensibly to protect the papacy. It was neither holy nor Roman, but even so the confederation survived for 850 years.

The Holy Alliance was formed in 1815 by the royal heads of state of Russia, Prussia and Austria, with Holland and then France joining later. Its stated object was "to manifest before the whole universe their unshakable determination to take as their sole guide the precepts of religion, namely the rules of justice, Christian charity, and peace." With republican movements fermenting in the southern states of Europe, the Holy Alliance had a deeper purpose, in pledging its troth to defend the divine right of kings.

From time to time attempts were made to curb the king's power. One of the earlier, if not the earliest, was the English Magna Carta - a feudal charter issued in 1215 by barons and church leaders. Over time the charter steadily grew in influence, leading to a parliamentary form of government, and in so doing, setting the example for reducing royal power to that of a symbolic head of state, but not devoid of all power.

Another example was King Charles V, grandson of Isabella of Castile and Ferdinand of Aragon, when he became the ruler of the four kingdoms that formed the nucleus of what would become Spain. At his coronation the assembly declared that it was a republic with an elective king. It served notice that, "we who are as good as you, make you, who are no better than we, our king. And we will bear true allegiance if you observe our laws and customs; if not, not." There is no evidence that the power of Charles V was curbed in any way, but this was the position towards which Europeans were heading.

Napoleon Bonaparte made a notable contribution in this regard. He hastened the extinction of feudal vestiges in central Europe and reduced the number of states from 300 to 36. He also treated kings and princes in a cavalier manner and was seen as a champion of the people. One of the first countries to jettison royalty was Portugal, doing so in 1910.

The so-called Great War could have been avoided but for three bumbling, totally inadequate kings who were cousins - King George V of Great Britain, Kaiser Wilhelm II of Germany, and Czar Nicholas II of Russia. This war would deliver the coup-de-grace to European royalty as a ruling force. Together with the United Kingdom, only Spain, Holland, Belgium, and the three Scandinavian countries have kings - all of whom are figureheads.

World War II ended the role of one of the last divine rulers. General Douglas McArthur, as temporary military governor of Japan, insisted that Emperor Hirohito, proclaimed as the one-hundred-twenty-fourth descendent of the Sun God, declare himself to no longer be divine. The last despotic kingdoms in Asia have only recently ended. The royal family of Nepal basically self-destructed, while the king of Bhutan took the lead in making himself the figurehead ruler of a new democracy. All but two of the god-kings have faded into history.

Besides the Dalai Lama, who is in exile, only one other god-king remains. These two relics of the bicameral era couldn't be more different in their fulfillment of their roles. The Dalai Lama, a humble and wise man, works tirelessly, not only for the betterment of Tibetans, but for all of humankind. The Pope, on the other hand, while claiming to do the same, is imperiousness personified, refusing to understand or accept the changes taking place in the world. The Pope rules over a postage-stamp-sized piece of real estate and yet he is treated in every way like the Incas and pharaohs of old. Cardinals, who have a proclivity for acting like gods themselves, are sycophancy personified when in the Pope's presence.

A strong case can be made that Kim Il Sung, who became leader of North Korea after World War II, came to assume the role of a god-king.

He maintained absolute control of all aspects of life, and the population was totally in his thrall. The nation was bereft and shattered when he died. He was succeeded by his son, Kim Jong Il, who has been able to maintain total control, despite being a painful example of dynastic decay.

The coming of people together in towns and cities created the conditions for the foundational myths such as those explaining how life started. Early mythologies expressed the gradual separation from nature which the new city dwellers were themselves experiencing. Biblical writers saw civilization as a separation from God as well, as taught in the story of the Tower of Babel. Civilization came to be seen as splendid but also unstable. The urban myths thus came to meditate on the continual struggle between order and chaos.

The foundation myth of Marduk, the city god of Babylon, is a classic example as it examines the human process of change. Marduk was at war with Tiamat (salt water), the goddess of chaos, whom he defeated. He then split Tiamat's massive corpse in two, creating the sky and the earth that would be inhabited by human beings. Marduk then created the first human by mixing the blood of a defeated god with a handful of dust. This showed that humanity and the natural world were all made of the same divine stuff.[4]

After his victory over Tiamat, Marduk founded Babylon with the ziggurat at the center - it being a copy of Marduk's shrine in the divine world. As the symbol of an infinite heaven, towering above all the other buildings, it becomes the gods' earthly home. The city is called Babiloni - the Gate of the Gods - the place where the divine enters the world of men. The city would thus replace the mountain, which had enabled the first human beings to climb up to the world of the gods.[5]

The book of Genesis tells us that the Lord God created Adam out of the dust of the earth and then breathed into the nostrils of this clay figure and it became the embodiment of a living spirit. The physical world was thus portrayed in these myths as something that was made - an artifact. As Alan M. Watts puts it, the earth was seen to be a ceramic creation. Clay is passive and has in itself no particular structure. It therefore has to be worked upon by an external force and intelligence if it is to assume an intelligible shape. The whole quest and motivation of Western scientific endeavor, initially, was to understand the nature of the physical world and thus the design in the mind of the Creator.[6] It was inevitable that the idea that humans and the earth are the same would die under the weight of scientific discoveries.

A major change that urbanization brought about was that of the gender of the dominant gods. The great river valleys - the Nile, Tigris-Euphrates, Indus, and Ganges - had been the world of the goddess. Ganges (Gangā), for example, is the name of a goddess. The goddess was also a very potent figure in the Mediterranean basin in Hellenistic times. The emergence of the city-states led to wars as they began to prey on each other. By the fourth millennium BCE, warfare became increasingly more devastating as massacres and deportations increased. These invasions brought warrior gods such as Zeus and Yahweh into the mythology. The invasion of the world of the goddess systems ended with the male-oriented mythologies becoming dominant. By about 1750 BCE, according to Campbell, the matriarchal society had ended.[7]

Evolution and change, being the hallmark of the ethos of humanity, would ensure that new developments would follow.

4

THE ORIGIN OF CONSCIOUSNESS

A reference to the breakdown of the bicameral mind was made in the preceding chapter. Two dynamics, with a see-saw relationship, were in play in this process. As the bicameral mind broke down, consciousness developed. It was a gradual process that started at different times in different parts of the world, the Americas probably being among the last of the geographic areas. The Near East led the way as its tempo of development picked up with the arrival of the second millennium BCE. The higher gods seemed to be receding into the heavens and by that period had disappeared altogether.

Consciousness, in this context, does not relate to the common understanding that to be conscious means that one is not asleep, nor in some kind of coma. This concept cannot be explained or defined in one sentence. Originally the search into the nature of consciousness was seen as a mind-body problem. It moved on from there to become the problem of the origin of mind. The brain, which developed through evolution, and consciousness are connected. It is not yet known, however, how the brain and consciousness are linked. If the latter is thought of as a "thing," then it must, like other things, have a location, but it actually does not have a location in a physical sense. This consciousness that is myself of selves is everything, and yet, in substance, it is nothing.

Consciousness began, not with matter, nor at the beginning of animal life, but at some specific time after human life had evolved. It could only commence once associative memory, or learning, had appeared and furthermore, could not have developed without language, which is not merely a means of communication but an organ of perception. Consciousness is generated and accessed by means of language. It follows, therefore, that it is of much more recent origin than has heretofore been supposed.

Humans have been aware of the concept of consciousness almost since it began. There is, however, a sense in which we shall never be able to understand consciousness in the same way that we can understand things of which we are conscious. Heraclitus (540 to 475 BCE), a Greek philosopher, called it an enormous space whose boundaries, even by travelling along every path, could never be found. "A millennium later the Christian theologian, Augustine, living among the caverned hills of Carthage, was astonished at the 'mountains and hills of my high imaginations,' 'the plains and caves and caverns of my memory,' with its recesses of 'manifold and spacious chambers wonderfully furnished with innumerable stores.'"[1]

Among other things consciousness is the difference between what others see and know about us and our own sense of our inner selves and the deep feelings that sustain us. Being conscious is an unfolding story that we tell ourselves, moment by moment, about what we are doing, feeling, and thinking. It is not only being aware, but being aware that we are being aware. Alone, of all species, we try to understand ourselves and the world at large, and this is accomplished by means of the dynamics of consciousness.

To aid in the understanding of how consciousness functions, some terms need to be defined: one of them is "analog." An analog is a model, which is at every point generated by the thing of which it is an analog.

A map, for example, is an analog of a given geographical area. The relationship is that of a metaphor, i.e., the use of a term for one thing to describe another because of some kind of similarity between them. The subjective, conscious mind is an analog of what is called the real world. It is active rather than passive, an operation or process as opposed to being a repository. It operates by way of analogy, by way of constructing an analog space with an analog "I" that can observe that space and move metaphorically in it. This is part of the process of spatialization - the process whereby we invent or assume mind-space inside our heads, as well as the heads of others. Mind-space is a part of what it is to be conscious and to assume consciousness in others.

Consciousness also has a need for order - it is constantly creating a narrative as it fits things into a beginning, a middle, and an end, thus providing a temporal sequence that makes sense of what is taking place. This process not only tells what happened, it explains why it happened. The knowledge and understanding that now would flow from the conscious mind would provide a totally different source of volition. In the bicameral mind volition was the result of an hallucinated voice, whereas with the development of consciousness, the mind would come to be intimately bound up with volition and decision. Free will would become an integral part of consciousness. The rigid behavior of the bicameral human would undergo a radical change accordingly. The old Sumerian proverb, "Act promptly, make your god happy," would no longer apply. Instead of being subject to hallucinations over which one had no control, consciousness would be learned on the basis of language. It would be introduced culturally, and would need, in turn, to be taught to each new generation. Consciousness would become something fundamental.

A crucial question arises from this development: "How could such a system, where the brain was structured into a bicameral mind, have its function change over so short a period of time, such that the admonitory voices would be heard no more?"

Writing itself would prove to be one factor. Initially it strengthened the gods by allowing a civil structure, such as that of Hammurabi's, to remain stable. But it was also gradually eroding the auditory authority of the bicameral mind. More and more, the accountings and messages of government were being placed on cuneiform tablets. Once the word of the gods became silent, written on clay tablets or incised into a speechless stone, the god's commands or the king's directives could be turned to or avoided by one's own efforts in a way that auditory hallucinations never could be. The word of a god now had a *controllable location* rather than an ubiquitous power compelling immediate obedience.

Another major factor that contributed to the breakdown of the bicameral mind was the profound and irreversible changes that occurred in the second millennium BCE. Vast geological catastrophes occurred. Civilizations perished. Half the world's population became refugees. Furthermore, wars, previously sporadic, came with hastening and ferocious frequency as this millennium staggered to its dark and bloody close. In this social chaos the gods could no longer tell people what to do. Or if they did, their volition led to death and an increase in the stress that physiologically occasioned the voices in the first place, until voices came in an unsolvable Babel of confusion. The story of the Tower of Babel in Genesis chapter 11 is probably a mythological explanation of those times.

There were two geological catastrophes that aided the transition to consciousness. The first occurred about 1500 BCE when a good part of Aegean land was suddenly a thousand feet underwater. This occurred in the vicinity of the island of Thera (now known as Santorini), some sixty miles north of Crete. It had been part of what Plato and later legend referred to as the lost continent of Atlantis. This collapse was accompanied by a series of eruptions of the volcano on Thera. Ash that was spewed two and a half miles into the stratosphere has been found as far as 500 miles away. Most of what was left of the island was covered with a 150-foot-deep crust of volcanic ash and pumice. Geologists have hypothesized that the black cloud caused by the eruption darkened the sky for days and affected the atmosphere for years. The air shock waves have been estimated as being ten times greater than those that followed the explosion that shattered the island of Krakatoa. A tsunami, towering 700 feet high smashed into the fragile coasts of the kingdoms along the Aegean mainland and its islands. Everything for two miles inland was destroyed. The Minoan civilization - the first to use writing - was brought to its knees.

The second geological upheaval occurred about 300 years later (some put the two events much closer together) when the whole of the Mediterranean, including Cyprus, the Nile delta, and the coast of what was then Canaan, suffered a universal calamity that dwarfed the Thera event. There was so much pumice floating in the Mediterranean Ocean that boats could not travel for years.

These events set off a huge procession of mass migrations and invasions which wrecked the Mycenaean empires, throwing the world into a dark age within which came the dawn of consciousness.

People, in what is known as the Dorian invasions, began pouring into Ionia (the western part of Asia Minor, now known as Turkey) and then south. The coastal lands of the Levant (eastern Mediterranean) were invaded by peoples from Eastern Europe, of whom the biblical Philistines were a part. The pressure of the refugees was so great in Asia Minor that in 1200 BCE the Hittite empire collapsed, causing the Hittites to be driven down into the Levant where other refugees were seeking new lands.

Assyria, being inland, was unaffected by the upheavals in the

Mediterranean basin. It thus found itself in a position to extend its control by taking advantage of the pervasive chaos. In three great phases, warring its way westward to Egypt and northward to the Caspian Sea, incorporating all of Mesopotamia, Assyria formed a very different kind of empire from any that the world had known before.

Prior to the emergence of this maelstrom of humanity, the coastal lands of the eastern Mediterranean, also know as Canaan, had evolved into about 25 well fortified city states with a rich culture and magnificent temples. The Canaanites were soon to find themselves part of the large amorphous masses of half-nomadic people with no fixed grazing ground, a common scene all through the Middle East. This mixture of people sometimes organized into unstable tribes, while others fought over waterholes or raided more settled lands as nomadic Bedouins occasionally still do today. Some, in the desperation of hunger, bartered control over their lives for bread and seed, as described on some fifteenth century BCE tablets unearthed at Nuzi, as well as in Genesis 47: 18-26. Egypt, for example, had escaped the turmoil. Citizens in these areas thought of these roving mobs collectively as robbers and vagrants. The word for vagrants in Akkad, the language of Babylon is *khabiru,* and so these desert refugees are referred to on cuneiform tablets. And *khabiru,* softened in the desert air, becomes *hebrew.* The Hebrews were the outcome of the collapse of Canaanite society - not the reason for it. They were in all likelihood originally Canaanites.

One of the notable Assyrian rulers is Tikulti-Ninurta I. He is referred to as Nimrod in Genesis 10: 8-10 and Ninos in Greek mythology. In about 1230 BCE he had a stone carving made of him kneeling before a throne. This scene was dramatically different from anything that preceded it in the history of the world: the throne before which Tukulti-Ninurta grovels is empty. No king before him in history is ever shown kneeling. And no scene before in history ever indicates an absent god. Other altar scenes of Tukulti are similarly devoid of gods. The bicameral mind had broken down, and that sometime since Hammurabi (eighteenth century BCE).

In the beginning of Tukulti's Epic (the next clearly dated and well preserved cuneiform document of note after Hammurabi), the gods of the Babylonian cities are angry with the Babylonian king for his inattention to them. They therefore forsake their cities, leaving the citizens without divine guidance, so that the victory of Tukulti's Assyrian armies is assured. The concept of gods forsaking their human slaves is impossible in the Babylon of Hammurabi. It is something new in the world and is found throughout the last three centuries of the second millennium BCE. An example is a tablet from Tukulti's time:

> One who has no god, as he walks along the street,
>
> Headache envelops him like a garment.

These words speak to the breakdown of the bicameral mind. Another tablet from the same era reads:

> My god has forsaken me and disappeared,
>
> My goddess has failed me and keeps at a distance.
>
> The good angel who walked beside me has departed.

Why have the gods left him? He goes on to catalog the prostrations, the prayers, and the sacrifices which have failed to bring them back. Priests and omen-readers are consulted, but still

> My god has not come to the rescue in taking me by the hand,
>
> Nor has my goddess shown pity on me by being at my side.

Another set of tablets from about 900 BCE, known as *The Babylonian Theodicy,* expresses the same sentiment but in the form of a plea:

> May the gods who have thrown me off give help,
>
> May the goddess who has abandoned me show mercy.

From here to the psalms of the Hebrew Scriptures is no great journey. Consider, for example, Psalm 27: 1, 2:

> My gods, my gods, why have you forsaken me?
>
> Why are you so far from saving me,
>
> so far from the words of my groaning?
>
> O my gods, I cry out by day, but you do not answer,
>
> by night, and am not silent.

There are no more poignant words than those found at the beginning of the forty-second Psalm:

> As the stag pants after the waterbrooks,
>
> So pants my mind after you, O gods!
>
> My mind thirsts for gods! for living gods!
>
> When shall I come face to face with gods?

The dominant theme of the soon-to-arrive world religions is here sounded for the first time. Why have the gods left us? Like friends who depart from us, they must be offended. Speech, even if incomprehensible, is man's chief way of greeting others. And if the other does not reply to an initiated greeting, a bracing of oneself to receive the others' hostility will follow. Because the personal gods are silent, they must be angry and hostile. Our misfortunes are our punishments for our offenses. We go down on our knees, begging to be forgiven. And then we find redemption in some form of the return of a word from a god.

Prayers, as the central important act of divine worship, only become prominent after the gods are no longer speaking to man "face to face" as Deuteronomy 34: 10 puts it in regard to Moses. What was new in the time of Tukulti becomes everyday during the first millennium BCE. A typical prayer begins

> "O lord, the strong one, the famous one, the one who
>
> knows all, splendid one, self-renewing one, perfect one,
>
> first-begotten of Marduk. . . ."

The general form of prayer, beginning with emphatic praise of the god and ending with a personal petition, has not really changed since Mesopotamian times. The very exaltation of the god, and indeed the very idea of divine *worship,* is in contrast to the more matter-of-fact everyday relationship of god and man a thousand years earlier.

The consequences of the disappearance of auditory hallucinations from human mentality are profound and widespread, and occur on many different levels. One example is the rules and dues that the world long had known. They had a divine source and people unquestioningly obeyed them. The idea of right and wrong, however, the concepts of goodness and of redemption from sin, only begin in the context of the uneasy questioning of why the hallucinated guidances can no longer be heard.

Another issue would be confusion about authority itself. What is authority? Rulers without gods to guide them are fitful and unsure. Cruelty and oppressions would become the means by which a ruler imposed his rule upon his subjects in the absence of hallucinations. Even the king's own authority in the absence of gods becomes questionable. Rebellion in the modern sense would become possible - as would treachery and deceit, which, among other things, would evolve in the struggle for survival.

By the end of the second millennium BCE, leaders would resort to a variety of devices such as omens and divination as aids to receiving messages from the gods. Hybrid human-animal beings such as centaurs and angels now appear in mythology. They are preserved to this day in tales, epics, and legends. Their role is that of intermediaries and messengers between the vanished gods and their forlorn followers. These supposed personnel of the celestial courts are found with increasing frequency in Assyrian cylinder seals and carvings. In early instances, such angels, or genii, are seen introducing an individual to the symbol of a god, but such scenes are soon replaced by angels in a countless diversity of situations, sometimes with humans, sometimes in various struggles with other hybrid beings.

But angels are not enough to fill in the vacuum left by the retreating gods, who in any event were usually associated with the king and his lords. For the common people, whose personal gods no longer help them, a very different kind of semi-divine being now casts a terrible shadow over everyday life. Demons fill the vacuum. Natural phenomena took on the characteristics of hostility toward people. For example, the sandstorm was seen as a raging demon sweeping the desert. In addition to plague-demons, others stood ready to seize individuals in lonely places, while sleeping or eating, or particularly at childbirth. They were also responsible for all the illnesses of humankind. Even the gods could be attacked by demons, and this sometimes explained their absence from the control of human affairs.

Protection against these evil divinities - something inconceivable in the bicameral age - took many forms. Dating from early in the first millennium BCE are many thousands of prophylactic amulets to be worn around the neck or wrist. The practice is still very much alive today, especially in Roman Catholic circles where amulets of various saints can be found dangling from bracelets, on necklaces, and from the rear-view mirrors in cars.

Innumerable rituals were devoutly mumbled and mimed all over Mesopotamia throughout this millennium to counteract these malign forces. The higher gods were beseeched to intercede. Medical treatment of illnesses, aches, and pains were primarily done by means of exorcism.

In bicameral times some gods were associated with celestial bodies, the greatest being Anu who lived in the sky; the majority of them were earth-dwellers along with the people. As the earth was being seen to be left to angels and demons, the dwelling place of the now absent gods was now believed to be with Anu in the sky. This is why the forms of angels are always winged: they are messengers from the sky where the gods live. The myth of the great flood served as an explanation for the departure of the gods from earth. The Gilgamesh epic has these lines:

Even the gods were terror stricken at the deluge.

They fled and ascended to the heaven of Anu.

The celestialization of the once-earthly gods is confirmed by an important change in the building of ziggurats from the beginning of 1000 BCE. It now has no central room whatever, and the statues of the major gods are less and less the centers of elaborate ritual. The sacred tower had now become a landing stage to facilitate the gods' descent to earth from the heavens to which they had vanished. The Ziggurat of Neo-Babylon, the biblical Tower of Babel, was built in the seventh and sixth centuries BCE. It soared 300 feet high, again with seven stages, pinnacling in a brilliant blue-glazed temple for Marduk. Its very name indicates this use: *Etemenank i* - temple of the receiving platform between heaven and earth. The Tower of Babel passage (Genesis 11: 2-9) only makes sense as a rewrite of a Neo-Babylonian myth of just such a landing by Yahweh, who in the company of other gods "come down to see the city and the tower," and thereupon "confound their language that they may not understand one another's speech." This sentence may be referring to the garbling of hallucinated voices in their decline.

If these voices were no longer adequate to the escalating complexities of behavior, something needed to take over their function in order for decisions to be made. The great solution of this dilemma would be subjective consciousness, which refers to the development, on the basis of linguistic metaphors, of an operative space in which an analog "I" could think through alternative actions to their consequences. But a more primitive solution, one that predates consciousness as well as paralleling it through history, is that complex of behaviors referred to as divination.

These attempts to divine the speech of the now silent gods work out into an astonishing variety and complexity. They can be categorized into four main types: omens, sortilege, augury, and spontaneous divination.

OMEN AND OMEN TEXTS

In contrast to all other types of divination the omen is entirely passive. If someone experiences B after A, he will have a tendency to expect B to follow the next time that A occurs. It is only towards the end of the second millennium BCE that omen texts proliferate everywhere and swell out to touch almost every aspect of life imaginable. At least 30 percent of the twenty to thirty thousand tablets in the library of King Ashurbanipal (± 650 BCE) at Ninevah come under the category of omen literature. A couple of examples follow:

> If a town is set on a hill, it will not be good for the dweller within that town.
>
> If a fox runs into the public square, that town will be devastated.

Omens were the beginning of meteorology and astronomy. By the fifth century BCE the use of stars to obtain the intentions of the silent gods, who now live among them, has become our familiar horoscopes. An omen forms part of the Gospel of Matthew's portrayal of the birth of Jesus, viz. the incident of the wise men following a star.

Humankind, deprived of its gods, like a child separated from its mother, is having to learn about its world in fear and trembling. Dream omens would become (as they still are) a major source of divination.

Omens, however, of whatever type, can only decide so much. One has to wait for the portent to occur. Novel situations do not wait.

SORTILEGE

Sortilege, or the casting of lots, differs from omens in that it is active and designed to provoke the gods' answers to specific questions in novel situations. It consisted of throwing marked sticks, stones, bones, or beans upon the ground, or picking one out of a group held in a bowl, or tossing such markers in the lap of a tunic until one fell out. Sometimes it was to answer yes or no, at other times to choose one out of a group of people, plots, or alternatives.

One is so used to the huge variety of games of chance, of throwing dice, roulette wheels, etc., all of them vestiges of this ancient practice of divination by lots (It is referred to 17 times in the Hebrew Scripture and 7 times in the New Testament.), that one finds it difficult to really appreciate the significance of this practice historically. The fact is that there was no concept of chance until very recent times. Therefore the idea of deciding an issue by throwing sticks or beans on the ground was an extremely momentous one for the future of humankind. For, because there was no chance, the result *had* to be caused by the gods whose intentions were being divined.

AUGURY

Augury is closer to the structure of consciousness. It was designed to divine a great deal more information from the unspeaking gods. Its earliest form, dating from about the middle of the second millennium BCE consisted of pouring oil into a bowl of water held in the lap, the movement of the oil in relation to the surface of the rim of the bowl portending the gods' intentions concerning peace, prosperity, health, or disease.

Augury in Mesopotamia always had a cultic status. It was performed by a special priest, surrounded with ritual, and preceded by a prayer to the god to reveal his intentions through the oil or whatever medium. Not only oil, but the movements of smoke rising from a censer of incense held in the lap of the diviner, or the form of hot wax dropped into water, or the patterns of dots made at random, or the shapes and patterns of ashes. The reading of tea leaves is a modern variation.

The most important type of augury during the first millennium BCE was extispicy - divining from the entrails of sacrificed animals. The idea of sacrifice itself originated in the feeding of the hallucinogenic idols. With the breakdown of the bicameral mind, the idols lost their hallucinogenic properties and became mere statues, but the feeding ceremonies now addressed to absent gods remained in the various ceremonies as sacrifices. The gods were now seen to be "writing" their message upon the entrails of the animal. The priest investigated, in traditional sequence, the animal's organs, looking for deviations from the normal state, shape, and coloring. Any atrophy, hypertrophy, displacement, special markings, or other abnormalities, particularly of the liver, was a divine message metaphorically related to divine action.

SPONTANEOUS DIVINATION

Spontaneous divination differs from the three preceding types only by being unconstrained and free from any particular medium. The gods recede into special people called prophets or oracles. Thus bicamerality becomes perpetuated in these certain persons. The prophets pertain mainly to the Hebrews, for whom they are very important, and the oracles to the Greeks. There is, however, reference to Assyrian oracles dating from the seventh century BCE.

These four types of divination - omens, sortilege, augury, and spontaneous divination, are successively closer and closer proximations to the structure of consciousness. They became the crucial aids to decision making only after the breakdown of the bicameral mind.

The story of the Hebrews has come down to us in their scriptures, usually referred to by non-Jews as the Old Testament. Jayne's thesis regarding the Hebrews to which he gives his attention is that this magnificent collection of history and harangue of song, sermon, and story, is, in its grand overall contour, the description of the loss of the bicameral mind and its replacement by subjectivity over the span of the first millennium BCE.

It needs to be borne in mind that the books covering the early Hebrew history were written much later than the times they cover. The majority of biblical scholars now date the literary composition of the patriarchal sages (Abraham, Isaac and Jacob) to the Judean royal court circa 900 BCE. Additions continued to be made in the seventh through fifth centuries until the text reached its more-or-less final shape in the late fifth or early fourth centuries with a possible final editing as late as Hellenistic times. Major impetus was given to the process with the discovery of the manuscript of Deuteronomy in Jerusalem in 621 BCE by King Josiah, after he ordered the temple cleaned and cleared of its remaining bicameral rites. It also needs to be remembered that the stories survived initially through oral tradition.

These varied activities would explain the many contradictions found in the Pentateuch or Torah. For example, the first two chapters of Genesis give two different creation stories. In the first the animals come first and in the second humans. Did Noah take the animals into the Ark two by two or seven by seven? Was the Torah given on Mount Sinai (Exodus 19) or Mount Horeb (Deuteronomy 5)? The Ten Commandments appear in Exodus 20 and 24 and Deuteronomy 5 with 30 minor variations. The three accounts of how Isaac received his name (Genesis 17, 18, and 21) differ as to who laughed and why. One should also ask why it is that Abraham pleaded for Sodom but not for his son Isaac. It is also seriously suggested that the story of the patriarchs, or at least many of its details, are probably not historical. There are too many recurring patterns, such as encounters at wells. Truth is always stranger than fiction.

A fresh, unworshipful reading of the Pentateuch is necessary in order to appreciate the magnitude of the mental struggle that followed the breakdown of the bicameral mind. Why were these five books put together? Was it not the nostalgic anguish for the lost bicamerality of a subjectively conscious people? Is this not the essence of all religious activities? Whatever their sources, the stories themselves, as they have been arranged, reflect human psychologies from the ninth up through the fifth centuries BCE - the period of decreasing bicamerality, as consciousness developed.

The Hebrew words for God - Elohim and Yahweh - speak to this transition as well. Elohim is the plural form of a noun. It could be used collectively taking a singular verb, or as a regular plural taking the plural form of a verb. It comes from the root of "to be powerful." Thus a better translation might be "the great ones, the prominent ones, the majesties, or the judges." Elohim is a general term referring to the voice-visions of the bicameral mind. The creation story of Genesis chapter 1 is thus a rationalization of the bicameral voices at the edge of subjectivity. "In the beginning the voices created heaven and earth!"

At the particular time in history when the pentateuch was assembled there were only a few remaining elohim in contrast to the large number that probably previously existed. The most important is one recognized as Yahweh - most often translated as "He-who-is." Evidently one particular group of Hebrews who were following only the voice of He-who-is, rewrote the Elohim creation story as found in chapter 2 in a much warmer and more human way, making He-who-is the only real *elohah* (simple form of elohim). These two stories then interweave with other elements from other sources to form the Pentateuch.

Other elohim are occasionally mentioned in the early Old Testament books. The most important of them is Baal, usually translated as the Owner. He is the predominant Canaanite deity. Each village had its own version, seen as being consorts of Baal. They were known variously as Anath, Ashtoreth, Ishtar, and Astarte.

The story of the Fall can also be seen as a myth of the breakdown of the bicameral mind. The Hebrew *arum*, meaning crafty or deceitful, an assuredly conscious subjective word, is only used three or four times throughout the Hebrew Scriptures. It is here used to describe the source of temptation. The ability to deceive is one of the hallmarks of consciousness. The serpent promises that "you shall be like the elohim themselves, knowing good and evil" (Genesis 3: 5), qualities of which only subjective conscious man is capable. When these first humans had eaten of the tree of knowledge, suddenly "the eyes of them both were opened" (their analog eyes in their metaphored mind-space), "and they knew that they were naked" (3: 7), or had autoscopic vision and were seeing themselves as others see them. And so was their sorrow "greatly multiplied" (3: 16) and they were cast out from the garden where He-who-is could be seen and talked with like any other person.

In the full bicameral period there was usually a visual component to the hallucinated voice; either the god-king itself hallucinated or the statue in front of which one listened did so. The Pentateuch consistently and successively describes the loss of the visual component. In the beginning, He-who-is is a visual physical presence, the duplicate of his creation. He walks and talks in the garden, shuts the door of Noah's ark with his own hand, speaks with Abraham at Sichem, Bethel and Hebron, and scuffles all night with Jacob.

By the time of Moses the visual component becomes very different. There is only one instance described where Moses speaks with He-who-is "face to face, as a man speaks to his friend" (Exodus 33: 11). The same chapter goes on to show He-who-is beginning to distance himself from Moses. "You cannot see my face, for no one may see me and live. There is a place near me where you may stand on a rock. When my glory passes by, I will put you in a cleft in the rock and cover you with my hand until I have passed by. Then I will remove my hand and you will see my back" (Exodus 33: 20-23). There is also a group hallucination when Moses and the seventy elders all see He-who-is at a distance as the Ten Commandments are about to be carved into stone (Exodus 24). In all the other instances the hallucinated meetings are less intimate. He-who-is is a burning bush, or a cloud, or a huge pillar of fire. And as the bicameral experience visually recedes into darkness, as at Mount Sinai, one approaches the greatest teaching of the Torah, that, as this last of the Elohim loses his hallucinatory properties, and is no longer a voice in the nervous system of a few semi-bicameral men, known as prophets, he becomes something written upon tablets, he becomes law, something unchanging - approachable by one and all. He-who-is becomes something that relates to all people equally, king and shepherd, universal and transcendent. Twenty-five hundred years have passed since this pivotal milestone was reached, and yet a huge proportion of the human race has still not claimed their full humanity by assuming personal responsibility for their journey through life.

The role of writing in the breakdown of the bicameral voices is tremendously important. What had to be spoken is now silent and carved upon a stone, to be taken in visually by one and all.

The dissonance of bicameral voices in this unorganized breakdown period inaugurates the importance of signs or magical proofs as to which voice is valid. Thus Moses was constantly compelled to produce magical proofs of his mission. He hallucinated his rod into a serpent and back again, and then his healthy hand into a leprous one and back again (Exodus 4: 1-7).

In the Pentateuch the bicameral voice can be petty and petulant - "I will have mercy on whom I will have mercy" (Exodus 33: 19). It is not a question of virtue or justice. He-who-is prefers Abel to Cain, and slays Er, the firstborn of Judah, having taken a dislike to him.

After the Pentateuch, the bicameral voice retreats even further. The voices are heard less frequently and less conversationally. Joshua is more spoken to by his voice than speaking with it; and, halfway between bicamerality and subjectivity he has to draw lots to make decisions. Lots are used to decide what to do or whom to destroy, and which tribe should get which land in Canaan. Devices, referred to as the Urim and Thummim, interpreted by the priests, were likely types of lots. Astrology (Isaiah 47: 13) and hepatoscopy (Ezekiel 21: 21) also came to be practiced.

Spontaneous divination provided by prophets came to play a significant role in Hebrew life as well. The Hebrew word for prophet is *nabi*. He was someone who had visions. They are also mentioned in Egyptian writings. Sometimes these prophets were "primed" through the use of certain drugs. This was consistently part of the activities of the Greek oracles. Such preparations led to ecstatic utterings and could have involved some sort of possession. In the book of Numbers the king of Moab consults with Balaam, a nabi who communicates with He-who-is.

Groups of prophets persisted into the seventh century BCE. They were often referred to as sons of the prophets, indicating that there was probably a strong genetic basis for this type of remaining bicamerality. Edgy kings consulted with them. In 835 BCE King Ahab rounded up 400 of them (I Kings 22: 6-10). They tell him what he wants to hear, but he doubts their information. They no longer speak for He-who-is, and no more is heard of such bicameral groups.

A transition to a different type of prophet now takes place. He invariably works alone as he speaks up for social justice. After dismissing the 400 prophets, Ahab consults with just such a person, Micaiah, who proceeds to tell it like it is. The prophet Amos was in the vanguard of this group. His utterances were very much in the bicameral mode, but more and more these prophets came to express the considered subjective thought of moral teachers.

These prophets are followed by the writers of Ecclesiastes, Ezra, and Nehemiah, who seek wisdom rather than a god. They study the law instead of roaming out into the wilderness "inquiring of He-who-is." By 400 BCE bicameral prophecy is dead. Zechariah 13: 4 says, "Every prophet will be ashamed of his prophetic vision." The preceding verse says that if parents catch their children prophesying, they are to kill them on the spot. That is a severe injunction. If it was carried out, it was an evolutionary selection which helped move the gene pool of humanity toward subjectivity. This decline of prophecy is part of that much larger phenomenon going on elsewhere in the world, the loss of the bicameral mind.

Once one has read through the Hebrew Scripture from this point of view, the entire succession of works becomes majestically and wonderfully the birth pangs of our subjective consciousness. No other literature has recorded this absolutely important event at such length or with such fullness. Chinese literature jumps into subjectivity in the teaching of Confucius with little before it. Hinduism jumps from the bicameral Veda into the very subjective Upanishads. Greek literature, like a series of steppingstones from the Iliad to the Odyssey and across the broken fragments of Sappho and Solon toward Plato, is the next best record, but is still too incomplete. And Egypt is relatively silent.

While the Old Testament, even as it is hedged with great historical problems of accuracy, still remains the richest source for our knowledge of what the transition period was like. It is essentially the story of the loss of the bicameral mind, the slow retreat into silence of the remaining elohim, the confusion and tragic violence which ensue, and the search for them again in vain among its prophets, until a substitute is found in right action.

But the mind is still haunted with its old unconscious ways; it broods on lost authorities; and the yearning, the deep and hollowing yearning for divine volition and service is with us still.

> As the stag pants after the waterbrooks,
> So pants my mind after you, O gods!
> My mind thirsts for gods! for living gods!
> When shall I come face to face with gods?
> (Psalm 42: 1, 2.)

The geological upheaval on Thera that contributed to the breakdown of the bicameral mind in the near East had an even greater impact nearer to the epicenter. Among other things it triggered the Dorian invasions which started about 1200 BCE and continued for the next two hundred years. The Dorians were a group of ancient Greeks who lived in the northwestern part of the Greek mainland. The invasions consisted of complex successions of migrations and displacements as they overran most of the southern peninsula of Greece. Mycenae had been the dominant Greek city-state, being the leading political and cultural center on mainland Greece from about 1450 BCE. All that the Mycenaean world has produced with such remarkable uniformity, everywhere came to an end and was never known thereafter. This ruin formed the soil for the growth of subjective consciousness in Greece. The breakdown of the bicameral mind resulted in an ever greater dispersion as all society broke down.

It was in this setting that the aoidoi came to play an important role. They might well have been the first of the bards. They were singers of narrative folk poetry delivered in dactylic hexameter - the structure of Greek heroic poetry. As they presented their long narrative chants from refugee camp to refugee camp, the newly nomadic people eagerly reached out for these lost certainties. The poems were rafts clutched at by people drowning in inadequate minds. Jaynes believes that this unique factor - the role of poetry in a devastating social chaos - is the reason why Greek consciousness specially flourishes into that brilliant intellectual light which is still illuminating our world.

The Greek alphabet was developed at the beginning of the first millennium BCE. This made possible the first writing in human history of which a reliable translation could be made - the epic known as *The Iliad*. Scholars believe that it was developed by the aoidoi between 1230 BCE when the events of the epic occurred and about 900 BCE when it could be written down.

The Iliad is a reflection of several stages of social development from bicamerality to literacy and consciousness. Iliadic people did not have subjectivity as we do. This epic is not imaginative creative literature but rather history, the history of the Greek gods webbed into the Mycenaean Aegean. *The Iliad* stands at the great turning of the times when every kingdom until then was in essence a theocracy and every person the slave of voices heard whenever novel situations occurred.

The poem was not created as poems now are. Its first three words are *Menin aedie thea* - "Of wrath sing, O Goddess." The entire epic which follows is the song of the goddess which the entranced bards heard and then chanted in the set metrical pattern of dactylic hexameter. In this regard Friedrich Schelling writes, "The crisis through which the world and the history of the gods develop is not outside the poets; it takes place in the poets themselves, it makes their poems."[2]

The characters of *The Iliad* do not sit down and think out what to do. They have no conscious minds and no introspections. It is invariably a god who initiates or who acts and gives orders - they take the place of consciousness. The Greek god simply leads, advises, and orders. The Trojan War was directed by hallucinations. And the soldiers who were so directed (in total contrast to us) were noble automatons who knew not what they did. The individual obeyed these hallucinated voices because he could not "see" what to do by himself.

After *The Iliad, The Odyssey.* A consecutive, fresh reading of these poems makes obvious the gigantic vault in mentality between them. *The Odyssey* followed *The Iliad* by at least a century or more, and, like its predecessor, was the work of a succession of aoidoi rather than any one person. But unlike its predecessor, *The Odyssey* is not one epic but rather a series of them.

The contrast with *The Iliad* is astonishing. Both in word and deed as well as character, *The Odyssey* describes a new and different world inhabited by new and different beings. The bicameral gods of *The Iliad*, in crossing over to *The Odyssey,* have become defensive and feeble. Other Greek poetry, such as the "Homeric Hymns," while celebrating the ancient Greek gods, also now show them with emotions such as anger, envy, and deceit - traits that humans only developed with the arrival of consciousness.

Seers and omens, these hallmarks of the breakdown of bicamerality, are more common. Semi-gods, dehumanizing witches, one-eyed giants, and sirens, reminiscent of the genii that showed the breakdown of bicamerality in Assyrian bas-reliefs a few centuries earlier, are evidence of a profound alteration in mentality. And the huge Odysseyan themes of homeless wanderings, of kidnappings and enslavements, are surely echoes of the social breakdown following the Dorian invasions when subjective consciousness in Greece first made its mark.

The overall contour of the story itself is a myth that speaks to the development of humanity. It is a story of identity, of a voyage to the self that is being created in the breakdown of the bicameral mind. The whole long song is an odyssey toward subjective identity.

The Greek poets in the seventh century BCE, as a group, are something like their contemporaries, the prophets of Israel - holy teachers of men, called by kings to settle disputes, resembling in some of their functions the shamans of contemporary tribal cultures. The new poetry expresses the present, and the person in that present - the particular individual with his unique differences - and celebrates that difference. Suddenly Greece is in the modern subjective age.

The sixth century BCE was made great principally by Solon (640-558 BCE), the morning star of the Greek intellect. He, more than any other, filled out the idea of human justice. With Solon the operation of consciousness is firmly established in Greece. The divine voices have been pushed aside into special places called temples, or special persons called oracles.

And so the Greek subjective, conscious mind was born, and that out of song and poetry. It would move out into its own history, into the narratizing introspections of a Socrates, the philosophy of a Plato, the classifications and analyses of an Aristotle, and from there into Alexandrian, Hebrew, Roman, and Christian thought. And thus into the history of a world which, because of it, will never be the same again.

Bicamerality, however, as in the Middle East, did not quickly fade.

Greek oracles became the central means for making important decisions, and they continued for over a thousand years after the breakdown of the bicameral mind. Oracles were subjectivity's umbilical cord, reaching back into the sustaining unsubjective past. The most famous is that of Apollo at Delphi, which was reputed to stand at the center of the earth.

Speaking through his priestess, but always in the first person, answering king or freeman, "Apollo" commanded sites for new colonies (as he did for present-day Istanbul), decreed which nations were friends, which rulers were best, which laws to enact, the causes of plagues or famines, the best trade routes, as well as which of the proliferation of new cults, or music, or art should be recognized as being agreeable to Apollo.

Such happenings are, at best, very hard to accept. A common reaction has been that these so-called oracles were really performances manipulated by others in front of an illiterate peasantry for political or monetary ends. It is possible that there was some chicanery in the oracles' last days, such as bribery of the subsidiary priests or priestesses who interpreted what the oracle said. But in earlier times, to maintain so massive a fraud for an entire millennium in the most brilliant intellectual civilization the world had yet known is plainly impossible. Nor can it gibe with the complete absence of criticism of the oracles until the Roman period. Nor with the politically wise and often cynical Plato reverently calling Delphi "the interpreter of religion to all mankind."[3] The whole Greek world believed in the oracle and had for almost a millennium. As many as 35,000 a day would come from all parts of the Mediterranean world.

Over the thousand years there was a steady decline in the efficacy of the oracle as the collective cognitive imperative of the bicameral mind grew weaker and weaker. The oracle of Delphi endured the longest. It is striking evidence for its supreme importance to the god-nostalgic subjectivity of Greece in its golden age that it lasted so long, particularly when it is recalled that in almost every invasion it sided with the invader: with Xerxes I in the early fifth century BCE, with Phillip II in the fourth century, and even in the Peloponnesian Wars, it spoke on the side of Sparta.

By the first century CE the oracle was approaching its end, as evidenced by failures to perform. Despite this, Delphi was still consulted by the tradition-hungry, Greece-haunted Romans. The last to do so was the Emperor Julian who tried to rehabilitate Delphi in 363 CE, three years after it had been ransacked by Constantine. Through his remaining priestess, Apollo prophesied that he would never prophesy again. And the prophecy came true. The bicameral mind had come to one of its many ends.

As the age of oracles slowly died away, there appeared here and there what might be called amateur oracles, untrained and uninstitutionalized persons who spontaneously felt themselves possessed by gods. Among such were those few but unknown number of women known as Sibyls (sios = god + boule = advice). In the first century BCE at least ten were known of in the Mediterranean world. They lived in solitude, sometimes in mountain shrines that were built for them, or in subterranean caverns.

Like oracles, the Sibyls were asked to make decisions on matters high and low up to the third century CE. So laced with moral fervor were their replies that even the early Christian Fathers and Hellenistic Jews bowed to them as prophets on a level with those in the Hebrew Scriptures. The early Christian Church, in particular, used their prophecies (often forced) to buttress its own divine authenticity. Even a thousand years later, at the Vatican, four of the Sibyls were painted into prominent niches on the ceiling of the Sistine Chapel by Michaelangelo.

And even centuries later, copies of these women with their oracular books open, looked down on Unitarians in a New England Sunday school. Such is the thirst of institutions for the authoritative voice.

The thirst for divine knowledge and guidance continues unabated. For monotheists, in particular, their scriptures came to be regarded as the ultimate, eternal, and unchallengeable message from Yahweh - God - Allah. The next chapter will draw attention to some of the pervasive vestiges of the bicameral mind.

The transition from bicamerality to consciousness impacted all aspects of life including, and especially, myth. As change occurred, people became more aware of the chain of cause and effect. They came to realize that they could have an influence on their environment and circumstances and that they were distinct from the natural world. Because there was now greater reliance upon human ingenuity, people began to see themselves as independent agents. They became increasingly more conscious of their own activities as the gods became more distant. History began to impinge on mythology. As Armstrong describes it, "Urban life itself began to change mythology. . . . Increasingly the old rituals and stories failed to project people into the divine realm which had once seemed so close. People were becoming disillusioned with the old mythical vision that had nourished their ancestors."[4]

It was in these circumstances that the epic came into play. It is the most archaic form of storytelling, poetic in form, and can be likened to an encyclopedia, being a compilation of knowledge on such subjects as politics, law, ethics, science, myth, and more. Literacy being nonexistent or rare when epics first formed, the stories were transferred by oral tradition. Redaction and editing took place as various stories were pulled together, constructed, and modified over time, with the goal of explaining life in a coherent way. In so doing, the epic taught that human beings could not revert to primitive spirituality, and that the quest for gods, as if they still dwelled in their midst, represented a cultural and spiritual regression.

Epics share certain characteristics. A hero, as described in chapter two, is the heart of the story. He (it is invariably a male) is a moral paragon who represents the group that produced the epic, chosen above others, and beloved of the gods. He embarks on a journey in the quest for something of great value; divine intervention is involved in the story, resulting in a homecoming that involves the triumph of the sacred over the profane. Epics also legitimized the powers that were, and reinforced the collective identity.

The oldest known such poem is the Epic of Gilgamesh, which predates any part of the Hebrew Scriptures. Our knowledge of it, however, is only a little more than a century old, when enough clay tablets were pieced together and translated. The protagonist, Gilgamesh, was a historical figure who lived about 2700 BCE: he is listed in the records as the fifth king of Uruk in southern Mesopotamia, who later became a folk hero. The final version of the poem, influenced by the rise of consciousness, was written in about 1300 BCE.

The story/myth of Gilgamesh narrates the inherent tension between the human and the divine as the epic explores the limits and meaning of human culture. Gilgamesh learns to reflect upon his own experience without divine aid. He declares his independence from the divine, saying that it is better for gods and humans to go their separate ways. He also learns that sooner or later he will die. This is the beginning of subjectivity. The story sheds light on the theme of searching for selfhood.

The epic of Gilgamesh exerted a strong influence on the biblical tradition, parts being borrowed into it. The narrative parts of the "Tanakh" (The Jewish title for Hebrew Scripture and an acronym for

Torah (Pentateuch), Nevi'im (Prophets), and Ketuvim (Writings)) have many of the qualities of an epic. This is particularly true of the Torah where separate stories are merged together to make a unified whole. It needs to be recognized that the Tanakh is an anthology, with texts written in different times and locations to meet different needs. The collective Hebrew people could be considered to be the hero of the Tanakh.

The biblical story spans from creation (Genesis 1 and 2) to Judaism's encounter with Hellenism in the wake of Alexander the Great (Daniel), and for each setting it provides a variety of literatures. Its subjects address such diverse questions as: Who are we? What is our history? What are our standards of morality? How do we relate to those outside our community? The first book itself - Genesis - explains why there are languages, rainbows, death, why women have sexual desire, why snakes are repulsive, etc. Archaeological research indicates that the Pentateuch recalls oral traditions going back to the early Bronze Age (± 3500 BCE).

The Garden of Eden, like the rest of primeval history (Genesis 1-11), is myth - a foundational story that undergirds cultural norms and explains community identity. The specific ways each culture tells its story permits understanding of the culture's values. The tree of knowledge of good and evil is prefigured in the epic of Gilgamesh. The wife of King Utnapishtim convinces him to tell Gilgamesh about the plant of eternal life. He obtains the plant, but it is eaten by a snake while he is bathing, which prefigures the serpent in Genesis. And as Eve was tempted by a serpent, so, too, was Enkidu tempted by a temple prostitute and Gilgamesh by Ishtar.

The stories of the Patriarchs (Abraham, Isaac, and Jacob) appear to be set in the late Bronze Age (± 1750 BCE), although the accounts were written centuries later, as evidenced by several anachronisms. The

Philistines, for example, did not arrive in Palestine until about 1200 BCE, as a result of the geological cataclysms in the Mediterranean basin, and camels only became domesticated at that same time.

Type-scenes are to be found throughout the Tanakh narratives, some being continued in the New Testament. They convey information about community heroes and values, and are told less for the sake of historicity. They can, in so doing, influence the presentation of history, because "what really happened" can be conformed to the plot. Such stories are composed of a number of set motifs such as being absent from home, being aided by a helper, being attacked by an opponent, the bestowing of a mark or brand - usually indicating maturation or survival, and in the end a transfiguration. Consider, for example, Jacob: he is sent away to escape his brother and to find a wife, is helped by God, wrestles with an angel who puts his thigh out of joint, causing him to limp for the rest of his life, and finally he has his name changed to Israel.

Other type-scene conventions in the Bible are birth annunciations, infertile women becoming pregnant, and the meeting of a woman at a well. In this last convention Abraham's servant, on behalf of Isaac, meets Rebekah (Genesis 24: 10-51), Jacob meets Rachel (Genesis 29: 1-14), Moses meets Zipporah and her six sisters (Exodus 2: 15-21), Saul goes to a well - not to find a wife - but to get water for his father's donkeys (I Samuel 9: 11, 12), and Jesus goes to Jacob's well where he meets a woman and discusses marriage with her (John 4: 4-17).

5

VESTIGES OF THE BICAMERAL MIND

For those who understandably may balk at the concept of the bicameral mind, there are the many continuing and undiminishing vestiges to consider. We are now in a position where we can look back and see the history of humankind in a new way and understand some of the main features of the last three millennia as vestiges of a previous mentality. In the sweep of evolutionary history, a thousand years is an exceedingly short period of time for so fundamental a change as from bicamerality to consciousness. Even now we are still, in a sense, deep in this transition to a new mentality and all about us lie the remnants of our recent bicameral past.

The most obvious carry-overs from the previous mentality are the vehicles and structures through which contact was made and maintained with the divine. We still have, and in ever-increasing abundance, our houses of the gods - our ziggurats. In Europe especially, these institutions continue to validate one's existence by recording the births and marriages of the local populace, receiving their confessions, interceding with the gods to forgive them their sins, and, finally, burying them.

The national mottos, such as "In God we trust," and hymns of state are usually divine invocations. Kings, presidents, judges, and officers begin their tenures with oaths to the now silent deities, taken upon the writings of those who were the last to hear them. American presidential candidates would disqualify themselves if they did not end every speech with the invocation, "May God bless America!" The president, in turn, constantly repeats the phrase. The practice began in Assyria where divination came to be built into the political state as an official means to generate decisions on important matters.

While the universal characteristics of the new consciousness, such as self-reference, mind-space, and narratization, have developed swiftly in the context of the grand sweep of time, the larger contours of civilization, the huge landscape of culture against which this has happened, can only change with glacial slowness. The substance of earlier ages of civilizations has survived into our era, bringing with it the older outworn forms in which the new mentality must live.

After the collapse of the bicameral mind, the world is still in a sense governed by gods, by statements and laws carved on stelae or written on papyrus that date back to bicameral times. But the dissonance is there. Why are the gods no longer heard and seen? "My mind thirsts for gods," say the psalmists as they cry out for answers. More assurances are needed than the relics of history or the paid insistences of priests. Something palpable, something direct, something immediate! Some sensible assurance that we are not alone, that the gods are just silent, not dead, that behind all this hesitant, subjective groping about for signs of certainty there is a certainty to be had.

Thus as the slow but certain receding tide of divine voices and presences has stranded more and more people on the sands of subjective uncertainties, the variety of techniques by which humankind attempts to make contact with its lost ocean of authority becomes extended. Prophets, poets, oracles, diviners, statue cults, mediums, astrologers, inspired saints, demon possession, tarot cards, ouija boards, popes, and peyote all are the residue of bicamerality which, as it progressively narrowed down, caused uncertainties to pile upon uncertainties. When these means have ceased to be effective, humans have searched for other ways of taking up the slack between heaven and earth, such as the countless new religions and a revival of paganism.

Following the disappearance of prophets and oracles, the latter lasting for a thousand years after the rise of consciousness, as if to replace them, a revival of idols similar to those in bicameral times took place. When the bicameral voices ceased in the transition to subjective consciousness, most idols were destroyed. The Hebrew Scriptures give many accounts of the destruction of idols, as well as placing imprecations on the heads of those who made new ones. By the middle of the first millennium BCE, idolatry had become unimportant, fitfully seen here and there. With the approach of the beginning of the Common Era, the oracles now mocked into silence for the most part, a very real revival of idolatry occurred. The temples of Greece and Rome were now crammed with more and more statues of gods. By the first century CE, Paul despairingly finds Athens full of idols (Acts 17).

There is no doubt that such idols at times "spoke" to their worshippers, but not often. In Rome Nero prized a statue which warned him of conspiracies. Cyprian, Bishop of Carthage in the third century, complained of the "spirits that lurk under statues and consecrated images."[1] The whole civilized world, in this effort to recall the bicameral mind after the failure of the oracles and prophecy, was filled with epiphanies of statues of every sort and description in this remarkable revival of idolatry.

The parallel development of the almost universal belief in an absolute dualism of mind and matter made belief in idols believable at this stage. Its thesis is that mind, or soul, or spirit, or consciousness, was a thing imposed from heaven on the bodily matter to give it life. (All emerging religions would believe this way.) If a soul could be imposed on so fragile a thing as flesh to make it live, how much more possible for life, divine life, to be imposed by heaven upon a statue consisting of unwrinkled marble or imperishable gold?

The evidence for all this would be much more obvious today had not Constantine, in the fourth century CE, sent his armies of Christian converts out with hammers to smash all idols. Every god is a jealous god after the breakdown of the bicameral mind. Yet idolatry survived, so vital is it to have some kind of authorization for one's behavior.

Medieval Italy and Byzantium believed in enchanted idols which had power to avert disaster. The Knights Templar was accused of taking orders from a gold head called Baphomet. In the late Middle Ages a Bull of Pope John XXII in 1326 denounced those who by magic imprison demons in images in order to obtain answers from them. Right up to the Reformation, and contributing to its birth, monasteries and churches vied with each other to attract pilgrims (and their money) by miracle-producing statuary.

Religious institutions still, on occasion, take advantage of the thirst for tactile contact with the gods. For more than 20 years, thousands of pilgrims flocked to Christ of the Hills Monastery, in the vicinity of Blanco, Texas, to witness a painting of the Virgin Mary said to weep rose-scented tears. Eventually it was discovered that, out of public view, the tears were applied with an eyedropper. Rose water was also dripped onto cotton balls which were then sold at $3.00 each, as tears that had dripped from the painting.

The discovery was precipitated by the complaint of a 14-year-old boy that he had been sexually abused by two of the monks two years earlier. The local community had always had their doubts about the monks but did nothing because the Virgin Mary brought tourist dollars into town. The monastery had been accepted by the Russian Orthodox

Church Outside of Russia for eight years. Ties were cut when the sexual abuses came to light.[2]

One of idolatry's original functions, that of being a socially cohesive force, contributes to the survival of this practice. In a less religious arena, parks and public gardens hold effigies of past heroic leaders. On appropriate occasions gifts of wreaths are given. In churches, temples, and shrines the world over, religious statues are still being erected and prayed to. Figurines of the Queen of Heaven dangle protectively from windshields. Teenage girls living in convents often sneak down to the chapel in the dead of night and excitedly claim to "hear" the statue of the Virgin Mary speak, and "see" her lips move or sometimes her eyes weep. Idols of Jesus, Mary, and the saints throughout the Catholic world are still being bathed, dressed, incensed, flowered, jeweled, and launched shoulder-high out of bell-ringing churches on feast day outings. Placing special foods in front of them still generates excitement and a sensation of divine presence. Such devotions mostly differ from similar divine outings in bicameral Mesopotamia 4,000 years ago only in the idol's relative silence.

A phenomenon that is peculiar to areas where the Roman Catholic Church has long held sway is that of apparitions of the Virgin Mary. The Virgin of Guadalupe is probably the oldest such reported sighting outside of Europe. Legend has it that she appeared twice to a poor Indian named Juan Diego in 1531. A shrine was built in honor of the event on the outskirts of Mexico City. It holds Diego's cloak on which a picture of Mary was said to appear. The Virgin of Guadalupe has been the patron saint of all of Spanish America since 1910. When the cloak is taken on tour, people fervently, if not frenziedly, flock to look upon and kiss it.

The Virgin Mary reportedly appeared to three young sibling shepherds near Fátima in Portugal in 1917. She appeared on the thirteenth day of the month for six consecutive months, starting in May. A shrine and basilica was erected in Fátima, and in 1932 the Church authorized devotion to Our Lady of Fátima, under the title of Our Lady of the Rosary. On October 13 of each year people flock to the shrine, some making pilgrimages on their knees, and walk repeatedly around her statue in adoration.

On the thirteenth of every month, for the last 20 years, upwards of a thousand assemble at a barren site 10 miles north of California City. It is known as Our Lady of the Rock. The pilgrims claim that the Virgin Mary appears and speaks to a woman named Maria Paula Acuña. Some visitors photograph the sun, saying that they see Mary in the images, and others seek miracles or say they want to feel closer to God.

Reported sightings of the Virgin Mary are widespread. Her image has been perceived in the mist on a window, on a stained wall, on gold nuggets, pieces of chocolate, on tortillas, a piece of pizza, and even a potato chip. The effect is always the same: people flock to see it, and gaze in wonder, in the fervent belief that a long absent god has once again revealed itself to people.

One of the two most enduring sources for information from and about the gods is that which was written down and purported to be divine communication. Thus the scriptures of various religions would come to be regarded as the ultimate conveyers of the mind and will of the gods. The medium of writing, which contributed to the breakdown of the bicameral mind, would also provide a permanent, fixed record of the divine. This development pertains especially to the monotheistic religions.

The Torah, Bible, and Qur'an came to be viewed respectively by Jews, Christians, and Muslims, especially as fundamentalism set in with the passage of time, as the unchallengeable mind and will of Yahweh/God/Allah. To challenge the orthodox interpretation and application of these scriptures would be to challenge the Ultimate. They came to be seen as a verbal incarnation of "God" and thus the object of worship. The irony of course is that all three of the sacred writings forbid the worship of idols and the making of graven images.

A vital part of any synagogue service is the removal of the Torah from the ark, the centerpiece of the sanctuary, by the rabbi. He then proceeds to carry it up and down the aisles, and the worshippers reach out as if to touch it. In the past, if the synagogue was in danger of being destroyed, as so often happened, great pains would be taken to rescue the Torah, and if it were not possible to flee with it, then to carefully hide it, with the hope of retrieving it at a later date.

In Christian churches a very large open Bible is commonly on display in the front and center of the sanctuary. Some Christians will not place any other book or object on top of their copy of the Bible. At the height of the battle by conservatives to take control of the Southern Baptist Convention, its then president said in an interview, "It is not people but God's literal word that is important!" One moderately conservative church's profile of itself as preparation to find a new minister stated, "The Scriptures are the center of our life, worship, and ministry." The circular argument is often made that proof that the Bible is of ultimate value is that there are more copies of it in circulation than any other book. This ignores the reality that the Bible is so widely available precisely because it is worshipped.

Conservative Muslims, if possible, exceed Christian zeal with respect to the Qur'an. When it was reported that Iraqi prisoners, being interrogated by American officials, were taunted by flushing a Qur'an down the toilet, the Muslim world was beside itself with apoplexy and rage. Two Afghanis were sent to prison for 20 years for publishing a translation of the Qur'an into an Afghan language. They had not put the original Arabic alongside and thus had modified the Qur'an, a crime punishable by death. Muslims regard the Arabic Qur'an as words given directly by Allah. A translation is not considered to be the Qur'an itself, and it is believed that a mistranslation could warp God's word.[3]

There is a Code of Hammurabi syndrome to be found in America today. This code - the judgments of a Mesopotamian god - was the first graphic presentation of such words. Despite having been forbidden by the highest courts in the land, attempts continue to be made to put the Ten Commandments on display in public places. This, despite the fact that only two and a half of them are part of American law. The chief judge in Alabama had the Ten Commandments carved into the side of a block of granite, which was then set up in front of the Alabama Supreme Court. This action blithely ignored the second commandment which forbids the making of any graven images. When ordered by a federal court to remove this item, the judge defied the ruling, losing his job in the process. Many showed up to protest the day the display was removed. An unforgettable image was that of a man on his knees wailing, "Leave our God alone," as it was being wheeled away. The Christian God has been reduced to a block of granite.

An enterprising idolator bought the display and placed it on a truck so that it could be taken to various places where people can gather to gaze and worship, even though the latter aspect would be vigorously denied.

There are some vestiges of the bicameral era that are not necessarily part of spiritual/religious activities. The most prominent of these is that of schizophrenia itself. Most of us spontaneously and sporadically slip back into something approaching the actual bicameral mind. As stated earlier, roughly one-third of normal people at some time or other hear hallucinated voices. "Hearing voices" is universal throughout all cultures. Jaynes believes that there is some usually suppressed structure of the brain that is activated in the stress of illness. Then there are those with overactive dopamine systems, or who lack an enzyme to easily break down the biochemical products of continued stress into excretable form, resulting in an even more harrowing experience.

One percent of the human population suffers from schizophrenia, a serious mental condition that causes hallucinations, apathy, dulled emotion, and cognitive problems. They hear voices of impelling importance that criticize and tell them what to do. Schizophrenics are disorientated with respect to time (one can only be conscious of time if it can be arranged into spatial succession), and they seem to lose boundaries of themselves. They become unaware of their behavior, and their mental space begins to vanish. They panic, and yet the panic is not happening to them. There is no them. It is not that they have nowhere to turn; they have nowhere. And in that nowhere they are automatons, not knowing what they do. In reality they have relapsed, at least in part, into the bicameral mind. It is not uncommon for schizophrenics to keep a copy of Jaynes's book handy, to make available to those who will have any kind of sustained contact with them, so that they may better understand the person so afflicted.

It is Jaynes's thesis that some of the fundamental, most characteristic, and most commonly observed symptoms of florid unmedicated schizophrenia are uniquely consistent with the description of the bicameral mind. This is supported by research that has revealed that schizophrenics have slightly greater activity in the right hemisphere of the brain than in the normally dominant left hemisphere.

The hallucinations of schizophrenics often have a religious/spiritual authority. This is because the neurological structure responsible for these hallucinations is neurologically bound to substrates for religious/spiritual feelings - the source of spirituality in modern humans but of gods themselves in the bicameral era. The sun itself, as the world's

95

brightest light, takes on particular significance in many unmedicated patients, as it did in the theocracies of bicameral civilizations. Even as schizophrenics cannot explain themselves, so too in bicameral times this was distinctly the function of the gods. The same dynamic is there when hallucinatory echolalia, where the patient repeats back the speech of others, occurs. This is essentially the same mental organization seen in the Hebrew nabi and the Greek aoidoi as they delivered the Homeric poems.

A study of the history of mental illness supports Jaynes's position because there is no evidence of individuals being set apart as insane prior to the breakdown of the bicameral mind. Before the second millennium BCE, *everyone* was in effect schizophenic. When insanity is first referred to in the era of consciousness, it is described in unmistakable bicameral terms. In the *Phaedrus* Plato calls insanity "a divine gift, and the source of the chiefest blessings granted to men." Paranoia, the ancient term for insanity, comes from *para* + *nous,* which literally meant having another mind alongside one's own. This concept describes both the hallucinatory state of schizophrenia and of the bicameral mind. The term died linguistically with other vestiges of bicamerality during the second century CE. Schizophrenia began in history as a divine quality and only came to be regarded as an illness around 400 BCE.

Thinking in terms of evolutionary dynamics, the question as to what biological advantage did the bicameral mind once have, needs to be asked. One advantage is that of tirelessness. Schizophrenics show less fatigue than normal persons and are capable of tremendous feats of endurance. This suggests that much fatigue is a product of the subjective conscious mind, and that bicameral man, building the pyramids of Egypt, the ziggurats of Sumer, or the gigantic temples at Teotihuacan with only hand labor, could do so far more easily than could conscious self-reflective moderns.

Not only are there great similarities between schizophrenia and the bicameral mind, there are great differences as well. The relapse is only partial. The learnings that make up subjective consciousness are powerful and never totally suppressed. The schizophrenic experiences a dissonance with the normal structure of interpersonal relations, together with a lack of cultural support and explanation for the voices. He thus has inadequate guides for everyday living combined with a need to defend against a broken dam of environmental sensory stimulation that is flooding all before it. This results in a social withdrawal that is a far different thing from the totally social member of bicameral societies. The florid schizophrenic is in an opposite world to that of the god-owned laborers of Marduk or of the idols of Ur.

The modern schizophrenic is an individual in search of such a culture. But he usually retains some part of the subjective consciousness that struggles against this more primitive mental organization in which the hallucination ought to do the controlling. In effect, he is a mind bared to his environment, waiting on gods in a godless world.

One of the best known and most familiar vestiges of the bicameral mind is that of hypnotism. It is widely used as a means of entertainment and in more recent times as a therapeutic tool. A person put through the induction procedures of hypnosis can, for example, be asked to taste vinegar as champagne, to feel pleasure when jabbed by a pin, or to stare into darkness and contract the eyes' pupils to an imagined light.

The very possibility of hypnosis seems to be a denial of one's immediate ideas about conscious self-control on the one hand, and scientific ideas about personality on the other. Hypnosis can cause extra enabling because it engages the general bicameral paradigm which allows a more absolute control over behavior than is possible with consciousness. The latter is a culturally learned ability, balanced over the suppressed vestiges of an earlier more authoritarian type of behavioral control, thus it can be, in part, culturally unlearned or arrested. Learned features, such as analog "I," can, under the proper cultural imperative, be taken over by a different initiative such as hypnosis.

Subjects are informed beforehand that certain manifestations will be expected of them, that there is a collective cognitive imperative about the proceedings. The hypnotized subject will therefore exhibit the phenomena which he thinks the hypnotist expects. This imperative is strengthened by crowds. The bigger the crowd the more effective the hypnotist will be.

A variety of techniques are used in the induction procedure. They are all means to achieve a narrowing of consciousness. What is essential to the operator throughout this procedure is that he must confine the subject's attention to his own voice. Succumbing to the hypnotist may only be achieved after repeated attempts, showing that the narrowing of consciousness is partly a learned ability. Unlike the bicameral era, the hypnotized subjects do not have true auditory hallucinations. That role is taken over by the operator. But there is nevertheless the same diminution and then absence of normal consciousness. It is uncritical and illogical obedience to the operator and his expectations that is similar to the obedience of a bicameral person to a god. Instead of the authorization being a hallucinated or possessing god, it is the operator himself who is manifestly an authority figure to the subject, who otherwise could not be hypnotized.

Paralogical compliance to verbally mediated reality takes place. It is paralogic because the rules of logic (an external standard of truth and thus not the way the mind works) are put aside in order to comply with assertions about reality that are not concretely true. The subject does not recognize any peculiarities in his behavior because he cannot introspect in a normal conscious manner.

There are other contexts in which different collective cognitive imperatives can be found. A very common example is those who gather together regularly to nourish their religious beliefs. They can, for example, change themselves through prayer and its expectancies much as in post-hypnotic suggestion. It is also well recognized that belief, political or religious, or simply belief in oneself through some earlier cognitive imperative, works in wondrous ways. And just as the crowd makes the hypnotist more effective, so, too, is religious belief and feeling enhanced by crowds in churches. It is not surprising, therefore, that people who have attended church regularly since childhood are more susceptible to hypnosis than those who have had less religious involvements. Some investigators of hypnosis seek their subjects in theological schools because such students have been found to be more susceptible.

An activity that has become in recent years increasingly more widespread in Christian churches is that of glossolalia. The apostle Paul called it "speaking in tongues." It consists of fluent speech in what sounds like a strange language which the speaker himself does not understand and usually does not remember saying. It began with the early Christian Church and, where recognized, is commemorated in the festival of Pentecost, the fiftieth day after Easter (Acts 2). Paul put it on a level with prophecy (I Corinthians 14: 27, 29).

From time to time in the centuries since Paul, glossolalia, which is in reality a search for authorization after the breakdown of the bicameral mind, has had its periods of popularity. Its current emergence, not just in theologically conservative churches, but also in mainline churches (including Roman Catholic communities), has caused glossolalia to come under scientific scrutiny with some interesting results. It has been found that glossolalia *always* happens in groups and always in the context of worship services. This speaks to the strengthening of the collective cognitive imperative which is necessary for a particularly deep type of trance. There is usually an induction, such as energetic hymn singing, followed by the exhortations of a charismatic leader, such as, "If you feel your language change, don't resist it, let it happen."

The worshipper, through repeated attendance at such meetings and watching others "speak in tongues," learns to enter into a deep-trance state of diminished or absent consciousness in which he is not responsive to exteroceptive stimuli. The trance is often accompanied by shivers, sweat, and/or tears. Then the participant may somehow learn to "let it happen." And it does, loud and clear, each phrase ending in a groan. The rhythm pounds, the way epic dactyls probably did to the hearers of the aoidoi, and this quality of regular alternation of accented and unaccented syllables, so similar to that of the Homeric epics, as well as the rising and then downward intonation at the end of each phrase, does not - and this is astonishing - does not vary with the native language of the speaker. If the subject is English, Portuguese, Spanish, Indonesian, African, or Mayan, or whatever he is, the pattern of glossolalia is the same.

At the end of the activity the subject opens his eyes and slowly returns from these unconscious heights to dusty reality, remembering little of what happened. He is then told that he has been possessed by the Holy Spirit. It is the ultimate authorization since the Holy Spirit is one with the highest source of all being. God has chosen to enter the lowly subject and has articulated his speech with the subject's own tongue. The individual has briefly become a god.

While the phenomenon is not simply gibberish, it has no semantic meaning. Tapes of glossolalia played before others in the same religious group are given very inconsistent interpretations. That the metered vocalizations are similar across the cultures and languages of the speakers probably indicates that rhythmical discharges from subcortical structures are brought into play, released by the trance state of lesser cortical control.

The ability does not last. It attenuates. The more it is practiced, the more it becomes conscious, which destroys the trance. An essential ingredient of the phenomenon, at least in more educated groups where the cognitive imperative would be weaker, is the presence of a charismatic leader who first teaches the phenomenon. And if tongue speaking is to be continued at all, and the resulting euphoria makes it a devoutly wished state of mind, the relationship with the authoritative leader must be continued. It is really the ability to abandon the conscious direction of one's speech controls in the presence of an authority figure, regarded as benevolent, that is the essential condition. As one might expect, glossolalists reveal themselves by the Thematic Apperception Test as more submissive, suggestible, and dependent in the presence of authority figurines than those who cannot exhibit the phenomenon.

An activity that often occurs in religious groups that practice speaking in tongues is that of being "slain in the spirit." This is a sequence that fully fits the profile of hypnotism. The minister, invariably an authority figure, is the operator. Congregants are informed beforehand of the manifestation that will be expected of them when the operator touches them - they will be "slain in the spirit," they will fall down. Again the congregation strengthens the imperative. Thus when the minister touches those who volunteer for the experience, they promptly collapse. Attendants are ready to catch them to prevent the possibility of injury. The "slain" person has an euphoric experience, and the operator usually demonstrates a smug superior air - he is being like a god.

A phenomenon that is somewhat similar to glossolalia (possibly taking it a step further) is that of possession. The oracles of Greece are a prime example. With possession, a complete domination of the person and his speech by the god-side occurs, but which does not allow him to remember what has happened afterwards. It has occurred throughout history and still takes place today. A good case could be made that at least some of the wandering nabi of Mesopotamia, Israel, Greece, and elsewhere did not simply relay to listeners something they were hearing in hallucination, rather that the divine message was coming from the nabi's vocal apparatus without any cognition on his part during the speech or memory of it after.

The most widespread current practice of possession takes place in Brazil where over half of its population participate in the Afro-Brazilian religions. It is believed in as a source of decision by persons of all ethnic backgrounds. The largest by far is the Umbanda religion. There are 4,000 Umbanda centers in São Paulo alone. Evidence that possession is a learned mentality is very clear. Some of the centers hold regular training sessions, where the procedures include various ways of making the novice dizzy in order to teach him or her the trance state, as well as techniques similar to those used in hypnosis. In the trance state, the novice is taught how each of several possible spirits behave.

The vestiges of the bicameral mind should not be considered as isolated phenomena that simply appear in a culture and loiter around doing nothing but lean on their own antique merits. Instead, they always live at the very heart of a culture or subculture, moving out and filling up the unspoken and the unrationalized. They become indeed the irrational and unquestionable support and structural integrity of the culture. A possession religion such as the Umbanda functions as a powerful psychological support to the heterogeneous masses of its poor and uneducated and needy. It is pervaded with a feeling of empathy and support which consoles and binds together this motley of political impotents, whose urbanization and ethnic diversity has stranded them without roots.

Blind, illogical commitment to people who claim to wear a divine mantle of authority has continually taken place in the West down through the two millennia of the Common Era. A major source of this phenomenon has been the Gnostic apocalyptic writings found in the book of Revelation. The longing to be reunited with God, or the gods, makes the masses very susceptible to the claims of those who insist that they have discovered, or been given, *the meaning* of these writings and consequently can explain when and how the end will come. All three monotheistic religions believe in the arrival or return of a messiah who could be God himself or who will unite the world with God. Practitioners of these religions are thus primed to favorably receive any claims that define when and/or where such a climactic event will occur.

Most, if not all, of these "prophets" lead lives that follow a typical arc. They may start out with a genuine desire to prepare people for the ultimate event, but the power and influence they experience invariably leads to corruption and/or abuse of the followers. The dictum that Lord Acton, a staunch Catholic, made with respect to religion has always been true: "Power tends to corrupt, and absolute power corrupts absolutely." The third phrase in this quote may well be the most significant: "Great men are almost always bad men."

A classic example is that of Pope Pius IX (1792-1878). He enjoyed the longest reign in papal history - 32 years. His early acts as pope promised a liberal and popular government for the Papal States: he pardoned political prisoners, admitted laymen to the government, and promised a constitution. Eighteen years into his reign he issued the Syllabus of Errors - a collection of propositions indicating opposition to all progress and to modern civilization. Five years later (1869) he assembled what is now known as the First Vatican Council that, among other things, established the doctrine of papal infallibility. This placed the teaching authority of the pope beyond all possible dispute for Roman Catholics. He was now a god in all but name.

It hasn't required the sanction of a religious sect to arrive at a position of absolute control over others. An early example began in 1534, when a charismatic, handsome tailor and sometime actor named Jan Bockelson proclaimed himself to be the "Messiah of the Last Days" and declared the German city of Münster to be a messianic kingdom. After a silent ecstasy, which lasted three days, he announced a new constitution for the city which was given to him by God. The citizens were required to hand over their gold and silver, submit to rebaptism, and comply with a strict code of sexual morality. Bockelson later revised the code to permit the practice of polygamy in imitation of the Hebrew patriarchs and kings, taking for himself a group of young women, none older than twenty. Those who defied him were condemned to death. Bockelson, seated on a golden throne, presided over the beheadings in the public square. The local bishop raised an army from the surrounding cities, which eventually brought a brutal end to Bockelson and his cohorts. The movement only lasted a year.[4]

In the last quarter of the twentieth century alone there have been three movements that made mind-boggling headlines. A man names Jim Jones started a church in the Midwest in the mid-1950s. In the next twenty years he twice persuaded his congregation to move with him to new locations in California. After several scandals and an investigation for tax evasion, he initiated a major move to 3,800 acres of jungle leased from the government of Guyana in 1974. Jonestown had a population of over 900 by 1977. The People's Temple members believed Jones's claim that it would be a paradise. Instead, most, including children, worked six days a week for the "People's Temple Agricultural Project" in an equatorial climate. Their diet consisted of rice and beans, and copious drugs were administered with detailed records of each person's drug regimen. Jonestown residents claimed the drugs were administered to control their behavior. There was day and night enforcement of obedience to Jones by armed guards. Children received communal care, only seeing their parents briefly at night. Jones helped himself to any woman who took his fancy. Up to $65,000 in monthly welfare payments to Jonestown residents were appropriated by Jones, whose own wealth was estimated to be at least $26,000,000.

The mass suicides that would make Jonestown notorious were rehearsed during "white nights." All would be given a small glass of red liquid to drink that supposedly contained poison that would kill them within 45 minutes. When none dropped dead, Jones would then explain that they had just been through a loyalty test, but that the time was not far off when it would become necessary to end their own lives. An investigative visit by Congressman Leo Ryan precipitated the unthinkable. Children were poisoned first. The poison caused death within five minutes. A total of 909 died or were shot.

The Branch Davidians are a sect which originated from a schism in 1955. "Branch" refers to the new name of Christ. The group established a settlement outside of Waco, Texas. In 1981 Vernon Howell joined the group. He was soon allowed to teach his own message drawn from Revelation. In 1990 Howell changed his name to David Koresh, invoking the biblical Kings David and Cyrus. The Branch Davidians built a large compound called Mount Carmel and cut themselves off from the population at large. Again the followers were typical citizens, who handed over their wealth to Koresh. Men were forbidden to have sexual relations with their wives, all of whom became in effect Koresh's harem, including girls who were underage. When it was rumored that the group had stockpiled illegal weapons, the U. S. Treasury Department's Bureau of Alcohol, Tobacco and Firearms (ATF) conducted a raid. The action resulted in the deaths of four ATF agents and six Davidians after the latter refused the demands of the federal agents. The Federal Bureau of Investigation then laid siege to Mount Carmel for 51 days, at which time federal agents released tear gas into the compound. Fires later broke out and spread quickly through the buildings, killing approximately 80 Branch Davidians, 21 of whom were children. Autopsies confirmed that many of the victims, including David Koresh, had died of single gunshot wounds to the head.

There was one lone survivor. He is one of less than a dozen followers who still live on the property, none of whom blame their leader. Instead they expectantly wait for him to be resurrected.

Then there was the Heaven's Gate, founded by Marshall Applewhite and Bonnie Nettles sometime before 1975. The two claimed to have arrived via a UFO from another dimension and would return via a secretive "Process," which was taught to cult members. The group was never large. Its structure resembled that of a medieval monastic order. Group members gave up their material possessions and lived a highly ascetic lifestyle. Six of the male members voluntarily underwent castration as an extreme means of maintaining this lifestyle. What made Heaven's Gate somewhat uncommon was the sophisticated level of its members' education. The cult funded itself by offering professional website development for paying clients.

The end of Heaven's Gate coincided with the appearance of Comet Hale-Bopp in 1997. Thirty-eight members, plus Applewhite, the surviving leader, were found dead in a rented mansion in an upscale San Diego community on March 26. Applewhite convinced them that their souls would take a ride on a spaceship carrying Jesus, which they believed was hiding behind the comet.

There are innumerable other groups who are in thrall to some prophet or other but are not well known because they have not yet been instructed to die for their cause. One of the better known, because of its size, is the Unification Church. It was started by Sun Myung Moon in Korea in the 1940s and legally established in Seoul in 1954. Members are found in over 50 countries, with the majority living in South Korea and Japan. Estimates of its membership total range from 250,000 to 3,000,000. Moon moved to the United States in 1971. The Unification Church believes that Jesus appeared to Moon on his fifteenth birthday and asked him to accomplish the work left unaccomplished after his crucifixion. He is thus viewed by his followers as being in some way divine.

During the first fifteen years of the church's growth in America, most members lived in what were called "intentional communities." The majority of members' marriages were arranged by Moon personally. In recent years this rule was relaxed, with parents often helping to arrange their children's choice of spouse and church leaders suggesting matches for members. Many members consider it the ultimate test of their faith to accept a match arranged by Moon, and the church's increasingly large "marriage blessings" have attracted much notice. Moon has presided over marriages of groups of thousands, or even of tens of thousands of couples at one time. He believes that his blessing cleanses believers of original sin. Moon also vehemently denounces homosexual activity.

The Unification Church owns or is deeply involved in numerous business interests such as News World Communications, which owns the *Washington Times,* True World Foods, fishing interests, and the firearms manufacturer Kahr Arms. Moon took full-page ads in major newspapers defending Richard Nixon at the height of the Watergate scandal. He vigorously campaigned for Ronald Reagan in 1980. Church missionaries, who decided to get involved politically, had to resign from church leadership positions (at least on paper) while conducting non-church political activities. Moon claims that his order to Unification Church members to support Reagan helped him win the presidential election. Moon also allied his constellation of civic organizations with evangelical Christians such as Jerry Falwell and Tim LaHaye.

In 1982 Moon was convicted by the U. S. government for filing false federal income tax returns and conspiracy and spent 13 months in prison. In the 1990s, thousands of Japanese elderly people successfully claimed to have been defrauded of their life savings by Moon followers' spiritual sales. His church was the subject of the largest consumer fraud investigation in Japan's history in 1997. Court decisions upheld a $300,000 payment to two women coerced into donating their assets to the Unification Church.

America has produced other homegrown versions of extreme control of people. The largest by far are the Mormons - The Church of Jesus Christ of Latter-day Saints. It was founded in 1830 in upstate New York by a charismatic farm boy, Joseph Smith, Jr., the sect's "prophet, seer, and revelator." He claimed to have received divine revelations from an angel named Moroni, who had visited him and directed him to restore God's true religion on Earth - to establish the new Zion in North America. Influence from the Book of Revelation is again in evidence here.

Smith inspired a holy war passion in many of his followers, who saw him as commander-in-chief of an "army of God." It was well trained and at one time was nearly a quarter of the size of the U. S. Army. Smith was shot to death in 1844 by an anti-Mormon vigilante mob. His successor, Brigham Young, led most of the followers to Utah where he sought to establish a new "Zion." The militant aspect continued: a group of settlers passing through their territory was massacred.

One of the Mormon doctrines is typical of these movements - that of polygamy. Smith had nearly 50 wives. This practice is no longer condoned; however, a prominent aspect of splinter groups is the return to polygamy. The original sect has become increasingly like typical

Christian groups. It is still, however, very difficult to break free of Mormon control. It is today one of the fastest growing religions with approximately 13 million members.

It is clear that in all these situations the consciousness of the participants has been diminished. An element of hypnotism is at work to make possible such control of people. Running through all this beneath the surface is the human longing for contact with the divine and, therefore, the hope that this prophet or that priest will bring it to pass.

An even more pervasive pattern that only differs in degree with respect to the behavior of those caught up in these sects is that of being in thrall to the priest. "Priest" is being used here in a generic sense and refers to mufti, mullah, sheikh, pastor, father, minister, rabbi, and higher echelon figures such as bishop, cardinal, patriarch, and pope. In the bicameral era it was the priest who communicated the messages from the gods or the god-king. And as the gods were seen to withdraw with the development of consciousness, causing humanity to ceaselessly strive for continued contact with them, it was the priest who came to be prized as *the* link with the gods.

So pervasive is the tendency to be in thrall to the priest that it could well be genetic. Richard Dawkins believes this to be true for a different reason: "Natural selection builds child brains with a tendency to believe whatever their parents or tribal elders tell them."[5] Daniel Dennett argues that because of this tendency it is not surprising to find religious leaders the world over using the title of "father" in order to take advantage of the extra authority so provided.[6]

Almost from the outset of Christianity, priests were promoted as having a divine calling. At the beginning of the second century CE, Ignatius of Antioch claimed that the local bishop was appointed by God and should be viewed in this light by church members. Such promotion of the priest has not diminished with time. A senior minister in the Unitarian Universalist Association, speaking at the installation of a new minister, stressed that ministers are "called." This man did not believe in the existence of God, so one has to wonder who "calls" the minister and how. Another minister from the same association attended a committee meeting wearing a clerical collar, an extremely rare practice. When asked the reason for the ecclesiastical accoutrement, he explained that he had just come from an event where not all would have known that he was an ordained minister, and he wanted to be sure that they did, so that he would be treated accordingly.

In *A Portrait of the Artist as a Young Man,* James Joyce describes a priest's understanding of his priestly role as he urges Stephen Daedelus, a character standing in for Joyce, to join the priesthood:

> To receive that call, Stephen, is the greatest honor that the Almighty God can bestow on a man. No king or emperor on the earth has the power of the priest of God. No angel or archangel in heaven, no saint, not even the Blessed Virgin herself, has the power of the keys, the power to bind or loose from sin, the power of exorcism . . . the power, the authority to make the Great God of Heaven come down upon the altar and take the form of bread and wine.[7]

In a similar but more derogatory vein, Friedrich Nietzsche wrote about "the legacy of the priest:"

> Having sacred tasks, such as improving, saving or re-deeming mankind - carrying the deity in his bosom and being the mouthpieces of imperatives from beyond - with such a mission a man naturally stands outside all merely intellectual valuations: he himself is sanctified by such a task, he himself is a type of higher order. What

is science to the priest? he is above that! And until now
the priest has ruled! He determined the concepts of
'true' and 'untrue.'[8]

Barzun reports about the augmentation of a priest's power by means of
a profusion of vestments. "Color and cloth, shape of hat or stole, gold
or silver ornament or piping [go] with rank or occasion and [make] up
an impressive show."[9]

The pervasive pattern of deferring to, if not being subservient to,
the priest can aptly be described as being priest-struck. And when
certain religious roles and activities are seen to be the sole preserve
of the priest, then adherents find themselves to be priest-bound. It is
not just religious people who are prone to become priest-struck; even
agnostics and atheists can suffer from this affliction. One context in
which the latter rub shoulders with priests is in Unitarian-Universalist
communities. As with those victimized by the more extreme sects,
people from all walks, classes, world views, and levels of education can
be, and usually are, subservient to the priest.

An example of the prevalence of unwarranted respect for priests
is that of a well-known comedian and TV host named Bill Maher.
He is noted for his irreverence and impiety and produced and starred
in a movie called "Religulous," which mocks religion. And yet he is
unfailingly deferential towards priests who appear on his programs.
George W. Bush, the forty-third president of the United States of
America, seemed to make a point of being casual, if not truculent when
in the presence of other national leaders. This was in sharp contrast to
his meetings with the pope. After an audience with Pope Benedict XVI
on June 9, 2007, he said, "I was in awe, and it was a moving experience.
I was talking to a smart, loving man." The following year when the same
pope was visiting America and had given a speech in Washington, D.C.,
President Bush rushed up to him and gushed, "That was awesome!"

The unwarranted elevation of priests has harmful effects. One of them is expressed in Lord Acton's dictum that power tends to corrupt. Instead of the minister being there to minister to congregants, the stage is set for the misuse and abuse of them. The people in turn tend to see themselves as ecclesiastical and spiritual peasants and thus reluctant to play an active role in their own spiritual journeys. Ralph Waldo Emerson made reference to yet another problem: "I have heard it said that clergy . . . are addressed as women; that the rough, spontaneous conversation of men they do not hear, but only a mincing and diluted speech. They are often virtually disfranchised."[10] A parallel situation is when one is in proximity to a representative of the law; there is a little unease and use of caution in one's conduct. The unhelpful aspect of this for priests is that they seldom see people as they really are - they are "virtually disfranchised."

There is no logical reason to behave in such a fashion. The priest is a fellow mortal. He may have studied at a seminary, but it is usually just another graduate school. Some practical experience is often required, and there are other hurdles for the candidate to clear which vary with each denomination. If an association becomes convinced that the candidate will preserve, preach, and promote its particular peculiarities, the candidate is approved for ordination. Upon the ceremony's conclusion the now priest is obsequiously addressed as "The Reverend Mr./Ms. X."

Americans are particularly priest-struck. It is somewhat ironic that in America, a country uniquely influenced by Thomas Jefferson's hope of a "natural aristocracy" based on ability rather than privileges of high birth, would be so in thrall to the religious "elite." Jefferson himself loathed the clergy, having concluded from history that "in every country and in every age the priest has been hostile to liberty." He called the work of the priests dark magic and avowed that the church would be better off dispensing with them altogether.[11]

A sad example of this American tendency occurred in Mississippi in 1964. Three civil rights workers were lynched by a preacher-orchestrated mob. At his trial one woman caused a hung jury because she could not and would not vote a minister guilty.

An illustration of how deeply entrenched deferment to priests is can be found in the Unitarian Universalist Association. It is a religious group that developed in America and thus has always been somewhat removed from European Christian influence. Unitarianism was strongly influenced by the Transcendentalist movement which believed that religious insight was gained through the spontaneous communion of the soul with the transcendent. A central part of Unitarian philosophy is the right of private judgment in religious and spiritual matters. People are to be responsible for and authoritative about their own spiritual journeys. It is customary, however, to give the minister sole say over the pulpit as part of the legal contract. The congregation mutes itself with respect to the content and emphasis of the worship service. When it was pointed out to one church that was revising its by-laws that this practice was in direct conflict with one of the Association's seven principles, viz. "the use of the democratic process within our congregations and in society at large," a member emphatically responded, "We choose not to be democratic about this."

Practitioners of religion would be far more vibrant if they tended to the attitude of a famous American free thinker. A *New York Times* obituary about Robert Ingersoll, who died in 1899, stated that he "lacked proper reverence, and what was worse, he gloried in it, gloried in having a hollow where the bump of veneration ought to be. It has justly been said that he was 'no respecter of parsons.'"[12]

There are other activities that have their roots in the bicameral era and because of this hold a great fascination for people the world over. One of them is magic. Much of one's enjoyment of magic tricks and prestidigitation is doubtless a holdover from the desire for signs that arose when the gods were seen to be withdrawing. Some part of the individual is enjoying the thrill of recognizing the magician as a possible bicameral authority.

A great example of signs or magical proof of validity is that of Moses confronting Pharaoh (Exodus 4: 1-7). Such "signs" continue to this day. The miracles that are required as one of the criteria for sainthood in the Roman Catholic Church are of precisely the same order. A big part of the incentive to canonize prominent religious figures is to strengthen the links with the god world.

The second ubiquitous activity, and related to magic, is that of gambling and games of chance. In ancient Assyria, as in Israel, as the gods were seen to be withdrawing, a major way of knowing their mind was through the casting of lots. It needs to be remembered that there was no concept of chance in that era, and thus the casting of lots *had* to be controlled by the gods. It was a substitute means of communication with them.

There is a widespread passive acceptance of life's ups and downs that is fostered by all religions. It is a belief in providence and predestination that everything should be accepted as being preordained. It is a major aspect of Christian theology. As Don Cupitt puts it, "A great cosmic purpose runs everywhere: it is there to be consulted, to be bowed to, to be collaborated with, to be accepted."[13] And yet at the same time there is an element of hope as one attempts to compel the gods to act in one's favor. This is done, for example, through games of chance, especially through gambling, for which there is a universal attraction. Undergirding these activities is the subconscious, if not conscious, longing that the gods will reveal themselves, will smile on us.

There has been an exponential growth of gambling in America. A century ago, gambling was a national vice almost universally outlawed. As recently as 30 years ago, legal gambling was only to be found in Nevada and Atlantic City. Now casinos are to be found in 32 states, and every one of them, except Hawaii and Utah, offer some form of legal gambling. And now the internet has made gambling available to one and all right in their homes. According to a *Parade* magazine article (Sunday, May 20, 2007), Americans will have gambled away $90 billion in 2007. The take for commercial casinos alone has more than doubled since 1995 from $16 billion to $33 billion. It is a sure bet that participation in games of chance will only continue to mushroom.

With the breakdown of the bicameral mind and the accompanying rise of consciousness, the stage was set for a major metamorphosis in human understanding of, and participation in, life.

6

THE AXIAL AGE

As chapter four revealed, the period of time straddling the second and first millennia BCE saw the rise of consciousness as the bicameral mind broke down. One was no longer informed and governed by the bicameral mind, causing human reasoning to awaken. As the theocratic framework diminished, people began to exercise their own will as they themselves became the source of their volition.

The old rituals now failed to project people into the divine realm, and so their mythology came to reflect the new circumstances. The Flood myth, for example, marked a crisis in divine-human relations. According to Armstrong, the Mesopotamian version of the Flood marks the beginning of the gods' withdrawal from the world.[1]

With the emergence of consciousness the stage was set for the archetypal hero to become, in a certain sense, incarnate. A legendary hero is one who becomes the founder of something - a new age, a new source, and way of life that would bring people to a more fulfilling and mature existence. In order to found something new, the hero has to leave the old and go in quest of a germinal idea that will have the potential to bring forth that new thing. Campbell defines a hero as one who has given his or her life to something bigger than oneself. But unlike the heroes described in the epics, these flesh and blood leaders played their roles with an absence of rancor or revenge.[2]

A hero such as this came to be identified as a prophet, a seer, a sage, or as Campbell prefers - a shaman. This role is not to be confused with that of a priest who, in post-axial times, has undergone preparation so as to serve the local religious community. The latter is a functionary who executes a defined role, whereas the former is someone who has had an experience or a vision or an insight. From time to time monks and mystics have played a similar role. More often than not the prophet's role now is to bring the people back to the sage's intent or to adapt it to a new understanding or situation.

As Campbell explains, the dynamic that the shaman or seer brought forth was something that was waiting to be brought forth in everyone. The rise of consciousness had prepared the masses for something new. When, therefore, the people heard the seer's words, they responded, "Aha! This is my story. This is something that I was wanting to say but wasn't able to do so." An interaction resulted. Change began to take place.[3] In similar vein, Emerson observed, "Every revolution was first a thought in one man's mind, and when the same thought occurs to another man, it is the key to that era."[4] The seer saw that the people had crossed a major threshold, setting the stage for a new era to emerge. He became a catalyst that initiated the process. In psychological terms the sage could be described as the one who perceived what could be achieved and showed the way.[5]

Over time there have been seers who have said things that people were not ready to hear and thus were ineffective. When they do come to be appreciated and understood, it is often observed that they were ahead of their time. This was true for not a few philosophers: Friedrich Nietzsche is a prime example.

It became the business of the sage to teach people how to find and have meaning in their individual lives. He gave the clues that led to a more spiritual life. There were more than one of them to emerge with the development of consciousness. They were contemporaries, or nearly so, who made their mark in various parts of the world. It was Peter Ernst von Lasaulx, a professor of philosophy, who first drew attention to the phenomenon in 1856:

> It cannot possibly be an accident that, 600 years before Christ, Zarathustra in Persia, Gautama the Buddha in India, Confucius in China, the prophets in Israel, King Numal in Rome, and the first philosophers - the Ionians, Dorians and Eleatics - in Hellas - all made their appearances pretty well simultaneously as reformers of the national religion.[6]

Further examination of this period has made clear that these figures were the formers, rather than the reformers, of religion.

Karl Jaspers explored this observation further:

> It would seem that this axis of history is to be found in the period around 500 BCE in the spiritual process that occurred between 800 and 200 BCE. It is there that we meet with the most deepcut dividing line in history. Man as we know him today came into being. . . . In this age were born the fundamental categories within which we still think today and the beginnings of the world religions, by which human beings still live, were created.[7]

The West, from about the sixth century CE onwards has dated its calendar from the birth of Jesus Christ. It saw that year as a central point, which divided history into two separate eras. But this axis of history is only valid in Christendom. The far more significant turning point actually occurred at least half a millennium earlier. It is now referred to as the Axial Age.

The great significance of the Axial Age is enhanced by the fact that the sages appeared in some five or six areas which were geographically isolated from each other. The oldest of the world religions is Hinduism which is rooted in the Indian subcontinent. It was initially a variation of animistic primal worldviews. Its first teachings, the *Vedas*, stretch back at least to the middle of the second millennium BCE. Prior to being written down they were preserved through memorization by priests and teachers who, in turn, passed them on to the next generation. The *Upanishads* were composed starting about 800 BCE, followed by the Bhagavad-Gita, which were written in two phases - fifth century BCE and the third century CE.

Zoroaster (660-583 BCE), also known as Zarathustra, spawned Zoroastrianism in ancient Persia. Gautama Buddha (563-483 BCE) was the founder of Buddhism, which started in India. Mahavira initiated Jainism in the same land mass in the sixth century BCE. Confucius (551-479) established Confucianism in China, where Lao Tzu and Chuang Tzu gave rise to the philosophy of Taoism. There is a lack of clarity as to when it began - it could be as early as the fifth century BCE, but definitely by the third century. Taoism, as a religion, began a century later.

The various prophets of Israel began their influence in the eighth century BCE and continued for the next two centuries. The Greek philosophers began making their mark in the fifth century BCE, the more prominent being Socrates (469-398 BCE), Plato (427-337 BCE), and Aristotle (384-322 BCE). There are two geographical clusters of people that are conspicuous for their lack of sages, viz. western Mesopotamia and Egypt. It would only be at the beginning of the seventh century CE that Muhammad would emerge in the former, whereas the latter came under heavy Hellenistic influence because of Alexander the Great (356-323 BCE).

There were three other prominent prophets/philosophers who fell outside the Axial Age, but because of the "Aha!" response that they generated in so many, they fully fit the profile of the Sages. They are Jesus Christ (6 BCE-30 CE), Muhammad (570-632), and Karl Marx (1818-1883).

The sages, each in his own way, taught that a sense of the sacred had to be assiduously cultivated. None of them saw a need or role for dogma in so doing. Looking back from our dogma-dogged and rigid worldviews makes the absence of a place for dogma in sage thinking all the more conspicuous.

Hinduism is unique among the historical religions in that it has no central text, no single major deity, no governing institution, and no definitive rites of practice.[8] Because of this, Hinduism absorbed and was influenced by other religions such as Buddhism and Jainism. Perhaps because of the lack of a central text, it does not, in contrast with the monotheistic religions in particular, worship its scriptures. Hindu rituals of sacrifice came to eclipse

> the gods to whom they were offered. [They] gradually retreated from the religious consciousness, and the ritual reformers of the eighth century BCE devised a new liturgy that put the solitary individual at center stage. Henceforth people would not rely on the gods for help; they had to create an ordered world for themselves in the ritual arena. The power engendered by these ceremonies, which was known as Brahman, was experienced as so overwhelming that it was thought to be the ultimate reality that lay beyond the gods and kept the world in being.[9]

To this day such rapture occurs at religious festivals. It is called *anya manos* - the "other mind." Hinduism is noted for its belief in reincarnation. Campbell explains that it, like heaven, is a metaphor. "It suggests that you are more than you think you are. . . . Your life is much deeper and broader than you conceive it to be here."[10]

Gautama Siddhártha, born the son of a king, was shielded from suffering while growing up. His exposure to human suffering and tragedy drove him to become a Hindu sadhu, an ascetic holy man. While meditating he had a transformational visionary experience which led to a set of principles for living, known as the Eightfold Path, which promised relief from suffering. Buddhists believe that ultimate reality is the final cessation of suffering in the blowing out of the candle of desire. This in turn leads to Nirvana (bliss) or Sunyata (emptiness).

The Buddha dismissed the gods and goddesses of Hinduism's supernatural domain. In so doing he founded the first atheistic religion in that there was no deity to revere. He further proclaimed that priestly hierarchies were only beneficial to the priests themselves. Gautama compared his teachings to a raft - its function was to help one cross the river. Once across, the raft had served its purpose - there was nothing to gain by then carrying it on one's back. Practitioners of his concepts were also urged to measure all teachings against their own experiences. (Socrates would later advocate the same practice.)

In the third century BCE Buddhism became the state religion in India under Asoka's rule. He succeeded in spreading it throughout the subcontinent, also sending missionaries elsewhere. Buddhism spread to China, Japan, Korea, Tibet, Vietnam, and Burma. In some of these countries Buddha, a man in India, became a deity. Buddhism later came to be reabsorbed by Hinduism in India.

Tao means "the way" where one finds the eternal, that which is beyond speech and description. The fundamental goal of Taoism is self-transformation and has nothing to do with the quest for objective knowledge. Any wisdom gained in this process cannot be turned into dogma which is seen as being counterproductive to the spiritual journey.

As the Axial Age exerted its influence in the East, demands were made for inner reflection and self-scrutiny. Central to man's evolutionary development has been survival, which has meant looking out for oneself. In order to move beyond survival pressures and demands, a different consciousness needed to be experienced, and this could be achieved through meditation. Hinduism, Buddha, and Confucius offered a path that demanded considerable time to follow, and in so doing had to diminish the ego. They cultivated a sense of the sacred by means of yoga. Lao Zi, the author of the *Dao De Jing*, relied on exercises of concentration similar to yoga. The goal of yoga was not to make one feel better about oneself, but to take one *out* from oneself to make one feel at peace.[11]

The role and significance of the gods changed drastically in the East as well. The Buddha ignored the gods, judging them to be irrelevant to the spiritual quest for human fulfillment. The gods were marginalized and eventually faded from Buddhist terminology. Hindu seers, in their respective ways, saw the gods as ephemeral reflections of a deeper and unfathomable reality. Even in the West the gods came to be seen in a very different light. The Greek philosopher Xenophanes subjected the gods to critical examination, condemning them for their immorality and poking fun at their anthropomorphic character. In the new Athenian ritual of initiating tragedy the gods were put on trial, with audiences as the judging tribunal. The Greeks began to question if the gods were fair and just.

The prophets in Israel openly attacked the gods of the region, warning people not to go after them, because in so doing they would hurt themselves. Later they went much further by poking fun at the gods. Effigies of Baal and Marduk were ridiculed for being man made. As for their own gods the Israelites retained the Hebrew word for the gods - *elohim* (plural in form) - as a singular. There was a measure of continuity but the word came to have a new meaning - the Holy One. "For the Jews henceforth, all divine power was believed to be concentrated in one unseeable spiritual force."[12] This made "God" radically different from the gods it replaced. As the ban on graven images makes clear, this god was beyond being visualized or objectified.

The concept of an abstract, transcendent God thus was born. Transcendent, not as meant in Christian theology where God is referred to as being beyond or outside the field of nature, but as that which is beyond all concepts and categories, including those of time, space, being, and nonbeing. This "God" cannot be personified.

> One problem with Yahweh, as they used to say in the old Christian Gnostic texts, is that he forgot he was a metaphor. He thought he was a fact. And when he said, "I am God," a voice was heard to say, "You are mistaken, Samael." "Samael" means "blind god": blind to the infinite Light of which he is a local historical manifestation. This is known as the blasphemy of Jehovah - that he thought he was God. . . . As the Buddha is reported to have said (with respect to the divine): "It both is and is not; neither is, nor is not." God as the ultimate mystery of being is beyond thinking.[13]

The search for personal contact with the Ultimate affected the way the world at large was viewed. Other-worldly expectations became increasingly important, and that at the expense of this world. The focus began to shift from being nature-oriented, from ensuring the continuation of the natural order of the earth, to ensuring the ultimate salvation of the true self, but not necessarily in the afterlife. The fact is that none of the Axial Sages were much interested in this aspect. Very few of them believed in the supernatural and did not provide their followers with obligatory doctrines in this regard.

The tangible world began to lose much of its earlier sacred quality. This gave humankind a new freedom to possess and use, and with the passage of time, abuse, the earth. The physical world of place, space, and time would become devalued in various ways. The Hindus, for example, would come to see the world as illusory - it needed to be transcended. The term for this is maya. For the Buddhist, existence in this world became identified with suffering. Later on Christianity would proclaim this as a fallen world, destined for ultimate destruction. So when nature is thought of as evil, one should attempt to control it rather than live in harmony with it.

The severance from the gods of the bicameral era was no more complete and permanent than it was with the southern kingdom of Judah. When Nebuchadnezzar, king of Babylon, conquered Jerusalem in 586 BCE and destroyed the Temple, he deported many of its inhabitants to Babylon, which, being devoid of the influence of sages, was still very much in the bicameral mindset. Even though they were exposed to the towering ziggurat and the rich liturgy of the city, these things had lost their hold on the Israelites.

The effect of the Axial Age upon Greece was to see *logos* (reason) come to the fore. It operates at a different level of the mind from mythos as it seeks to "establish the truth by means of careful inquiry in a way that appeals only to the critical intelligence."[14]

The first physicists appeared in Ionia (Turkey), but the first scientist of note was Pythagoras of Samos (580-500 BCE). He envisaged what would eventually become the modern science of physics. It was only in the sixteenth and seventeenth centuries CE that his theories would flower. Then there was Leucippus of Miletus who originated the atomist theory of matter in the fifth century BCE. Aristarchus should also be mentioned for concluding in the third century BCE that we live in a helio-centric universe.

Logos, as it evolved in Greece, was more than academic in nature. It could also have an intense spiritual component.

> Plato insisted that the philosopher train his mind by the discipline of philosophy, especially mathematics, which would teach him to turn from the external world and concentrate on the inner abstract laws and forms of existence. He would then wake up to a more profound level of his own nature, to an ecstatic union with the divine.[15]

The man who triggered purely philosophical thinking was Socrates of Athens (470-399 BCE), who brought attention to man as an individual. Up until that time one only had identity as being part of a clan, a tribe, or a city-state. You were who your community was, even as a leader. Socrates said "know thyself," suggesting that there was something unique within every human being. As the Austrian philosopher Frank Bretan stated, "He tore the individual out of his historical context."[16] "Socrates gave us the discrete human psyche, in essence inventing psychology and human potential. We owe the entire notion of introspection as it is understood in the West to Socrates."[17] The West thus also came to see the importance of meditation.

Two millennia would pass before a society would figure out a way to foster and sustain the individual and yet have him live in community in a mutually beneficial way. As man began to take the initiative in his personal spiritual journey, he was limited by being in thrall to the king and his perceived divine right. Man's humanity could not be fully realized.

It took the geographical conditions of colonies weeks removed from their king on the far side of a vast ocean, resulting in the dissipation of the king's power and influence, for the colonists to resent their situation. The king's hold on them had to end. They had to be free. It is no coincidence that at the height of the Age of Reason the profound concept of government of the people, by the people, for the people, was distilled.

From the very beginning it was deeply flawed in its execution because of the continued practice of slavery, together with the lack of appreciation of the aborignials as people. It nevertheless remains the ideal to which people everywhere aspire.

Those who formulated this idea, the founding fathers of the United States of America, went a very important step further by building a wall of separation between religion and the state. And yet two hundred years later there are those Americans who insist that this ideal was inspired by the Christian God, thus making America a Christian nation. The wall of separation has come increasingly under attack as certain religious leaders unabashedly give voice to the goal of reducing America to becoming a fully fledged theocracy. This trend is not unique to America. In more and more Muslim states, Sharia, a law code distilled from the Qur'an, is becoming the law of the land. The bicameral mindset still runs very deep.

Divination continued to play a major role throughout Europe into the twentieth century. In most, if not all, states now, even though the Church continues to receive financial support from the government, it has no say in the affairs of state. And where the Church still seeks to influence, if not control, certain issues, it finds itself being increasingly ignored and defeated.

A major change brought about by the development of consciousness and the breakdown of the bicameral mind was the cessation of acting like automatons in response to the hearing of voices - of communications from the gods. Action would now take place by one's own volition. Behavioral instructions written on stelae, like Hammurabi's Code and the Ten Commandments, were no longer effective in controlling behavior.

The Hebrew prophet Samuel had already said that it would no longer be sufficient to meticulously perform the conventional rites (I Samuel 15:22). Jeremiah would later write that Elohim would put the law in people's minds and write it on their hearts (Jeremiah 31:33). People would understand what to do in a new way and they, as individuals, would be responsible for acting with justice and equity. The concepts of ethics and morality would emerge with the rise of consciousness. Chapter 12 addresses this topic.

As mentioned earlier, an essential aspect of the universal hero's profile is that of leaving the life one knows in order to find a way to bring one's people to a richer and more mature state. The sages discovered that the quest itself resulted in a better and more fulfilling life. One of the Buddha's teachings was that we are most fully ourselves when we give ourselves away. In the Gospels, Jesus is credited with saying something similar. Scholars doubt that he himself actually said such things, but it was an acknowledged truth. John 12: 24, 25 has Jesus saying, "Unless a kernel of wheat falls in the ground and dies, it remains a single seed. But if it dies it produces many seeds. The man who loves his life will lose it, while the man who hates his life in this world will keep it for eternal life." Matthew 16: 25 expresses a similar sentiment. The parable of The Sheep and the Goats (Matthew 25: 31-46) teaches that to reach out to those in great need is to commit a divine act.

Karen Armstrong found that all the sages came to a similar realization regarding the primacy of compassion. Humanity has found no greater insight. Its central dynamic is summed up in the various expressions of The Golden Rule. This was another way to assault the ego. Greed and selfishness are a major cause of personal misery. Egotism imprisoned people in an inferior version of themselves and impeded enlightenment. The disciplined practice of compassion demands the dethroning of the self from the center of one's universe and placing others there. *Ekstasis* is a Greek word meaning "stepping outside." It is not an exotic state of consciousness but rather the freedom gained by stepping outside the prison of egotism, selfishness, greed, and envy. Compassion and kindness bring one into the presence of what monotheists call God, but which is also known as nirvana, Brahmin, and the Way.[18]

Scientific study of people has led to a similar conclusion with respect to human activity. Charles Darwin, in the *Descent of Man*, described "Homo Sapiens as a socially oriented species whose survival has depended at least in part on the development of behavior that is characterized by compassion." Ludwig von Bertalanffy, the father of General Systems Theory, agreed with Darwin, concluding in his study of modern man, that "humanity's fulfillment depends on our becoming aware of the rules of life so that we can live our life to the utmost."[19]

Every year in ancient Greece, during the three-day festival of Dionysios, all Athenian citizens were required to attend the performance of a variety of tragedies. It was a course in Axial empathy. Suffering was put on stage, and the audience learned to identify with the pain of others whom they normally would have considered beyond the pale, thereby enlarging the scope of their sympathy and humanity.

The Golden Rule was first enunciated by Confucius in about 500 BCE. "Do not do to others as you would not have done to you." He taught his disciples to get into the habit of Shu - likening to oneself. They had to look into their own hearts, discover that which gave them pain, and then vigorously refrain from inflicting this suffering upon other people.

In the Buddha's version he advised his monks and lay followers to undertake meditative exercises called The Immeasurables. They had to send out positive thoughts of compassion, benevolence, and sympathy to the four corners of the earth. By practicing compassion, Buddhists would reach a release of the mind.

The Hebrew prophets insisted that ritual and practice were pointless unless the Israelites take care of the orphans and the widows. This was the segment of society that otherwise would be without protection and provision. As this message was repeated by prophets over a period of two hundred years, it became integral to Hebrew life. A major reason that the Jews survived the last two millennia of oppressions was their orientation towards providing for one another.

Rabbi Hillel, an older contemporary of Jesus, taught The Golden Rule in a particularly emphatic way. When a skeptic asked him to sum up the whole of Jewish teaching while standing on one leg, Hillel assumed the stance and replied, "That which is hateful to you, do not do to your neighbor. That is Torah; the rest is commentary; go and learn it." This is an extraordinary statement: the Rabbi did not mention any of the doctrines that seem essential to Judaism. Jesus himself taught The Golden Rule in this way: he told his disciples to love even their enemies and never to judge or retaliate. The apostle Paul would later reinforce this message by writing that people could have faith to move mountains, but if they lacked love then it was worth nothing (I Corinthians 13: 2).

Some seven hundred years later Muhammad would commit Islam to the ethic of compassion. The bedrock message of the Qur'an is an insistence that it is wrong to build up a private fortune and good to share one's wealth fairly in order to create a just and decent society where poor and vulnerable people are treated with respect. On the Last Day, the one question that Allah will ask Muslims is whether they have looked after the widows, the orphans, and the oppressed, and if they have not they cannot enter Paradise.[20]

It has already been noted that as humans changed from being hunters and gatherers through various stages to becoming city dwellers, the transition was accompanied by an evolution, a series of mutations, in mythology. Campbell has noted that

> Man, apparently, cannot maintain himself in the universe without belief in some arrangement of the general inheritance of myth. In fact, the fullness of his life would even seem to stand in a direct ratio to the depth and range, not of his rational thought, but of his local mythology.[21]

In the world at large the basic mythological worldview had been that of a universe not progressing to any end but rather

> of the endless, spontaneously self-generating cosmic cycle of Eternal Return. . . . There was never a time when time was not, nor will there be a time when time will have ceased to be; for the daily round of the sun, the waxing and waning of the moon, the cycle of the year, and the rhythm of birth, death and new-birth in the organic world, represent a principle of continuous creation that is fundamental to the nature of the universe.[22]

Not surprisingly, this worldview gave rise to a contemplative and fatalistic approach to life: nothing can be gained, either for the universe or humankind, by means of individual effort and originality. Man's first duty, therefore, is to fulfill his given role - along with all heavenly bodies and the various animal and plant species. One needed to identify with "the inhabiting essence of the whole."[23]

Life was viewed in this way from the far East through Southeast Asia, Mesopotamia, and Egypt. Certain aspects of the Greek and of the Celto-Germanic mythological systems belonged to this contemplative order of thought. It remains the basic view of much of the Orient to this day.

The dividing line between the tradition of the Eternal Return and more recent Occidental concepts runs through what is today known as Iran. The first formulation of the new mythology upon which the Occidental worldview was to be founded appeared in the reforms of one of the earliest Axial sages - the Persian prophet Zoroaster. He not only presented a fundamentally new concept of history but also challenged people as *individuals* to become *voluntarily* engaged in the furtherance of the Kingdom of God (Ahura Mazda).[24] In so doing, he introduced ethics as a function of humanity.

Zoroaster's reform broke the dreamlike spell where light and darkness were seen as alternating in an eternal dance. It radically separated them, assigning to each an ethical value,

> the light being pure and good, the darkness foul and evil. Before the creation of the world these two were apart. But the violent powers of the dark overwhelmed the light, and a cosmic battle ensued - which was, precisely, the universe. Hence the universe was to be known as a compound of wisdom and violence, light and dark, wherein good and evil were contending fiercely for the victory. Man, who being himself a part of creation, was a compound of good and evil. His privilege was to elect, voluntarily, to join the battle in the interest of the light.[25]

Zoroaster believed that he made this announcement 12,000 years following the creation of the world and that he himself would return after another 12,000-year period as the Messiah Saoshyant. This would trigger a cosmic conflagration, through which he would annihilate all darkness, utterly. All would then be light, history would come to an end, and the Kingdom of God would be realized forever.[26]

If all this sounds more than a little familiar, it is because it is. All three monotheistic religions believe in the return of a Messiah. Furthermore the phrase "Kingdom of God" or "Kingdom of Heaven" is widely used in the Gospels of Matthew, Mark, and Luke. The term was part and parcel of people's worldview at that time. Several times the Gospels tell of Jesus being asked to talk about it. The themes and schemes of a final showdown are also repeated and enlarged upon throughout the book of Revelation, which is itself currently impacting the West's worldview more than ever.

Myth and liturgy were affected on the local level by the teachings of the various sages. The prophets of Israel found the existing anthropomorphic myths to be incompatible with their Axial reform. They mocked the effigies of Baal and Marduk. When a myth no longer provides understanding of the transcendent, it ceases to be a myth. The Hebrew people gradually became estranged from the mythical worldview of their neighbors, becoming fulfilled instead with Judaism as it came into being.[27]

Greece was unique in that its Axial Age was fuelled by *logos* (reason), which, again, operates at a different level of the mind from myth. The latter requires emotional participation and/or some kind of ritual imitation. There was, however, the imitation of tragedy, a unique Greek ritual, which reenacted the ancient Greek myths. But in these procedures the gods and their actions were queried, and the myths came to be seen as out of touch with the new realities of the city-states.

Plato and Socrates played down the role of myth, believing that concepts of love, beauty, and justice could only be achieved through the reasoning powers of the mind. For all his impatience with myth, Plato allowed it an important role in the exploration of ideas that lie beyond the scope of philosophical language. There was, therefore, a contradiction in Axial Western thinking. Greek *logos* seemed to oppose mythology. Despite this tension, philosophers continued to use myth, either seeing it as the primitive forerunner of rational thought, or regarding it as indispensable to spiritual discourse and thinking.[28]

And so the Axial sages set the stage for a new and different world. The profile of humankind's spiritual journey would be unique to each geographical area, and would be a force to reckon with, even until now.

7

THE RISE OF RELIGION

Religion, as a categorizing label of people, only came about after the development of consciousness and the emergence of the Axial Sages. Spirituality, the seeking after the transcendent, did not diminish in this process. The means and methods of meeting one's spiritual needs would be shaped by the teachings of the particular sage under whose influence one fell. And this was directly related to geographic location.

People in each location developed beliefs, rituals, and a code of behavior that stemmed directly from a particular Axial prophet. These spiritual activities became an identifiable entity which could be named. In its earliest phase religion offered a structure to nourish and sustain the participant in his life's journey, rather than to provide a body of beliefs and practices. With the passage of time, religion would help shape one's social, political, and economic views as well, as it came to play a dominant and extraordinary role in people's lives. In fact one of these would be that of contributing to survival. As Jared Diamond has noted, "Shared ideology or religion helps solve the problem of how unrelated individuals are to live together without killing each other - by providing them with a bond not based on kinship."[1]

The influence of religion has gone even deeper. Many followers have been willing to set aside their natural needs and desires in devoting their entire lives to furthering the interests of their religion. In the words of Daniel C. Dennett,

> Our ability to devote our lives to something we deem more important than our own personal welfare - or our own biological imperative to have offspring - is one of the things that sets us aside from the rest of the animal world. . . . Probably more people have died in the valiant attempt to protect sacred places and texts than in the attempt to protect food stores or their own children and homes.[2]

Unlike all other creatures, humans have the ability to transcend their genetic imperatives.

Each of the religious paths that led from the Axial Age would transcend the exclusively ethnic limitations of the cultural traditions of the past. Each body of beliefs, rituals, and code of behavior was shaped by followers of a particular sage more than the local milieu, thus a religion could become disengaged from the context in which it originated and cross ethnic and even geographic boundaries. This migration of worldview was greatly aided by the fact that the Axial teachings appealed to the needs of the universal human condition.

Not all the religions possessed the penchant for expansion. Judaism, Hinduism, and Confucianism have remained more ethnic in character, more pragmatic, and almost totally passive regarding proselytizing activities, and yet Hinduism provided the context for the birth of Buddhism, and Judaism for Christianity and Islam. The latter two would become militant in their missionary zeal. And yet these offspring could not replace their parent religions.[3]

The ebb and flow of the religions would finally result in the Christian West, the Islamic Middle East, the Hindu subcontinent, and the Buddhist Orient. Buddhism started in India where it flourished at first, only to be reabsorbed by Hinduism. But it was able to establish itself alongside Confucianism and Taoism. What is now Pakistan and Bangladesh became Muslim by military conquest. In contrast, Iberia remained Christian. There were few converts so that when the Moors were driven out, so was Islam. The latter did, however, succeed in putting down roots in what is today known as Bosnia.

One notable exception of large-scale conversion from one historical religion to another has taken place in South Korea in the last century. The Korean peninsula, like China, embraced both Confucianism and Buddhism. It came under Japanese control in 1910, becoming at one stage annexed by Japan. It was under these conditions that Christianity took root, as becoming a Christian came to have a nationalistic flavor. It was a way to resist Japanese influence. When Korea became divided after World War II the Communist North crushed all religious activity. In contrast, Christianity continued to flourish in South Korea, becoming by far the most Christian nation in East Asia. Thirty percent of the population is Christian. In America, 80 percent of the people of Korean ancestry are affiliated with a Christian church.

The traditional worldview of prescientific people the world over is commonly referred to as animistic. Animism is concerned with the pervasive presence of spirits, especially those of one's ancestors, who are often worshipped. This description also applied to bicameral times as well. The advances that Axial religions with proselytizing tendencies have made have taken place primarily among animists. In the first few centuries following the Axial Age, only Buddhism was so inclined. China, Tibet, Sri Lanka, Mongolia, Japan, Indo-China, Burma, and Thailand came to embrace this religion. Geographical and travel barriers prevented further expansion. Sub-Saharan Africa, the Americas, and the Pacific Islands would only become Christian in the last two or three centuries of the second millennium CE as the West expanded its influence. Islam would claim Indonesia, the Malay peninsula, and parts of Sub-Saharan Africa as well.

A prime example of the vulnerability of the worldview of animists has taken place in Papua-New Guinea and Irian Jaya. Until sixty years ago most tribes living there were totally isolated. During World War II some groups were suddenly exposed to totally new things and people. Huge amounts of war material were dumped in their midst. The only way to explain the materials was to say that the gods had put them there. A cargo cult developed. A shaman would announce that the gods were about to deposit some cargo in a certain place. All would follow the leader with great anticipation.

Further exposure to modernity shattered the worldview of many of the tribes on this island. A common outcome was mass conversions to Christianity where entire tribes would declare themselves to be Christian. In order to make such a happening conform with Evangelical Christian theology, mission leaders explained that a series of multi-individual decisions to convert had been made. This was wishful thinking to say the least.

Hinduism takes credit for being the first historical religion, based, of course, in India. This population group had, from early times, established trade with various Southeast Asian populations such as Java, Sumatra, and Bali, which have remained Hindu, Cambodia, Burma, and Thailand. This, together with political conquests, caused Hindu culture to spread throughout this area. According to Chinese dynastic chronicles, a Hindu kingdom called Tunan, the most powerful state in the area for several centuries, was founded in Cambodia in the first century CE. It was conquered five centuries later by the Khmers, which founded the largely Hindu Angkor dynasty in the ninth century. The city of Angkor became the largest preindustrial metropolis in the world, with a population approaching one million spread over more than 115 square miles. It covered parts of what is now Laos, Thailand, and Vietnam. This achievement was made possible by a sophisticated technology for managing the water supply. The Angkor Wat temple was built in the twelfth century. It, together with a number of other temples, contains images of Buddha and figures from Hindu mythology.

Hinduism and Buddhism existed side by side, as they did in India at first. Their achievements in Southeast Asia were built on a joint inspiration. The role of Hindus in that area is similar to that of the Jews in relation to Christianity: they gave birth to Buddhism but, in the long run, did not accept it in India. According to K. M. Sen, "India's role is similar to that of Greece and Rome vis-à-vis Western culture. It provided the techniques and basis of inspiration on which a flourishing culture was developed by the native genius of south-east Asia."[4] With the migration of many people in the twentieth century, Hindu communities have been formed outside of India. Hindu temples can thus be found in such places as South Africa and America.

Buddhism was brought to China in 520 BCE by Bodhidharma where it became an authentically indigenous Tao-influenced Buddhism. It was initially called Ch'an but later was identified as Zen Buddhism - one of four major schools. It also wanted to be distinguished from Indian Buddhism, mocking the latter for the class prejudice that infused it. Zen Buddhism centers on the notion of emptiness. Bodhidharma said that the first principle is, "It is empty. No-thing is sacred." Largely due to persecution, the character of Zen Buddhism began to change in the ninth century CE. It gradually became more structured until it dissolved into the Chinese Buddhism at large. Zen Buddhism reemerged in Japan in the twelfth and thirteenth centuries, where it split into two movements - state-sponsored and independent.

Gautama Buddha, who eschewed all concepts of a divine being, came to be treated as a god, portrayed in hosts of three-dimensional images. Most show him as a plump, serene being. In real life he probably more closely matched the silhouette and mien of Mahatma Gandhi. Bagan, the former imperial capital of Myanmar (formerly known as Burma) once had more than 4,000 temples and monuments, of which 2,217 have survived to the present. They were built from the eleventh through the thirteenth centuries. One temple, Ananda, housed several twenty-foot-high golden Buddhas.

Each religion that emerged from the Axial Age has, and had, unique characteristics. From modern times the tendency is to look back and think of Judaism as beginning, if not with the Patriarchs, then definitely with Moses and the Exodus. Judaism, as it is known today, came to birth when the people of Israel no longer had a land of their own. The religion gelled during and immediately after the Babylonian Exile and came to play a vital role. The Hebrews had ceased to be a people united by a dynasty and possession of their own country. The uniqueness of Judaism is that, together with cultural tradition, it held the Jewish community together for over two thousand years. Except for a brief period under the Maccabees (142-63 BCE), Jews would not rule themselves until the establishment of modern day Israel in 1947.

It would not be long after the establishment of their faith that Jews would have to learn to do without their Temple. Even before its final destruction in 70 CE, the Temple and its priesthood began to be replaced by the synagogue, an entirely new kind of lay, non-priestly institution, and the Hebrew Scriptures. The synagogue existed for prayer, fellowship, and the celebration of their tradition. It became the prototype of both the Christian church and the Muslim mosque.

Part of the priestly functions would be taken over by the heads of households as they led each family in the Sabbath rituals. The role of rabbi emerged as well. He became the teacher and scholar of Jewish civil and religious law and later an ordained leader of Jewish congregations. Rabbinic Judaism and Christianity started at about the same time.

The Christian religion emerged directly from Judaism and was basically Jewish for its first one hundred years. Tensions grew between the two religions until Christianity would maintain a permanent hostility towards, and persecution of, Jews, which would culminate in the Holocaust starting in the mid 1930s. James Carroll estimates that but for the Christian-inspired anti-Semitism, there would be two hundred million Jews in the world today instead of approximately thirteen million now alive.[5]

The next chapter will be a survey of Christianity and Europe. A brief comment about animism in Greece needs to be made. The monumental achievements of Greek philosophy and nationalism had little local effect on primal practices. People continued their animistic rituals and practices until the sixth century CE. That was when the Emperor Justinian forcibly imposed Christianity upon the populace.[6]

Islam, the third major monotheism, started 600 years after the death of Jesus. If there was a common link, it was with Judaism rather than Christianity, and in similar fashion became both a religious and a social system. Mohammad (570-632) was the founder of Islam. He was born in Mecca and had a vision at the age of 40. He began preaching with great effectiveness and stressed belief in the one god - Allah.

Muslims (ones who submit) trace their heritage back to Ishmael and the Patriarchs. As with the Axial religions, Islam (submission) began among animists but didn't stop with them. Becoming like Christianity after Constantine, a warrior religion, Islam spread rapidly. Within a century all the Middle Eastern countries (formerly Christian, Jewish, or Parsee), Northwest India, the North African seaboard, and Iberia were incorporated into Islam. It later withstood the onslaught of the

Crusades (1069-1291). Further inroads were made into India in the eleventh century.

From Islam's beginning, Persian and Arab merchants maintained trade with India. Their knowledge of Islam went with them, finding fertile soil. Indian converts made Islam acceptable to people in the Malay Peninsula and what later became known as Indonesia. Under the Ottomans, Turkey and Constantinople became Muslim by 1453, and the Balkans soon followed as did southern Russia.

It wasn't just conquest of land and people that motivated Islam but also a voracious thirst for the knowledge offered by other cultures. The Abbasid dynasty, founded in 750, absorbed the Hellenic legacy at a time when Europe, under Charlemagne, intellectually withered. Islam, however, rejected the ideas of ancient Greece. By the thirteenth century, the Muslim lands were the richest in the world and the most sophisticated in virtually every branch of learning. They extended and developed what would come to be known as Arab and Islamic sciences. These included medicine, cartography, agronomy, linguistics, evolutionary theory, and philosophy. Many mosques engaged a full-time astronomer. A ninth-century Baghdad mathematician, Muhammad al-Khwarizmi invented algebra and developed the use of algorithms, the term itself being derived from his surname.

These lands also possessed the world's highest levels of literacy among the general population. Nearly every village had at least some men (and only men) who could read the Qur'an and interpret Muslim law. By comparison, only priests could read in Europe and India, and only government bureaucrats in China. The Muslim world was also superior in having sophisticated commerce and technology.

The Muslim world, at its best, ranked well above Christian Europe, but this would not prevent it from declining as it followed the cycle of all previous civilizations. Genghis Khan and the Mongols began the process. He started his military exploits in 1206. As his power steadily grew, the Muslims of modern day Kyrghystan and Kazakhstan asked for Mongol protection in 1220. During the next four decades the Mongols conquered every Muslim kingdom and city. Only the Arabian Peninsula and North Africa escaped. In the last two years of that period the Mongol army accomplished what the European Crusaders had failed to do in two centuries of sustained effort - it conquered the heart of the Arab world, viz. Baghdad and Damascus.

8

CHRISTIAN EUROPE

Jesus Christ, even though he lagged five hundred years behind the heart of the Axial Age, was an arch exemplar of its essence. Like his predecessors, he probably had little idea of the host that would come to claim him as their spiritual leader and/or inspiration.

Armstrong has succinctly summed up the uniqueness of Jesus:

> That Jesus was radically different was soon obvious to all who crossed his path. . . . He is constantly shown consorting with the wrong people, antagonizing the establishment, violating purity conventions, even belittling the sacred institution of the Temple, without which the religious life of Israel was at that point unthinkable.[1]

All this was very appealing as the Jews constantly suffered under Roman restrictions. The religious leaders, if anything, were appeasing Rome rather than sustaining Judah. He inspired hope, and his untimely death by crucifixion (along with many thousands of others) did not end his influence.

One zealous Pharisee, named Saul, at first did what he could to counter the influence of Jesus, but soon found himself won over to the cause. He was known as Paul after his conversion and became Christianity's second prophet. He came to have a post-death view of

Jesus, showing little interest in his public ministry, focusing on his death instead. Later on, orthodoxy would follow Paul, largely passing over the life and teachings of Jesus. Paul devoted his life to informing the Jews settled around the eastern end of the Mediterranean basin about Jesus.

There was no one clear understanding of, or teaching about, Christianity in the first three centuries CE. A variety of understandings of various issues flourished. The vitality of primitive Christianity was made evident in the countless ways that one could be a follower of Jesus Christ. One way, itself very divergent, was a movement known as gnosticism. The Greek word - *gnostokoi* - refers to those who understand divine matters, knowing what the gods know. Gnostics consisted of a number of rebel groups that "prized wisdom and insight; they were adept in taking earlier traditions and turning them upside down. Everything was fair game - including how one talked of the divine."[2] Jesus himself had blazed a similar trail, especially in his use of parables.

One major piece of evidence of the strong interest in the life of Jesus is the number of books, the great majority non-narrative in content, written about him and that which he promulgated. There are currently over 20 gospels, complete and incomplete, that are available, including three Jewish-Christian writings. There are at least a further ten gospel writings to which references are made. A majority of these seem to be the work of gnostics, who made major use of myth in their writings.

The Jewish-Christian rift was one of the aspects of primitive Christianity that would have long-term horrific consequences, and in so doing would reduce the religion to remaining primitive in the worst sense of the word. Both Jews and the first Christians faced many challenges in the first one hundred years that followed the death of Jesus. The Jewish revolts of 115 and 133 CE and the Roman oppression that followed them, together with Judaism's rejection of Christianity, encouraged the

Gentile believers in Jesus to distance themselves from Judaism. In this early period Christians had referenced Hebrew Scripture. A distinctly Christian canon was now needed. Marcion, an early second century Christian philosopher, slammed Judaism as a lesser religion with a lesser God. He proposed a canon consisting of the letters of Paul and the Gospel of Luke - minus the early chapters because of their connection to Judaism. Justin Martyr (100-165), a Samarian Christian apologist, reconceptualized Jesus as the "Word," referencing Hellenistic thinking. Jesus the Gallilean prophet became removed from his historical Jewish context and continues to be seen in this way, even until now.

Jewish Christians themselves began to separate from Judaism. Fasts were moved to different days, and rituals were given different meanings. The Passover, for example, became Easter. The Gospel of John, written about 100 CE, clearly reflects the intensification of intra-Jewish sectarian conflict. The loaded phrase "the Jews" appears a total of sixteen times in the first three Gospels, while in John it appears seventy-one times.

And so Christianity would come to highjack Jewish rituals and scriptures as it saw itself superseding Judaism. James Carroll shows how the Catholic mass, to this day, continues to make this claim:

> When the priest in the consecration says, "This is the cup of the New Covenant," he is pronouncing the Old Covenant superfluous. Its job, after Jesus, is to leave the sanctuary. The Jews' job is to disappear. From a Christian point of view, just by continuing to exist, the Jews dissent. Because of the threat it poses to the faith of the Church, that dissent can be defined by Christians as the core of Jewish belief, which of course continues to insult.[3]

Protestants may not be conscious of this claim, but they, too, put down Judaism every time that they celebrate Communion.

There is no clear understanding regarding the number of primitive Christians. Early Christian writers had little interest in statistics as such, and secular writers from that period barely even acknowledged the existence of Christianity in their midst. In *The Rise of Christianity* Rodney Start, the author, estimates that there were 7,500 adherents by the end of the first century CE. This nucleus would grow into a thriving movement of over 200,000 in the next century. Constantine's embrace and promotion of Christianity in the fourth century did not cause immediate further growth.

Constantine, in his total commitment to the reintegration of the divided Roman empire, used a Christian symbol to inspire his army in a crucial battle. This led to his embracing Christianity as the religion of Rome. Although his conversion took place in 312, resulting in his seeing himself as "the vice-regent of God," he was not baptized until 25 years later in the last months of his life.

Carroll calls the conversion of Constantine

> the second greatest story ever told, at least concerning
> ... Western civilization. ... When the power of empire
> became joined to the ideology of the Church . . . [it]
> became an entity so different from what had preceded
> it as to be almost unrecognizable.[4]

Christianity went from being a private apolitical movement to being the shaper of world politics. Among other things it began to retreat from its trademark radicalism. The most harmful effect, however, would be that Europe, by becoming a theocracy, would be dragged back 1500 years to the bicameral era.

Spiritual and allegorical treatment of the Bible dominated Christianity into the fourth century. There were blurred lines of mystical feeling and spiritual paradox. Orthodoxy - derived from a Greek word meaning "right thinking" - began to emerge as early as the second century. It was the first attempt to eliminate diversity. The canon formula that was hammered out at the Council of Nicea in 325 had this as its primary purpose.

Constantine summoned 250 bishops of the Church to Nicea. He himself presided over the event, and he would not let the bishops go until they produced, by voting, a formulaic statement of belief. The few bishops who would not agree were exiled. To this day millions of people regularly recite the formula known as the Nicene Creed. And thus Christian orthodoxy came to be defined.

A major negative legacy of such a development is what Carroll calls the first law of exclusion: "you can't say who is out unless you can say what it is to be in."[5] There is a proverb that says, "No heretic without a text." After Nicea, Christianity would become characterized by obedience, orderliness, conformity, and, above all, literalism. This would all be at the expense of vitality and spirituality. The foundation had been laid for the later development of fundamentalism.

The legends, myths, and traditions that had been passed on from generation to generation as they nourished and sustained Christianity until Nicea were now frozen by embedding them in the Creed. With the passage of time there would be increasing intolerance of any deviation from its declarations. The credal would come to be seen as cardinal truths that had to be believed in, in order to avoid chaos and confusion on earth and to be assured of divine acceptance after death. Islam would later follow a parallel path.

Christianity would not be forced upon the Roman Empire until Theodosius I (346-395) established it as the state religion in 391. Church officials became, at a stroke, officers of the empire. The populace was encouraged to destroy all religious property that was not for Christian ends. The vandalism involved in the destruction of the ancient pagan temples was possibly only matched by the Spaniards in Mexico. Less than a century after Theodosius's move, when the last emperor ruling from Rome was deposed, a remnant of imperial power devolved upon the most important church official in the West: viz. the Pope. And for several centuries, successive popes would maintain quasi-imperial jurisdiction over the princes and kings of Europe. By the sixth century, Christianity, a religion originally based on acceptance, would become tyrannically intolerant.

There is a tendency in Christendom to assume that the crucial doctrines of Christianity were defined and understood as ineffable truth from, or near, the beginning of the religion. It is extremely difficult to find Jesus framing a single doctrine in all that he is recorded as saying. He seems to have been consistently indifferent about Jewish religious practices, nor did he make definitive pronouncements on any of the dogmas long held to be essential to the Christian faith. Most of them, in fact, evolved centuries after his death.

The doctrines of the Incarnation and the Trinity were the product of the Council of Nicea (325). The concept of Original Sin was formulated by St. Augustine (354-430). It was he who would secure the Church's place as the indispensable agent in charge of Christian souls. He was "the dark genius of imperial Christianity, the ideology of the Church-State alliance, and the fabricator of the medieval mentality."[6]

The evolution of new doctrines also caused existing doctrines to be drastically changed. Paradise, for example, was the dominant image of early Christian churches, and it was something other than "heaven" or the afterlife. Paradise was, first and foremost, this world, permeated and blessed by the Spirit of God. Images of Paradise in the earliest churches were represented by sparkling mosaics in vivid colors. Congregants stood in a three-tiered sacred cosmos. The top tier was either a night sky or multihued clouds, representing the heavens, where celestial beings hovered. The intermediary was where the living Christ presided, accompanied by the departed saints. The lowest tier was the floor of the church where worshippers stood in God's garden on earth. Christians thought that paradise had always been here on earth. Jesus Christ had reopened the portals that had been closed by sin. The Eucharist, the giving of thanks, was a meal celebrated as the feast of life. It bound humanity to the glory of life in "this present paradise."[7]

A thousand years would pass before Christians focused on the death of Jesus. No representation of his death is found in the catacombs, in Rome's early churches, in the Basilica of Saint Apollinare in Classe, a sixth century church in Ravenna, Italy, nor in Istanbul's great sixth century cathedral Hagia Sophia. Images of Jesus's crucifixion did not appear in churches until the tenth century. They proliferated in the eleventh century, becoming increasingly grotesque. "The needs of empire - and theologies that justified, and then sanctified, violence and war - transformed Christianity and alienated Western Christians from a world they had once perceived as Paradise."[8]

In 830 a theologian named Paschasius Radbertus introduced the doctrine of transubstantiation that claims that the elements of bread and wine, when consecrated in the Mass, are changed into the body and blood of Christ. The Eucharist came to be seen as a reenactment of Christ's execution. It became heresy to deny this view. His execution came to be seen as being repeated in full-blown holy war as well. Pope Urban II launched the First Crusade in 1095. And three years later Bishop Anselm of Canterbury introduced the doctrine of the Substitutionary Atonement that taught that Christ died to pay the price of humanity's sins and thus make possible reconciliation with God. It would become the central doctrine of conservative Protestant Christianity. Humanity was now divided into the saved and the damned. With the advent of Crucifixion-centered theologies, paradise was lost, postponed to the hereafter, or secularized as a land to be conquered.[9]

Armstrong believes that these dogmas were very inventive ways of making the Christian tradition address the circumstances of the theologians' own times and that they seemed to be good for those times. But Christianity has not handled them as Buddha urged regarding the use of the raft: they helped one to get across the river, but Christians continue to carry an accumulation of them on their backs.

The next turning point in Europe after Constantine's embrace of Christianity was the fall of Rome in 410. A series of inept emperors caused Rome to implode. Alaric, a Vizigoth mercenary, led in the sacking of the city. Wave after wave of invaders occurred in the fifth century.

For a while the Roman Empire endured in the East (Constantinople), having split from the West in the third century. The East had the most resources. Rome's glory was gone. The coup-de-grace was the first of several bubonic plagues, it being the most virulent in history. Perhaps as many as one hundred million were struck down in the empire. As many as half the city dwellers were killed. In Constantinople 5,000 to 10,000 people died each day. When the city ran out of room for burials, the dead were piled on boats and taken out to sea. There were further outbreaks of the plague in the seventh and eighth centuries.

Rome's glory was gone. The "Dark Ages," a term coined by Petrarch, a fourteenth century Italian scholar, began. It would last for seven centuries. There was decline throughout the Continent as the scale of life got smaller. People now lived in shacks built of stones removed form Roman structures. Economic activity shrank as trade came to a standstill. Subsistence living was in place. Half the children died in childhood. Europe had reverted to what it had been a thousand years before. It became divided by Barbarian warlords. Pagan practices became rife. Even literacy disappeared. There were 28 public libraries by the time of Constantine's reign. All continental libraries would go out of existence in the emerging feudal systems. Even the memory of them would be erased, together with the habits of mind that encourage thought.[10]

The Irish would become mainly responsible for the rebirth of European literature and civilization, Christianity being the vehicle that made this all possible. But it would not have happened without St. Patrick.

Patricius was born into a Roman family in Britain. At the age of 16 he was captured and carried into slavery in 401, serving as a shepherd for one of the many kings that then existed in Ireland. The island had remained beyond the reach and influence of Rome and was still very much in the bicameral mode. Patrick found himself desperately isolated and sought solace in prayer, becoming something of a mystic. After six years in slavery he escaped to the Continent before making it home to Britain. Patrick was ordained a priest and bishop after entering a monastery in Gaul. He then returned to Ireland, becoming in effect the first missionary bishop.

Responding as the masses did in the Axial Age, the Irish were transformed as they embraced the teaching of their sage. "While Roman lands went from peace to chaos Ireland went even more rapidly from chaos to peace."[11] Its Christianity had the added advantage of being unencumbered by Romanization, the first such development in Christian history. Furthermore, Ireland became the only land into which Christianity was introduced without bloodshed.[12] Irish Christianity also paralleled the development of primitive Christianity in the Mediterranean basin as it came to teem with variety.

There being no population centers at that time in Ireland, the monasteries that St. Patrick established became the first cities. They became hubs of unprecedented prosperity, art, and learning. The first Irish Christians became the first Irish literates. Much copying of any and all available books took place. They devised Irish grammars and wrote down all the oral history, the first vernacular to be so preserved. This would explain why so much of Irish mythology has remained a part of their culture. Within a generation they mastered Latin and became very familiar with Greek, together with some Hebrew.

These monasteries began to draw students from Britain and the Continent. When a center of learning became too large, a group of twelve plus one would move on and establish a new one. Some were led by women. The Irish then went on to establish monasteries across Scotland and England, and then moved on to what is now France, Belgium, and Germany, making a southwesterly sweep into the Italian peninsula. The Irish monks reconnected barbarized Europe to the traditions of Christian literacy.[13]

In the sixth century a new power center would emerge at some distance west of Rome. Clovis (466-511), king of the Franks, had become a Christian, doubtless because of the influence of the Irish monks. In the context of endemic civil wars and vendettas, Christianity was the only common thread. Its message became increasingly attractive, causing many to convert. This helped Clovis to cement his power as he launched holy wars. He conquered most of what would eventually become France over a fifteen-year period. This led to an alliance with the Roman Catholic Church.

In the eighth century, the Franks found themselves challenged by an invasion from the south. The Moors, inspired by Islam, had conquered the Iberian peninsula. They penetrated into France in 730. Charles "the Hammer" Martel, leader of the Franks at that time, rose to the challenge. By means of Church funds, he formed a full-time army, driving the Moors back across the Pyrenees in 732.

Martel became the savior of Christendom in Europe. His grandson, Charlemagne, would become the first leader of the Holy Roman

Empire. It was neither Roman nor holy, but it would last for a thousand years, waxing, waning, and mutating throughout that timespan, until Napoleon ended it in 1806. Charlemagne was crowned emperor in 800 by the Pope, the Church having become the supreme authority. He was the first emperor in three centuries. Through fifty military campaigns, Charlemagne came to conquer and control most of Europe - from the North Sea to the Mediterranean. Those he conquered had to choose between embracing God or meeting him.

Charlemagne took time out from warfare to foster creativity and learning, establishing schools on a grand scale. He was a Renaissance man seven hundred years before its time. The arrival of the Vikings in his final years would provide Charlemagne with his greatest challenge. They started raiding the British Isles in 793, their favorite targets being the monasteries which were like defenseless banks. The Empire ended up having to pay the Vikings protection money. It would take until the end of the first millennium to be rid of them. Six hundred years after the fall of Rome, Europe was desperate for a new dawn.

Several different developments would contribute to a new day in Europe. Roles such as knights and troubadours, the Crusades, the warming of the climate in the eleventh and twelfth centuries, population growth, and the construction of bigger buildings, especially the cathedrals, all made their mark.

After the Viking period, Europe teamed with unemployed soldiers. Many became private armies to local counts. The English coined the term "knight" to describe French mounted soldiers who first came to England after the Norman conquest of 1066. They were at that stage merely warriors that had been equipped and trained to fight on horseback. Knights were more brigand than Sir Lancelot at this stage. There was no central law in those times. Everyone was looking out for himself, leading to great violations everywhere. The Church, in an attempt to reign them in, made the knights swear to abide by certain rules. They became cast into the role of servant, protector, and rescuer of women.

The Crusades were a series of military expeditions made by the knights of Western Europe to free the Holy Land from Muslim control. Unspeakable atrocities were often inflicted upon Jewish communities en route. The first of eight different Crusades began in 1096. They would continue in all their gore for the best part of the next two centuries. Not only did the Crusades ultimately fail in their objective, but the knights' deleterious effect upon the Byzantine Empire made it possible for the Turks to conquer Constantinople in 1453.

The Knights Templar was one of the most prominent orders involved in the Crusades. It was founded in Jerusalem in 1119 and assumed responsibility for the defense of the Holy Sepulchur and Christian pilgrims while they were in the Holy Land. The Pope took this order under his special protection. Its name stemmed from being quartered by Baldwin II, King of Jerusalem, in his palace, built on the site of Solomon's Temple. Over time the Knights Templar gained fame as one of the richest and most powerful groups in Christendom. It came to suffer false accusations by various jealous kings, causing this order to be abolished by Pope Clement V in 1312.

The death knell of the Knights as a fighting force was sounded by the Mongols. They only made one foray into Western Europe when they conquered Hungary, Germany, and Poland in 1241. Europe lost 100,000 soldiers - the core of their knights and aristocracy. The era of walled cities and the role of heavily armored knights was about to end. Knights tried even heavier armor after the development of gun powder, but it proved to be more burdensome than helpful. All that would be left would be the ceremony and the playing of war games such as jousting and tilting.

The most beneficial development of the twelfth and thirteenth centuries was a civilizing force mediated by women. They became the focus of a band of artists known as the Troubadours, a class of poet-musicians often of noble birth or knightly rank. The movement was influenced by Sufi devotional expressions and Moorish poetry and music and began in Provence in the south of France.

The impact made by the Troubadours was out of all proportion to the number of performers involved, which is estimated to be about four hundred through the two centuries that it was in play. It contributed to the Albigensian movement that would come to be seen as a threat to and by the Church. Similar Troubadour-inspired artists appeared in other parts of Europe. In Germany they were known as Minnesinge - *minne* being a medieval German word for love.

For the first time Europeans not only wrote and talked about love but also about respect for women as they became elevated to the level of men. Women in Provence came to have the right to inherit, own, and run property themselves. This development was aided by the severe loss of men due to the Crusades.

The Troubadours' love of womankind rose to the level of religious devotion. Inspired by such spiritual thinking, their fresh and unprecedented songs soon caught and seduced the ears of Europe. In later centuries it would become the stuff of theater and opera.

As Campbell observed, "One of the most important mutations of human feelings and spiritual consciousness [emerged] . . . a new way of experiencing love came into expression."[14]

> The troubadour movement was the beginning of the romantic idea of the Western individual taking matters into his/her own hands. They decided to be the author and means of their own self-fulfillment, that the realization of love is to be nature's noblest work, and that

> they were going to take their wisdom from their own experience and not from dogma, politics, or any current concepts of social good. [This is] the beginning of the romantic idea of the Western individual taking matters into his or her own hands.[15]

For the first time love was thought of as a person-to-person relationship - a natural opening of the human heart to another human being. It would become a hallmark of the West.[16]

Pairing and marriage had long been dictated by economic and political agendas. The notion of romantic love had been totally absent. The Greco-Roman myths about stormy romances between the gods and goddesses had long been neglected, gradually being supplanted by Christendom's romantically arid theology.

The emphasis on the individual was a return to one of the ideals and concepts promoted by the Sages. The beginning of individuality in Europe would be in complete contrast to everything that the Church had come to stand for. Instead of the function of the individual being that of supporting society, a radical change was set in motion that would mark the function of society to be that of cultivating the individual.

The early centuries of the second millennium CE also witnessed the construction of cathedrals. "Cathedral" is derived from the Latin noun *cathedra* - meaning a seat or chair. It refers to the presence of the bishop's or archbishop's chair or throne. It in turn symbolized his role as teacher or ruler. The seat is the preeminent church of a given diocese, which could be a city and its environs, a county, or an even larger area. By this time the church leaders had long been a variation of the god-kings of the bicameral era.

The earliest church buildings tended to be small and modest structures, the Hagia Sophia in Constantinople being a glorious exception. The architecture of the first cathedrals, appearing in the eleventh century, was based on the old oblong-shaped Roman basilica, only they were bigger and taller. Early in the twelfth century, Gothic architecture began to be preferred. The style was Germanic, but it spread throughout Europe, flourishing into the fifteenth century. These structures paralleled the Babylonian ziggurats. They are generally enormous, with large stain-glassed, story-telling windows and towers, spires, or domes to enhance their symbolism. Many such buildings took centuries to build and decorate, many artists, and countless artisans contributing to the truly monumental tasks. They displayed myth and biblical stories in pictorial form and continue to constitute a major cultural investment for the cities in which they were erected.

At their best they were seen as a representation of spiritual images that put the worshippers in touch with the essential archetypology of their spiritual journeys. As myth degenerated into dogma, the images no longer connected people to the sacred. And without this catalyst, the looming cathedral makes the worshipper feel insignificant and in thrall to the Church and its leaders - shades of the bicameral mindset.

9

Mysticism and Myth in Religion

There are several elements common to the spiritual vehicles formed by the various followers of Axial Sages. Two of the most vital are those of mysticism and myth, which are inextricably linked.

The words *mysticism* and *mystery* are related to a Greek word meaning "to close the eyes or the mouth." Both words refer to experiences that are obscure and ineffable, because they are beyond speech and relate to the inner world rather than the external. Mystics make a journey into the depths of the psyche by means of the disciplines of concentration that have been developed in all the religious traditions and have become a version of the hero's mythical quest. Because myth charts the hidden interior dimension, it is natural for mystics to describe, at times, their experiences in myths that seem inimical to the orthodoxy of their religious traditions.[1]

Within most, if not all, spiritual vehicles there are adherents who seek after and experience ecstatic and uncommon experiences. It has always been so, even in bicameral times. To this day,

> in spite of all that rationalist materialist science has
> implied since the Scientific Revolution, mankind as a
> whole has not, does not, and perhaps cannot relinquish
> his fascination with some human type of relationship

to a greater and wholly other, some *mysterium tremen-dum* with powers and intelligences beyond all left hemispheric categories, something necessarily indefinite and unclear, to be approached and felt in awe and wonder and almost speechless worship, rather than in clear conception, something that for modern religious people communicates in truths of feeling, rather than in what can be verbalized by the left hemisphere. . . .[2]

This call to a deeper, description-defying awareness of the very act of living itself is the essence of all mystic traditions.

In bicameral times, the shaman was, and still is in premodern societies, the specialist in ecstatic activities. He still can be found from the northern tip of Siberia and Alaska down through the Americas to Tierra del Fuego and around the globe. Traditionally, shamans have played the role of the priest with the major difference that his authority comes out of a psychological experience rather than a cultural ordination. The shaman is the expert in spiritual matters. He has been somewhere others have not, and he explains it to them the best way he can. Images usually have to be used, but, as Campbell says, there is more reality in an image than in a word.[3]

The whole complex of shaman activities represents what is now called mysticism and mystical experiences. Mysticism, as it is found in the monotheistic religions, is the continuation of shamanism.

All people can meditate, but not everyone can be a mystic. As with practitioners in Buddhism and Hinduism, special temperaments . . ., great discipline, and application is required, often with the aid of one-on-one training. During the First Great Awakening in New England (1734-1740), many attempted to become mystics and achieve alternative psychic states. Such attempts often led to mass hysteria and even mental illness. A similar syndrome had occurred earlier in the Puritan movement. Many had tumultuous conversion experiences which they were ill equipped to handle. As a result, a large number fell into a state of depression, and some even committed suicide.[4]

It is not clear as to which monotheistic religion was the first to develop a mystical component. The Jewish form, known as Kabbalah, has one tradition that traces its roots back to Abraham, Melchizedek, and Moses. One of the two books that form the basis of Kabbalah was written before the sixth century CE. The practice remained obscure until a small explosion in popularity occurred in thirteenth century Spain. It was revived in the sixteenth century with the deportation of Jews from Spain. The Kabbalist Isaac Luria (1543-1572) initiated what would become a mass movement that helped Jews to cope with the forced migrations. Lurianic Kabbalah spread throughout the European Jewish communities and even further afield. Two centuries later Israel ben Eliezer (1700-1760) brought about a renaissance in Judaism when he founded Hasidism in Poland. It means "the devout ones" and was a protest against authoritarian rationalism. Hasidism emphasized the ecstatic element of Judaism and had a democratizing effect by making Kabbalism accessible to the Jewish population at large. The Kabbalah Center was established in Jerusalem in 1922.

Kabbalah's goal is to give one the tools needed to achieve happiness and fulfillment and to bring "the Light of the Creator into one's life." Its teachings have been passed from master to student over many generations. At one time the movement was condemned and suppressed by Jewish religious leaders. Today Kabbalah has become popularized, even gaining many non-Jewish followers. Traditional Kabbalists say this new development is more New Age than Jewish.

The mystical element in Islam is known as Sufism. Muhammad was himself a mystic. Seventh century Muslim mystics attracted followers because of their personal saintliness. This dynamic led to

163

the establishment of formal communities called Sufiyay in the eighth century, and by the late thirteenth century Sufi orders were a notable force among Arabs and in India.

Sufism focuses on the divine qualities of love and generosity, offering a mystical interpretation of the psychological experience of love between the lover and the beloved. The Sufis' passion for the human subject of their ardor represents the intensity of their desire for union with God. Sexual love isn't about self-gratification, the goal being to lose the self, the ego, in one's passion for God. Sufism helped inspire the troubadours in Europe.

Many Sufis acknowledge the divine genesis of all religions and reject claims of superiority or exclusivity on the part of any, including Islam. A number of Sufi masters have worked within Jewish and Christian traditions. According to the *Jewish Encyclopaedia*, Kabbalah is rooted in Sufi practices. Sufism also inspired Saint Francis of Assisi (1181-1226) to promote a radically pacifist Christianity during one of Europe's most religiously inspired epochs of violence. Similarly Roger Bacon (1220-1292), an English Franciscan philosopher, influenced by meetings with Sufis, subverted the religious authority of his time by laying the groundwork for the "scientific method."

It shouldn't be surprising to learn that Sufis oppose authoritarianism. They don't acknowledge any human as an absolute spiritual authority. Rather, Sufism affirms that any person has the potential to be divinely inspired. It is not surprising therefore that Sufis would come into conflict with fundamentalist Muslim scholars. Muhammad Ibn 'Abd al-Wahhab (1703-1792), the founder of the puritanical Wahhabi movement, which has long controlled Arabia, vigorously denounced Sufism. Suppression reached a contemporary historical peak during the Ayatollah Khomeini's rule in Iran's 1978 revolution.

Christian mysticism did not become as well-defined and widespread as it did in Judaism and Islam, failing even to earn an identifying label. Some founders of monastic orders, such as Saint Francis of Assisi, were mystics. Many nuns and monks, because of their disciplined lifestyle, became mystics. They do not figure prominently in the writings about Christian developments and activities.

Probably the best known Christian mystic was Meister Eckhart (1260-1327), a German theologian. He wrote about his experiences and their implications, and, not surprisingly, his observations tended to break out of the shackles of orthodoxy. He was accused of heresy, and Pope John XXII issued a papal bull in 1327, declaring seventeen of his positions as being heretical. Eckhart's serene response was to say, "Those are wrong who take the way rather than God."

Nicholas of Cusa (1401-1464), a German philosopher, was another prominent mystic. He abhorred religious wars and wrote of the hope of seeing a universal religion emerge. He also anticipated Copernicus and Galileo in teaching that the earth is round and not the center of the universe.

Aspects of the Christian charismatic movement, viz. speaking in tongues, which began near the beginning of the twentieth century and has grown and thrived ever since, may have some of the mystical attributes. However, the motives of the participants could be at variance with mysticism's profile. The accompanying feelings of euphoria could be at least as sought after as communication with the divine.

There are vitally important commonalities to mysticism as practiced in the monotheistic religions. One of these is that they cannot be shackled by traditional dogma. It could be said that mystics have worn a badge of honor in being condemned and even persecuted by their respective religions.

They have also all tended to transcend religious and even ethnic myopias. They have in fact revived the spirit of the Axial Sages. The essence of this quality is personified in Rumi (1207-1273), also known as Mevlana, a Muslim philosopher and mystic, but by no means orthodox. His teachings advocated unlimited tolerance, positive reasoning, goodness, charity, and awareness through love. Looking with the same eye on Muslim, Jew, and Christian alike, his peaceful and tolerant teaching has appealed to people of all sects and creeds. Part of a Rumi poem says it all:

> I am neither a Muslim nor a Hindu,
>
> I am not Christian, Zoroastrian, not a Jew,
>
> I am neither East nor West
>
> I am of the divine whole.

Appendix B provides a brief synopsis of meditation practices, which are integral to mysticism in the Eastern religions as well as that found in Gnosticism. The latter was a bridge between the East and the West. These are passages taken from *Code Name God* by Mani Bhaumik.

The need for, and role of, myth did not fade with the arrival of the various religions. Humanity still needed (and continues to need) a symbolic portrayal of ultimate truth, which is the role of myth. Myth functions as a translation device that transports us from the physical three dimensional world to the realm of ultimate truth and meaning. It enables us to gain an understanding of things unseen that otherwise would remain unknown, and in this process to become spiritually nourished. But myths need to be flexible. As Campbell says, "Myths are so intimately bound to the culture, time and place that unless the symbols, the metaphors, are kept alive by constant re-creation through the arts, the life just slips away from them."[5] The emergence of the historic religions made such work a necessity.

In her book entitled *A Short History of Myth,* Karen Armstrong has sketched the role and place of myth in the various religions. In

Hinduism, history is regarded as ephemeral and illusory, and therefore unworthy of spiritual consideration. Hindus therefore feel very much at home in the archetypal world of myth. Similarly, Buddhism, a deeply psychological religion, finds mythology, an early form of psychology, quite congenial. In Confucianism, on the other hand, ritual has always been more important than mythical narratives.[6]

Because adherents of the three monotheistic religions believe that their god is active in history and can be experienced in actual events in this world, they have a somewhat ambivalent attitude towards myth. The influence of Plato and Aristotle on the Western mind has also periodically resulted in attempts to make their religions conform to the rational standards of philosophy. They have invariably returned to an appreciation of the complementarity of myth and reason (of mythos and logos).[7] In fact, monotheists are compelled to use myth.

Unless a historical event is mythologized it cannot become a source of religious inspiration. A vital part of that which defines a myth is that it is an event that, in some sense, happened once, but which also happens all the time. An occurrence needs to be liberated, as it were, from the confines of a specific period and brought into the lives of contemporary worshippers, or it will remain a unique, unrepeatable incident. Not only must the myth be freed from its historical setting, it cannot be correctly understood without a transformative ritual, which brings it into the lives and hearts of generations of worshippers. A myth calls for action.

We do not know if it actually happened that the Israelites escaped from Egypt because the story has been written as a myth. The rituals of Passover have for centuries made this story central to the spiritual lives of Jews, who are told that they must consider themselves of the generation that escaped from Egypt. The myth of the Exodus demands that Jews cultivate an appreciation of freedom as a sacred value and refuse to be enslaved or enslave others. The Seder causes it to remain a living reality.[8]

Judaism had a paradoxical attitude towards the mythology of other peoples, sometimes drawing upon foreign myths to express the Jewish vision. The book of Revelation is a prime example. Although it is part of the Christian New Testament, it is Jewish in origin. Its writers were influenced by Zoroaster's apocalyptic vision and the prevailing myths of the Roman Empire, resulting in a full inventory of ancient cosmological motifs. For most of the last two millennia, Christianity has been heavily influenced by those who have attempted to interpret and apply the myths found in Revelation in a literal way.

Christianity itself is another of the Jewish-inspired myths. Jesus and his disciples were Jewish and strongly rooted in Jewish spirituality, as was the apostle Paul, who probably more than anybody else transformed Jesus into a mythical figure. This is a classic example of a historical event becoming mythologized in order to become a source of spiritual inspiration. In this case the mythologizing process was aided and abetted by the Greco/Roman custom of declaring that an outstanding person was fathered by the appropriate Greek god. Furthermore, they take on an enduring, if not eternal, quality. The disciples of Jesus thought that he had in some sense risen from the dead. This tendency to resurrect the dead continues to the present era: for the longest time stories circulated that President Kennedy and Elvis Presley were still alive after they had died.

Paul was not much interested in the teachings of Jesus, which he rarely quotes, nor in the events of his earthly life. In a letter to his Corinthian converts, Paul wrote, "Even if we did once know Christ in the flesh, that is not how we know him now" (II Corinthians 5: 16). What was important was the "mystery" (a word which has the same etymological root as the Greek word *mythos*) of his death and resurrection. Paul had transformed Jesus into the timeless, mythical hero who dies and is raised to new life. After his crucifixion, Jesus had been exalted by God to a uniquely high mode of being (Philippians 2: 9).

Everybody who goes through the initiation of baptism enters into Jesus's death and will now share his new life. Jesus is no longer a mere historical figure but becomes a spiritual reality in the lives of Christians by means of ritual and the ethical discipline of living the same selfless life as Jesus himself. Christians could not know him "in the flesh" but would encounter him in other believers, in the study of the Scriptures, and in the Eucharist. They know that this myth is true, not because of the historical evidence, but because they had experienced transformation. Thus the death and "raising up" of Jesus is a myth: it had happened once to Jesus and was now happening all the time.[9]

Rudolf Bultmann came to see that the whole Christian worldview, presupposed in the preaching of Jesus and in the New Testament generally, as mythological: the world as being structured in three stories - heaven, earth, and hell - the intervention of supernatural powers in the course of events, miracles - especially that of the intervention of supernatural powers in the inner life of the soul, and that people can be tempted and corrupted by the devil and possessed by evil spirits. This mythological concept of the world stands in contrast to the world which has been studied and revealed by science (logos) since its inception in ancient Greece and which has been accepted since the Great Western Transformation.[10]

Many Christian terms and concepts only make sense and have meaning in a mythological framework. Seeing oneself as being "born again" is to summon the aura and essence of myth. The concept of the Trinity was a myth designed to remind Christians that they should not even attempt to think of the divine in terms of a simple personality. As Gregory, Bishop of Nyssa (335-395) explained, the three persons of the Trinity were not objective ontological facts but rather terms used to express the way in which the "unnameable and unspeakable" divine nature adapts itself to the limitations of the human mind.[11]

When the Roman Empire in the West was collapsing, Saint Augustine, bishop of Hippo in North Africa, reinterpreted the myth of Adam and Eve by developing the myth of Original Sin. Because of Adam's disobedience, God had condemned the entire human race to eternal damnation (an idea without biblical foundation). The inherited guilt was passed on to all Adam's descendents through the sexual act, which was polluted by "concupiscence," the irrational desire to take pleasure in mere creatures rather than in God. Remorse for his youthful licentious practices probably fueled Augustine's reasoning. This vision of reason dragged down by a chaos of sensations and lawless passion was disturbingly similar to the spectacle of Rome, source of rationality, law and order in the West, brought low by the barbarian tribes. Original sin became essential to the faith of orthodox Western Christianity.

The Greek Orthodox Byzantium, where Rome did not fall, have never fully endorsed this doctrine, do not believe that Jesus died to save humankind from the effects of Original Sin, and have asserted that God would have become human even if Adam had not sinned. In the view of Greek Orthodox Christians, the study of theology cannot be an exercise in rationality. Using reason to discuss the sacred is about as futile as trying to eat soup with a fork. Theology is only valid if pursued together with prayer and liturgy. The icons in Orthodox churches are pictorial myths - representing holy figures and events, they provide access to the divine. By making visible that which is invisible, icons enhance the viewers' understanding of God.[12]

Traumatic events have not only inspired the creation of new myths, they have also caused radical reinterpretations of long-standing mythical narratives. The deportation of Jews from Spain by the monarchs

Ferdinand and Isabella in 1492 led to just such a development. Many could no longer relate to the calm, orderly creation myth in the first chapter of Genesis so the Kabbalist Isaac Luria (1534-1572) told an entirely different creation story. It was one full of upheavals which resulted in a flawed creation, where everything was in the wrong place. Far from shocking the Jewish people by its unorthodox departure from the biblical story, Lurianic Kabbalah became a Jewish mass-movement. It reflected the tragic experiences of sixteenth century Jews. The myth, however, did not stand alone. Luria devised special rituals, methods of meditation, and ethical disciplines that gave life to the myth and made it a spiritual reality in the lives of Jews all over the world.[13]

Mythology has played a central role in Islam as well. The Qur'an has no problem with myth. Every single one of its verses is called an ayah - a parable. All the stories about the prophets - Adam, Noah, Abraham, Moses, or Jesus - are ayat, "parables," similitudes, because one can only speak about the divine in terms of signs and symbols. The Arabic word *qur'an* means "recitation." The scripture is not to be perused privately for information, like a secular manual, but recited in the sacred context of the mosque, and it will not reveal its full significance unless a Muslim lives according to its ethical precepts.[14]

In Islam mystics also evolved myths of separation and return to God. It was said that Muhammad had made a mystical ascent to the Throne of God from the Temple Mount in Jerusalem. This myth has become the archetype of Muslim spirituality, and the Sufis use this mythical journey to symbolize the Prophet's perfect act of *islam* or "surrender" to God. Shii Muslims developed a mythical view of the Prophet's male descendants who were the *imams* ("leaders"). Each Imam was an incarnation of the divine Ilm ("knowledge"). When the line died out, they said that the last Imam had gone into a state of "occultation," and that one day he would return to inaugurate an era of justice and peace - the Muslim version of the Messiah myth.

The myth of the Imamate, which might seem to flout Muslim orthodoxy, was a symbolic way of expressing the mystic's sense of sacred presence, immanent and accessible in a turbulent and dangerous world. The Hidden Imam had become a myth; by his removal from normal history, he had been liberated from the confines of space and time, and, paradoxically, had become a more vivid presence in the lives of Shiis. The story expresses our sense of the sacred as elusive and tantalizingly absent, in the world but not of it.

When Plato and Aristotle were translated into Arabic during the eight and ninth centuries, some Muslims tried to make the religion of the Qur'an a religion of *logos*. They evolved "proofs" for the existence of Allah, modeled on Aristotle's demonstration of the First Cause. It remained a minority pursuit. By the eleventh century, Muslims had decided that philosophy must be wedded with spirituality, ritual and prayer, and the mythical, mystical religion of the Sufis became the normative form of Islam until the end of the nineteenth century.[15]

In the eleventh and twelfth centuries, Christians in Western Europe rediscovered the works of Plato and Aristotle that had been lost to them during the Dark Ages that had followed the collapse of the Roman Empire. Just at the moment when Jews and Muslims were beginning to retreat from the attempt to rationalize their mythology, Western Christians seized on the project with an enthusiasm that they would never entirely lose. They had started to lose touch with the meaning of myth.[16] The old myths were beginning to be interpreted as though they were factual (*logoi*), a development that was doomed to disappoint such practitioners because these stories were not, and never had been, historical events.[17] Disappointment would be the least harmful effect of such a change in the use of myth.

10

The Best Laid Plans . . . .

The expression "the proof of the pudding is in the eating thereof" certainly held true for the religions that issued from the Axial Age. The fact that they not only survived but thrived and spread is undeniable proof of their meeting the needs of people. This could happen because the emphasis of the Axial Sages was on spiritual development and had nothing to do with doctrine and dogma. Armstrong has stated that humanity has never gone beyond the spiritual insights of the sages, but, sadly, we have failed miserably to be sustained by them.

The religions should not have become static because they were all about individual initiative and growth. Change was fostered from within the traditions themselves. Despite, however, the earth-changing groundwork that was laid, religion has shown a dismaying tendency to ossify and fossilize. In his book *From Dawn to Decadence,* in which Jacques Barzan has analyzed Europe in the second half of the second millennium CE, his observations about its major institutions speak aptly to religion for most of the post-Axial period. It is their nature to ossify because of their aim to form a common mind and/or will. They therefore all "need periodic overhaul, a re-injection of the original idea that got lost in routine."[1] Many of the Sages' teachings did not survive for long, including three of their most radical concepts, viz.

personal responsibility, individualism, and compassion. The vestiges from the bicameral era (see chapter 5) probably aided and abetted this deterioration.

Post-Axial religions sooner or later developed their own conservatism, and eventually, especially in monotheism, their own fundamentalist wing. The priest, whose role of sanctifying and defending the norm, would come to have more influence than the prophet, who has always been needed to play his vital role of renewal and advocating for change. There would be no distinctively new religious developments until the advent of the modern era, which in turn had to await the disintegration of medieval Christianity.

As the last paragraph of the previous chapter suggested, the diminishing understanding and appreciation of myth would play a decisive role. In the search for meaning and understanding there have always been the two vital roles of mythos and logos. As Campbell says, "Every religion is true in one way or another. It is true when understood metaphorically. But when it gets stuck in its own metaphors, interpreting them as facts, then you are in trouble."[2] Mythos is poetry, and by comparison logos is prose. Western Christianity, especially, started turning poetry into prose.[3] "A literal understanding would be a mistake in the reading of the symbol. That is reading the words in terms of prose instead of in terms of poetry, reading the metaphor in terms of denotation instead of the connotation."[4] Religious adherents began to hear concretely rather than metaphorically. Furthermore, whenever a myth "has been dismissed as a mere priestly fraud or a sign of inferior intelligence, truth has slipped out the other door."[5]

In analyzing the modern era Armstrong makes a similar lament:

Today we have lost the ability to think mythologically. . .

. . In the eighteenth and nineteenth centuries scientific rationalism made such huge strides . . . that reason and logic became the only valid means of arriving at truth.

The more intuitive approach was discredited.[6]

The turning of mythos into logos was, without doubt, aided by the influence of the Greek philosophers, but the event that laid the foundation for this retrograde change was the Council of Nicea. All bishops in attendance had to agree in the formulation of a defining statement of beliefs. The Emperor, Constantine, permanently silenced, by means of exile, those who did not agree. The Nicene Creed would lead to orderliness, conformism, and, above all, literalism, and in so doing the metamorphosis of poetry into prose. Truth would now be defined by, and limited to, a statement that had been removed from its mythical context. A belief now had to be understood and accepted in concrete terms.

With the passage of time these statements of belief would become absolute and immutable dogma. And dogma would come to hold sway - at the expense of spiritual vitality. All three monotheisms would come to be defined and confined by laws. Myth would be turned into dogma, which in turn would stifle and subvert followers in their spiritual journeys rather than sustain and renew them.

Religious leaders, locked into their doctrines, interpreting a text as a judge does a law, would consistently take extraordinary measures to stamp out activities that could result in fresh thinking and experience as opposed to blindly adhering to dogma. As Nietzsche later wrote, "The snake that cannot shed its skin perishes. So do the spirits who are prevented from changing their opinions; they cease to be spirit."[7]

With time the stifling dynamic of turning poetry into prose would come to be applied to the three monotheistic scriptures. For many centuries they were heard rather than read. The liturgical sound and ambiance of such ritualistic readings fostered worship. As Armstrong has observed, "Before the modern period Jews, Christians and Muslims all relished highly allegorical interpretations of scripture. The word of God was infinite and could not be tied down to a single interpretation." The various scriptures would come to be interpreted in a wholly literal way.[8]

The demythologizing of the scriptures was, ironically, aided and abetted by the development of the printing press and the rise of literacy. As people came to read the holy books for themselves, they tended to read them more literally. Instead of being open to the inspiration that derives from poetry, the scriptures would come to be seen as stark statements. As people continued to read scripture, they would become increasingly convinced that they *knew* the mind of their god. Different groups within a religion came to conceive of their god in different ways, each convinced that their interpretation was the correct one. Warfare became inevitable. People began killing each other because they believed in a different abstract idea. Christians have warred against Christians and Muslims against Muslims. For two millennia Christians have attacked Jews. Over a period lasting for two hundred years they executed a procession of crusades against Muslims. In very recent times Muslims have gone after Jews only to be repeatedly driven back. And now in the Holy Land some Jews are doing to Muslims what was done to them by Christians because they are totally convinced by their scriptures that the land was given to them by Yahweh. Muslims have now turned on Christians who are responding in kind. Monotheists have waged war with an intensity and purpose never witnessed in polytheistic cultures. Mayhem and murder continue to take place in the name of "God."

Religious warfare has not been the only pervasive activity to negatively impact the populace. The religious vehicle itself came to burden people rather than lighten their load and enlighten their lives. No religion has been worse than Christianity in this regard.

The Church has taught that unity with God is the supreme spiritual goal. And yet most people came to believe that such an experience of oneness was beyond their grasp and that only the experts, such as the priests, could know this. The best that could be hoped for was a somewhat removed comfort, derived from ritual and music. An impenetrable barrier between priest and people has long been in place.

The priest came to be presented as, not only the mediator between God and man, but also of value and truth. Failure to follow their concepts and precepts came to be seen as a "sin." A "catch 22" was constructed. The Church, through the priest, defined and decided that which is a sin. And sin has focused on the struggles of the individual rather than societal oppression. Reconciliation with God has only been attainable through the priest, who forgives and prescribes the penance. This has guaranteed more thorough submission to the priest, who alone redeems. As Nietzsche wrote:

> Psychologically considered, 'sins' become indispensable in any society organized by priests: they are the real handles of power. The priest *lives* on sins, it is essential for him that people 'sin.' Supreme principle: 'God forgives those who repent' - in plain language: those who submit to the priest.[9]

Campbell describes how these circumstances have caused people to live inauthentic lives. The idea of the supernatural as being something over and above the natural was bad enough. By the Middle Ages the world had become a wasteland. People were not "doing anything they truly wanted to because the supernatural laws required them to live as directed by their clergy. In a wasteland, people are fulfilling purposes that are not properly theirs but have been put upon them as inescapable laws."[10]

The American Revolution was as much about opposing religious oppression as political despotism. Thomas Jefferson himself loathed the clergy, concluding from a study of history that "in every country and in every age the priest has been hostile to liberty." He called the work of the priest dark magic, avowing that the church would be better off dispensing with the clerical office altogether.[11] Ethan Allen, another founding father, saw that

> Notions of the depravity of human reason were cherished by priests because, if ordinary human beings were assumed to be perfectly capable of reasoning for themselves, the clergy would be out of work. "While we are under the tyranny of Priests . . . it will ever be in their interests to invalidate the law of nature and reason, in order to establish systems incompatible therewith."[12]

The Church in Europe, long before the term was coined, created the conditions for the Stockholm syndrome to develop. It refers to an incident that took place in that city in 1973. Kristin, a Swedish bank teller, was held hostage in a vault for several days. She became enamored with Olsson, her armed assailant, breaking off her engagement to her fiancé after her release.

In Stockholm syndrome there is a sudden, terrifying capture. (At one time both Christianity and Islam literally made converts in this way.) The hostage is shocked and often certain that he or she will die. But then, little by little, small acts of kindness by the captors evoke feelings deeper than relief. As one ex-hostage has said, "We knew they were killers, but they gave us blankets, cigarettes." He came to feel warmth and compassion toward the men who chose not to kill him. The attachment goes both ways. The captor often develops reciprocal feelings towards the hostage.

There are two other ways in which people become adherents of a particular religion. One is that of willing conversion in which the convert enthusiastically embraces its requirements and teachings, often as a means of reinforcing their decision. Most people, however, are born into their religion. They usually feel the same towards it as to their parents.

The Stockholm syndrome is the essence of Fyodor Dostoevsky's parable of the Grand Inquisitor, as found in *The Brothers Karamazov*. It is examined in chapter 12, but one quote will reveal its thrust. The Grand Inquisitor is talking to Jesus who has returned to earth at the height of the Spanish Inquisition and been thrown into prison for his efforts:

> For fifteen centuries we have been wrestling with Thy freedom, but now it is ended and over for good. . . . Now, today, people are more persuaded than ever that they have perfect freedom, yet they have brought that freedom to us and laid it humbly at our feet.[13]

Islam now holds a similar sway over its followers as Christianity once did. When a religion so controls, it becomes far more impregnable than any prison. Bars and chains aren't needed to hold the follower because the religion has imprisoned the soul, the intellect, the person; and one feels no need to be free in spirit. Rather one fears it. This is the ultimate prison.

A measure of how completely Christianity had imprisoned the soul is seen in the Church's historical approach to scholarship and learning. Prior to Constantine the aspects of logos that addressed the understanding of humanity and the world at large were embraced by Christianity. One crucial area was the understanding of the universe.

Aristarchus, a third century BCE Greek astronomer, taught that the earth revolved around the sun. A century later, Hipparchus postulated the opposite. In the second century CE Ptolemy (Claudius Ptolemaeus), Greek astronomer and geographer of Alexandria, wrote the *Great*

Collection in support of Hipparchus's geocentric view of the heavens. He also wrote *Geography,* which remained the standard geographic work throughout the Middle Ages.

At first glance anatomy and medicine would seem to be, at best, obliquely related to religion. In Christian theology, however, the condition and destiny of the human body has played a crucial role. It is not surprising, therefore, that the early church embraced the work and writings of Galen (130-200 CE). He studied medicine in Alexandria, the leading place to study this subject. Cadavers could be examined there, and he either did so or studied the drawings of those who did. Galen learned to treat the whole person. He became a doctor to athletes and gladiators before becoming physician to Marcus Aurelius. He pioneered neurosurgery and also performed cosmetic and eye surgery. He and other doctors used hand-crafted instruments, whose function doctors today would understand. Above all, Galen wrote profusely on medical matters, averaging at least three pages a day. Research stopped with his death, his writings being regarded as definitive.

With the passage of time the Church leaders came to equate the writings of Ptolemy and Galen with that of Holy Scripture. It became heresy to express anything that conflicted with their work. Medieval physicians, for example, knew almost nothing about the fundamental causes of illness. It was understood that the plague was contagious, but the Jews were singled out as being deliberate agents, even though they were dying as well. The killing of Jews was regarded as a prophylactic measure, and in 1348-1349 large numbers were hanged, burned at the stake, or even rolled into rivers in wine casks. The Muslims in Spain had a knowledge of medicine far in advance of European Christians. Ibn al-Khatib of Granada declared that the role of contagion in spreading the plague was established beyond all doubt. He was imprisoned and murdered by a mob for this heresy.

A system known as scholasticism was developed. All knowledge was divided into four strictly delineated areas - theology, philosophy, jurisprudence, and medicine - with an equally specific list of approved scholars as the unquestioned authorities for each. It was heretical to question the overall veracity of the source - only the meaning of a particular passage or phrase could be discussed. Proscribed interpretations were weeded out. Canon law, as set down by the Pope and other Church leaders, was irrefutable, even more irrefutable than the word of a king. With the arrival of the Renaissance and the accompanying increasing challenges to the ideas of Ptolemy and Galen, the Church continued to restrict the sciences of astronomy and medicine to the ideas and findings of these two men.

The agent that was sorely needed to counter the ossifying of spirituality in Europe was of course the prophet. In the early stages of the post-Axial religions, it was the prophet who countered the priest as he promoted change from within the tradition itself. There was the occasional prophet in medieval Europe, but he invariably met with fierce opposition and failed to gain a following.

The priest proved to be enormously effective. Opposition came not only from the Church leaders but also from the population at large, which was totally caught up in the Stockholm syndrome. Church thinking and beliefs had come to be deeply rooted in their lives. Primo Levi, a noted Italian holocaust survivor, summed up the problem that was still pervasive in modern times: "Monsters exist, but they are too few in number to be truly dangerous. More dangerous are the common men, the functionaries ready to believe and to act without questions." The structure of ecclesiastical authority was protected by the claims of revelation and tradition. God was the ultimate source, thus putting dogma and practice beyond human questioning.

One of the earliest voices raised in protest and challenge was that of a theologian named Tertullian (160-220). He "grew increasingly troubled by the ostentatious excesses and the dearth of Christian spirit he witnessed in the Orthodox clerical class." He finally broke with the Church, becoming Christianity's first "Protestant."[14] These negative traits developed at a very early stage. If not constantly addressed, they would (and did) become cancers that would transmogrify the Church into the very opposite of what Jesus was about.

Peter Abelard (1079-1142), of Abelard and Heloise fame, was a French scholastic philosopher who urged the use of logic in order to understand and defend Christianity. He endured much persecution for his efforts. William of Ockham (or Occam) (1285-1349), a Franciscan monk of independent thought, was critical of Scholasticism and of the temporal power of the papacy. He opened the way to the Reformation by distinguishing between faith and reason. He was one of the first Christian thinkers to advocate for the separation of Church and State. He asserted that humankind has no knowledge of God, even by intuition, and that it was impossible to give any cogent proofs of his existence. He was excommunicated as a result.

Challenges to Church-sanctioned positions did not just arise from the occasional scholar. A variety of innovations in Christian belief emerged in the eleventh century. Their source is traced back to Bogomil - a tenth century Bulgarian village priest. He taught a variation of dualism which has its roots in the gnosticism of the early Christian era. This version claimed that there are two sources of divine power in the cosmos, one good and the other evil, and that the world was created by the fallen angel Satan. The cross, as a religious symbol was rejected along with the authority of both the Orthodox Church and the Roman Catholic Church.

Bogomil's ideas appeared in different parts of Europe and were known by a variety of names, none of them flattering. Followers were to be found in Cologne, Liege, Italy, Flanders, and in southern France where it was centered in the town of Albi. Practitioners were known as Albigensians. At large they were best known as Cathars.

The Dominican Order was founded in 1205 to combat this heresy, and the Pope declared a crusade against them in 1209. Campbell called it one of the most monstrous crusades in the history of Europe. Mass genocide took place. The Troubadour movement in Provence was extinguished in the process.

To put this event in context, it needs to be remembered that there was a time when a government killing its own people was unthinkable. An early incident of this aberrant behavior was the Roman persecution of Christians. In comparison with the Albigensian Crusade, it was done half-heartedly, sporadically, and with ambivalence. The event in Provence

> was not a war about land, revenge, or even an alien religion. For the first time in human history a governing group carried out mass genocide against its own kinsmen because of abstract theological ideas about a religion both held in common.[15]

Or as Armstrong puts it, "For the first time in Europe a pope was calling on Christians to kill other Christians: precedent for a new kind of holy war that would become an incurable disease in Europe."[16]

The crushing of the Cathars launched the Inquisition, which in three different phases would last for 600 years. The medieval phase functioned across Western Europe. After finishing off the Cathars it expanded its scope of operations to heretics such as radical Franciscan priests and women accused of witchcraft. The Spanish Inquisition began in 1478, its goal being to detect and punish Jewish and Muslim converts to Christianity (known as *conversos*) who were suspected of secretly clinging to their former faiths. The third phase is referred to as the

Roman Inquisition and operated mostly in Italy. It was created in 1542 to fight against the Protestant Reformation as well as the impact made by the Renaissance. Napoleon himself issued the decree that abolished the Spanish Inquisition when his army entered Madrid in 1808. The inquisitors took their last human life on July 26, 1826.

The word "inquisition" is derived from *inquisito*, the form of dealing with crime that permitted one person to perform the roles of investigator, prosecutor, and judge. Conrad of Marburg (1180-1232) was the first to carry the title of Inquisitor into Heretical Depravity. He is noted for saying, "We would gladly burn a hundred if just one among them were guilty."[17]

The Inquisition was intended to achieve a critical mass of terror by making examples of people who dared to think for themselves. The mere existence of free thinking people was regarded by the ecclesiastical authorities as an intolerable threat. People were guilty of wrongful thoughts rather than wrongful acts. The sole means of proof was obtaining a confession, and massive use of torture was applied in order to achieve it. "The ordeal" became the medieval equivalent of the modern lie detector test.[18]

The witch hunts, which were actually women hunts, began in 1460 and lasted through the eighteenth century. Eighty-five percent of those executed were female. Married women and widows ranging from fifty to seventy years of age represented the greatest number of victims. A kind of madness seemed to seize the collective imagination, with some people clamoring to confess that they were indeed witches.[19] At a later stage Protestants also became ardent practitioners of witch hunting. It amounted to mass murder on an apalling scale. Estimates of the numbers put to death (drowning was the most widely used means) vary from 100,000 to three million. Archives reveal that between 1591 and 1680, in one Swiss canton, 3,371 victims were tried and executed on charges of witchcraft. By the time the trials were over (in 1585), in the bishopric of Trier, Germany, two villages were left with only one female inhabitant each.[20] In more than one French village all the inhabitants were put to death. In order to cover the expenses of the mock trials and executions, the properties of the accused were seized and sold. The disposal of such property became a cottage industry. A lack of learning was not a factor. Germany, with the fastest rise in literacy rates, was where the witch craze was most monstrous. "It was not the poor who did the killing. Ermine-cloaked prelates, shiny-armored police, and well-fed magistrates were the instigators and perpetrators of the purge."[21]

This indiscriminate slaughter of women is without equal in human history. At the outset pregnant prisoners were not tortured, but they too became victims starting in Nuremburg in 1576.

> In some places, after the women most vulnerable to accusation had been executed, the inquisitors turned on children, convinced that witches passed their dark art on to their daughters. In the crowning grotesquerie of the entire episode the prince-bishop of Würzburg executed forty-one girls, ages seven to eleven, between 1623 and 1631. There is no other incident in all of recorded history in which a community was seized with a psychosis so extreme that it tortured and killed its own children.[22]

As Blaise Pascal would later observe, "Men never do evil so completely and cheerfully as when they do it from religious conviction."

The Spanish Inquisition was, if possible, even more horrific. Although the victims included Muslims, Protestants, mystics, and other eccentrics, the vast majority were of Jewish ancestry. Children as young as ten were charged by the tribunal at Toledo. Here a new and far more dangerous principle emerged, one that sought purity of blood as opposed to that of belief. It would reach its most horrific expression with the Holocaust in the twentieth century.

Autos-da-fé (acts of faith) occurred everywhere. Human sacrifice had never before been practiced on such a large scale in such an allegedly civilized society. The most prominent location for these ceremonial incinerations was the Plaza Mayor in Madrid where the Spanish sovereigns and their courts would be among the enthusiastic spectators.[23] Juan Antonio Florente, a general secretary of the Inquisition from 1789 to 1801, estimated that, beginning in 1480, forty thousand heretics had been burned at the stake and another 400,000 had suffered "heavy penance."[24] Another forty thousand were persecuted by the Portuguese tribunals. Fifteen percent of Spain's population was affected by the Inquisition.

By the time that Martin Luther nailed his 95 Theses to the door of the Castle Church at Wittenberg on October 31, 1517, the Inquisition was operating creakily at best in most of Western Europe. The Reformation stirred up a renewed spasm of violence in the papal attempts to combat heresy. Pope Paul III established the Sacred Congregation of the Roman and Universal Inquisition in 1542. One example of its desperate measures was to condemn every word of the reformer named Erasmus. Another was to require special permission from an inquisitor if one wished to read a translation of the Bible.[25]

The Inquisition even impacted the new world. In addition to the Salem witchcraft trials that led to the execution of 19 "witches," Quakers, who refused to recognize clerical authority, were flogged and expelled. Those who defied expulsion were tried and hanged by the civil courts of Massachusetts.[26]

> The long history of the Inquisition teaches that the
> machinery of persecution, once switched on, cannot be
> easily slowed or directed, much less stopped. Nor does

the machinery require the high technology of a modern industrial state.[27]

That long history succeeded in establishing a model of authoritarianism that continues to the present time in most of Christendom.

The Inquisition also left behind a huge negative legacy that has only dissipated in very recent times. A lack of progress remained pervasive in the areas where it held the greatest sway. In broad geographic terms, northern Europe became undeniably superior to southern Europe with respect to scholarship, science, technology, and commerce. While Galileo's writings were being banned in Italy, they were being published in Holland. Spain, in particular, lagged behind the rest of Western Europe. As Cecil Roth wrote in *The Spanish Inquisition,* "The Dead Hand of the Holy Office was pressing slowly on the vital arteries of Spanish intellectual life."[27]

Christianity is not the only Axial religion to abuse women or fail to accord them equal status. They have all remained essentially male spiritualities. Armstrong has found that Confucius, for example, seemed to be entirely indifferent to women. In India the Jain and Buddhist orders were pacific forms of the ancient Aryan military brotherhoods, and though nuns were permitted to join, in a second-class capacity, many felt that the presence of women was inappropriate. Even the Buddha, who usually did not succumb to this type of prejudice, declared that women would fall upon his order like mildew on a field of rice.[28]

Hindu women have no say as to their partner in marriage. They move into the husband's household where they are often treated as slaves. If they fail to produce a son, they can be maimed or even murdered. To this day in Orthodox Jewish marriages the wife becomes the property of the man. There is the ancient Hebrew prayer in which a man thanks God that he is not a gentile, a dog, or a woman. The Christian New

Testament teaches that women should remain silent in church and always honor their husbands. A Muslim woman has none of the rights and privileges of the man, and even in Paradise she can only look forward to being part of the heavenly harem of some misguided mass-murdering "martyr."

Another negative trait that is common to the Axial religions is that of child abuse. Their various scriptures are adult books, written by adults, for adults. To shove them down a child's throat, which is what the monotheistic religions, in particular, are noted for, is unquestionably child abuse. Great pressure is put on Buddhist boys to become monks. In preparation for this role they are relentlessly drilled in Buddhist schools. The same thing happens in Orthodox Jewish institutions and Muslim madrasses. Christian schools, especially the more conservative ones, force children to follow rigid codes which they are told are demanded in the Bible and/or by God.

A Hindu child often learns of its caste limitations the hard way: a young schoolgirl wanted a drink of water. Because she was an outcaste, she was not supposed to pour the drink herself. The teacher struck her so hard when she picked up the jug that she lost an eye. When Muslims force their children to follow the fasting rituals of Ramadan, they are being subjected to abuse. And the Bris can only be a traumatic experience for male Jewish babies.

A third common religious trait is that of fatalism. The failure of the Axial religions to foster personal responsibility and individualism helped this to remain an entrenched characteristic.

Fate is not to be confused with destiny. Those who have a sense of destiny are inspired to achieve it. Fate is a passive resignation to one's situation as being the way things are meant to be: The gods are omnipotent - one's fate is unchangeable. The caste into which a Hindu is born determines the parameters of his life - it is not going to get any better than that. The Buddhist says that life is just a valley of suffering - it is to be stoically endured. In addition, it is Karmic law that determines one's fate. Christianity has two theological terms, viz. foreordination and predestination. They both mean that our fate is determined by God. A practicing Christian spends his or her entire life asking, "Why, God, did you do this to me?" Or if it is something so bad that he or she cannot see God as being the initiator of the event, "Why, God, did you allow this to happen to me?" Muslims have a term that conveys the same idea - kismet - which means "This is the will of Allah." Axial religions, over time, have come to focus on preparing one for dying rather than living.

The tsunami that devastated the coasts of the Indian Ocean on December 26, 2004, painfully highlighted the fatalism inherent in the various worldviews. Animists, Hindus, Buddhists, Christians, and Muslims alike saw the natural disaster as a divinely initiated event punishing the cumulative wrongs that had been committed. The devastating loss of family members and possessions was only augmented by feelings of guilt. The survival of various religious structures was all the evidence needed that this was an act of God. The fact that the buildings remained standing because of their mass and size, together with the scientific explanation of the event, was totally lost on them.

If there is any validity to the saying that it is always darkest before the dawn, it certainly held true for Christian Europe.

11

RENAISSANCE AND REFORM

One measure of how bleak and backward Europe was in the Middle Ages was the Mongolian disgust at what they found when they conquered the territories now known as Hungary, Germany, and Poland in 1241. They didn't bother invading more land. The most valuable assets that the Mongols took with them were the tents and furnishings of the Hungarian king's camp together with various craftsmen.

Technology was less advanced in Europe than any other civilized area of the old World. The populations failed to generate a single significant scientific, literary, or philosophical idea. And yet Europeans, who had been cut off from the mainstream of civilization since the fall of Rome in 476, in the end suffered the least, while acquiring all of the advantages of contact with the Mongols. In the fifty years following the Mongolian invasion of Europe, civilizations that had once been separate worlds unto themselves had become part of a single intercontinental system of communication, commerce, technology, and politics.

The Mongol war routes were gradually transformed into commercial arteries. A merchant navy was developed to expand and speed up the supply of goods being moved. And the Mongolian armies guarded against robbers and pirates. Western scholars later designated the fourteenth century as the Pax Mongolica. It would take the plague, known as the Black Death, to end this vital period.

The plague is believed to have originated in Inner Mongolia and was carried westward by Tatar traders and warriors. A fleet of Genoese merchant galleys loaded with infected rats and sailors imported the plague to Sicily from the Crimea in the Fall of 1347. Europe was thrown into turmoil. Twenty-five million--a third of the population of the pre-plague continent--perished in four years, effecting lasting social and economic change, contributing, for example, to the demise of the feudal system.

The ideas and assets of the Mongol Empire triggered an awakening in Europe which was every bit as significant as the events giving rise to the Renaissance would be and, in fact, influenced those developments. Jack Weatherford in *Genghis Khan and the Making of the Modern World* writes that naissance applies more accurately to the Mongol impact because "it was not the ancient world of Greece and Rome that was being reborn: it was the Mongol Empire, picked up, transferred and adapted by the Europeans to their own need and culture."[1] New paths of intellectual discovery were opened, leading to new ideas and experiments. Two of these that would take several centuries to be adopted were the primacy of the State over the Church and freedom of religion.

"The Mongolian answer to the pernicious enmity among the religions of the world was that simple religious concord could only be produced by subsuming all religions under the power of the State."[2] Genghis Khan himself decreed complete and total religious freedom for everyone. In order to promote religious activity he exempted religious leaders and their property from taxation and from all types of public service. It would be the new nation of the United States of America that would set an example for Europe to follow by putting these ideas into practice at the end of the eighteenth century.

In countless ways European life was improved by the technology and ideas flowing from the Pax Mongolica. In 1620 the English scientist, Francis Bacon, would designate printing, gunpowder, and the compass, all inventions from the orient, as the technological innovations on which the modern world was built. Printing with moveable letters began in China in the twelfth century. The Mongols adopted and greatly expanded the technology. Johannes Gutenberg in turn adapted the Bible to print in 1455. The printing press made the availability of books one of the most potent forces of public life. This in turn made it possible for ordinary citizens across Europe to connect with each other. "They read what they wanted, which meant that they could think what they wanted. Most of all, they had the power that came from the knowledge that there were others who thought like them."[3]

By 1500 six million volumes had been produced. They stimulated the revival of the Greek classics, written forms of language, the growth of nationalism, the outbreak of the Protestant Reformation, the birth of science, and virtually every aspect of life and learning. The impact of cathedrals would also be diminished. In 1831 Victor Hugo, while reflecting on the storytelling walls and windows of Notre Dame with a book in hand said, "This will kill that."[4]

The Renaissance itself is recognized as starting at the beginning of the fourteenth century and was the product of several sources of stimulation and renewal. It started in the Middle Ages and lasted for three centuries as it brought Europe to modernity. It took, however, another hundred years for people to begin to be freed from restraints such as ignorance and superstition. The Europe of the Middle Ages consisted of great feudal estates owned by wealthy noblemen. The population at large consisted of serfs who farmed the land for these feudal lords.

The Italian peninsula was a major source of the Renaissance, the city-state of Florence being the cradle. It began in a time of change and disruption. Charles Nicholl, in his biography of Leonardo da Vinci, writes that old beliefs were crumbling in a climate of "venal political strife, of economic boom and bust, of outlandish reports from hitherto unknown corners of the world."[5] The Pax Mongolica made possible the arrival of these reports. Venice and Genoa stood at the crossroads of Western Europe and the Near East. Their merchants set up trading posts in the Black Sea and developed a long and lucrative trade with the Mongols. People like the Polo family preceded the exchange of envoys between the Mongol Khans and the popes and kings of Europe.

The period became marked with a loss of certainty in tandem with a palpable excitement. Rule-books were being rewritten, and everything now seemed to be possible. The Renaissance man emerged "as a trader in doubts and questions and with them self-doubts and self-questionings."[6] Da Vinci's manuscripts "reveal that everything is to be questioned, investigated, peered into, worried away at, brought back to first principles."[7] The new ideas and forms that emerged were often old ideas and forms reexamined in a new and modern light. The emergence in the city-states of a wealthy, leisured class of merchants and bankers made secular patronage of men of genius possible. If medieval painters did think of secular subjects, they certainly did not paint them. But now they felt free to paint portraits, landscapes, and scenes form everyday life. Renaissance art showed that the artist could and should belong to the ranks of scholars, philosophers, and scientists. No one epitomized the multi-disciplinary "Renaissance man" more than da Vinci himself.

It was not just the fine arts that were revolutionized. Architecture came to center on humanity and its needs. And literature too would begin to emphasize individual personality. New forms, such as essays and biographies, (more and more in the local language) became important.

The artisans' guilds, for example, opened up as they began to publish their own manuals, giving the latest developments in techniques. This in turn caused them to rely more on talent than on secrets to protect the value of their services, thus becoming individuals who felt free to innovate. The gaze of Europeans was being diverted from the vertical to the horizontal. They began to look with new eyes on the natural world around them - it no longer appeared to them as fallen. People were beginning to discover their capacity for creativity and with it vital progress towards emancipation.

Another contribution to the Renaissance came from the Muslim world. Arabic science, for example, much of it based on the Greek classics, had been percolating into Europe, via Iberia, since at least the twelfth century. For centuries a series of Muslim scholars had preserved the works of Aristotle that would in time lay the foundation for the secular logic and science that would usher in the new world.

There were two intellectual giants in particular that must be acknowledged. They were contemporaries, both born in the Spanish city of Cordova - the one a Jew, the other an Arab. Maimonides (Rabbi Moses ben Maimon, 1135-1204) was a physician, theologian, and philosopher who sought to reconcile biblical and rabbinic teaching with Aristotelian philosophy. He held that there exists a single truth, and that faith, properly understood, never can conflict with reason. Averröes (ibn Rushd, 1126-1198) was a Muslim writer on medicine and much esteemed commentator on Aristotle, who profoundly influenced Scholasticism. In contrast to Maimonides he held that there were two truths - that of revelation and that of the natural world, and that there was no need to reconcile them. His thinking continues to negatively impact the Muslim world to this day as revelatory "truth" continues to dominate.

The influence of the Greek classics would be greatly augmented by the conquest of Constantinople by the armies of the Ottoman sultan Mehmet II in 1453. This key event caused a stream of refugee scholars to fan up through Italy with their bundles of rescued manuscripts containing the stored-up wisdom of Greek science and philosophy. The Orthodox Church, unlike its Catholic cousin, did not become separated from these roots.

The revival of the language, philosophy, and literature of ancient Greece and Rome inevitably led to humanism - a movement of the fifteenth and sixteenth centuries which aspired to restore the human values of antiquity. The Latin writer Terrence had said in the second century BCE, "I am a man, and nothing human is foreign to me." Humanism came to teach that all human beings have dignity and worth; therefore they should command the respect of their fellow men. Humanism was destined to break away from Scholasticism as the former encouraged free enquiry every bit as much as the latter discouraged it. Some of the popes were, however, passionate humanists, beginning in the mid-fifteenth century with Nicholas V, a sincere Christian who made his court an art center.

One sign that humanism impacted the Roman Catholic Church was the late medieval development of one-on-one confession for the laity. This was a concession that every peasant had a mind and conscience of his own.

Humanism, in contrast to Christianity, focused "on the goals that could be reached on earth, individual self development, action rather than pious passivity."[8] Humanists came to look outward, to the realm of human experience and values. This in turn led to broad scholarship. Humankind, rather than God, would come to be seen as the hub of the social universe. Reason would come to be seen as being as important as faith, and people would be urged to claim responsibility, free of clergy, for their own lives. With the growth of Christian fundamentalism in the twentieth century, humanism would become a buzz word in conservative circles, especially when preceded by the epithet "secular"!

Jacques Barzun made a sad and ironic evaluation of humanism:

> On the whole, the Humanists were perhaps more truly Christian than the run-of-the-mill priests and monks or the fanatic Evangelicals (Protestants) who lived by violence, yet deemed themselves saved by faith. . . . In filling their minds with the facts of the two ancient civilizations, the Humanists were forced to settle the perennial questions that precede religious belief: What is life for? What is man's duty and destiny? What is the significance of death?[9]

Desiderius Erasmus of the Netherlands (1466-1536) is regarded as the prince of Humanists. He was made a monk against his will by his guardian but gained exemption from monastic life possibly because "from his earliest days he denounced the monks, discredited the saints and declared 'almost all Christians wretchedly enslaved by blindness and ignorance.'"[10]

The printing press magnified the influence of Erasmus in a manner that had never been seen before. "Nothing like his sway over the minds of contemporaries has been seen since: not even Voltaire or Bernard Shaw approached it."[11] He was the first person to earn his living by his writings. In them he aimed at bringing Christian thought into harmony with Greek philosophy. He produced his own Latin edition of the New Testament: it included comments on errors, omissions, and unauthorized additions to the Vulgate.

The Renaissance took place apart from, if not in spite of, the Church. If these developments were encouraged at all, it was for mercenary reasons. Direct taxation, in the guise of the tithe, was the law of the land. Priests therefore encouraged the acquisition of secular technical information because it would lead to more wealth, and thus larger tithes.

Four centuries after Erasmus Friedrich Nietzsche would evaluate the Renaissance as being "the *revaluation of Christian values,* the attempt, undertaken with every means, with every instinct, with all genius, to bring the *countervalues,* the *noble* values to victory."[12] Barzun believes that Europeans should refer to their heritage as being Graeco-Roman-Judeo-Christian, rather than just Judeo-Christian. "To cite but one item, the endless effort to change society for the better, which is characteristic of the last five centuries, comes from the Graeco-Roman tradition."[13]

The crucial religious event that precipitated permanent and progressive change in Western Europe was the Reformation. Although Constantine was responsible for giving Christianity a dominant role in Rome, it was not until 391 that Christianity became established as the state religion by Emperor Theodosius. This move immediately made Church leaders officers of the empire. Thus, less than a century later, when the last emperor ruling from Rome was deposed, a certain imperial power devolved upon the pope. For the next millennium, successive popes maintained quasi-imperial jurisdiction over the kings of Europe. Gradually, as powerful nation-states took shape, their rulers sought to subordinate Church authority to their own. This desire would play a vital role in the birth of the Reformation.

The term "perfect storm" has perhaps become overused in referring to the confluence of various events, but key elements and forces did indeed combine to create the tumult that made possible the Reformation. Four of the most significant factors, in addition to the ambitions of certain rulers were, the printing press, humanism, a succession of notorious Church leaders who became known as the Renaissance popes and, most important of all, Martin Luther.

The press's impact on European life in general has already been noted. It has been said that its arrival can only be equated with the internet in its impact on life. The writings of Erasmus and Luther would have only had minimal impact but for their proliferation through printing.

It is doubtful that the Reformation would have taken place without the unwitting aid of the Renaissance popes. There were six in all, their reigns starting in 1471 and continuing for the next 63 years. Despite the fact that this was a glorious period in European history, these leaders brought about the steepest regression of papal moral authority in all of the Church's history. There has been no comparable decline in all the other religions of the world.

None of these popes exhibited the slightest awareness of their spiritual mission, as they successively embraced such vices as avarice, extreme nepotism, brutality, and depravity. They sold offices and indulgences, unwaveringly preferring power and personal gain to establishing badly needed reforms. The nadir was reached under Pope Alexander VI when depravity not seen in Rome since the reigns of Nero and Caligula took place. This lack of moral force in Rome left the Church at large demoralized and in disarray. The situation was ripe for radical change.

Martin Luther, the son of a miner, was born in 1483 and lived for 63 years. He studied law but had an epiphany when he was knocked off his horse in a thunderstorm. This experience caused him to enter an Augustinian monastery, which in turn resulted in his becoming, in 1507, a teacher of theology at Wittenberg University. His new profession was more than just a career. He studied the Scriptures in earnest and came to the conviction that salvation was attained by faith alone and that consequently the mediation of the Church was unnecessary.

Luther made a pilgrimage to Rome where he became appalled at the corruption and meaningless execution of religious rituals. He became particularly incensed at the practice of selling indulgences. This was instituted by Pope Leo X under whose reign the Protestant break occurred. In order to support his profligate lifestyle, Leo X signed documents that were supposed to expiate sins in exchange for money. One could even purchase proxy release from purgatory for deceased relatives - or release for sins that the buyer might commit in the future. That the public would be taken in by this hoax indicates the extreme degree to which Europeans were in thrall to the Church. Luther attacked this practice and other long-held teachings by nailing his 95 Theses to the cathedral door at Wittenberg.

At the Church trial triggered by this act, the reformer took an extremely bold stand and refused to recant his teachings. He continued his attack on papal authority, including the doctrine of papal supremacy over secular rulers and was excommunicated by the pope in 1521. He was protected by the Elector of Saxony, the emperor of a major German territory, who placed him in Wartburg Castle where he translated the Bible into German.

Luther taught that no one had the right to come between an individual and God, that priests weren't needed to administer the sacraments, and that each person had the ability and right to interpret the Bible according to his private judgment. He said, in so many words, "every man is a priest."

Luther not only fulfilled the role of a prophet, he also became a pioneer of German philosophy. Immanuel Kant and George Hegel were influenced by him. He was instrumental in fashioning the German idea of freedom; he tied it to the individual. Some believe that this was his greatest contribution. Luther was the bridge between the static society of the Middle Ages and the modern ideas of the rights of man. He was, however, contemptuous of the doctrine of reason, as established by the Greeks, stating that "reason was the devil's whore."

To make the concept "every man is a priest" absolute, he added the principle he called Christian liberty. "A Christian man is a perfectly free lord, subject to none." Luther meant it strictly as a religious concept, but many, to his horror, applied it to all aspects of life. This resulted in peasant revolts, and, among other activities, churches were ransacked and images of saints destroyed. Luther encouraged the ruthless crushing of such rebellion. He did not intend to promote anarchy and accordingly stated the counterpart to liberty: "A Christian man is a perfectly dutiful servant of all, subject to all." He had in mind the secular society ruled by princes.

There was much other shedding of blood that stemmed from Luther's initiatives. A third of the German population died in the wars spawned by the Reformation. Often it came down to the murder of neighbor by neighbor. As bad, or worse, was to follow in England, France, and Holland. In the latter, Calvinists ended up killing Calvinists.

Luther was not at first antisemitic. In his early writings he urged that "heathens" (Jews, Turks, and Moors, among others) be treated with respect. When he saw that the Jews, in particular, did not embrace his teachings, he demonstrated "splenetic bigotry, more extreme and explicit than that which the Church had practiced."[14] The things that he urged be done to Jews would later be literally carried out by the Nazis. It was as if he wrote their handbook.

Although Martin Luther blazed the trail that led to the Reformation, he was not alone in establishing it. He was supported by an ever-growing list of theologians and teachers. The name that is most often linked with his is John Calvin (Jean Cauvin, 1509-1564). He spread the Protestant Reformation in France (the converts becoming known as Huguenots) and Switzerland.

Calvin established himself in Geneva in 1541 where he developed a form of church government known as Presbyterianism. He started writing *Institutes of the Christian Religion* in 1536, adding to them for the rest of his life. To this day Calvinists hold his writings in only slightly less esteem than the Bible. Shlain does not paint a bright picture of his legacy:

> John Calvin introduced little that was original. He simply appropriated the harshest ideas from Judaism and Catholicism, excluded many wise, conciliatory words of the Jewish prophets, and negated all the mitigating and compensatory images, rituals, and sacraments of Catholicism. When this shredding was over, the religion that remained was dark, gothic, and forbidding. Calvin, along with other Reformation figures, stalled the Humanist movement and ended the glory of the Renaissance. He turned the clock back by several centuries with his medieval views, and he delayed the Enlightenment. Summing up his dour outlook, he wrote, 'The best is not to be born, one should mourn and weep at births and rejoice at funerals!'[15]

Calvin sought to establish the ideal city of God, causing Geneva to become "notorious as the most repressive police state in the history of religious movements.[16] There were even laws regulating how many dishes could be used at a meal. All children had to be given biblical names (a man was jailed for four days for not so doing); Calvin's stepson and daughter-in-law were separately convicted of adultery - all four were put to death. The height of brutality occurred when elders ordered the beheading of a child for striking his parents. He also discouraged excessive charity because it weakened moral fiber. Will Durant charitably summed up Calvin's life by saying, "We shall always find it hard to love the man who darkened the human soul with the most absurd and blasphemous conception of God in all the long and honored history of nonsense."[17]

The emergence of Luther, Calvin, et al., shattered the West's unity of belief. One way that this happened was the Reformers' undermining of the other-world by, e.g., the rejection of Purgatory. They emphasized the finality of all actions performed in this world and of implying that most vital aspects of life belong in this world only.

The continued splintering of beliefs came to reveal the various church structures and belief systems as being human in origin rather than divine. Church government itself, it can now be clearly seen, mirrored that of the state in which the denomination was formed. The Roman Catholic Church continues to have the equivalent of an emperor. Presbyterianism drew upon the Swiss Canton system, and later denominations have followed the democratic forms of modern times. The emergence of denominationalism itself, combined with the principle of the priesthood of all believers, has foreshadowed individualism as a political, social, and religious right. Ever more people are choosing their own paths in seeking spiritual fulfillment.

T. H. Huxley, the man who coined the term "agnostic," would later say "The Reformation was the scraping of a little rust off the chains that still bind the mind."[18] But, by providing the Renaissance, and its rediscovery of human potential, with religious alternatives, the Reformation led the West right up to the threshold of a door, on the other side of which was to be found a whole new world - a world that it was not prepared to embrace.

> The theology of Luther and Calvin was formulated just before the rise of the modern historical consciousness and just before the take-off of modern science. They missed some of the most essential features of modernity, even though it was already beginning in their time.

Their new Protestant confessions and church polities made no provision for the coming knowledge explosion and the vast cultural changes that it would bring about. . . . The result has been the steady decline of Protestantism into pietism, literalism, and (eventually) fundamentalism. What began as the most progressive force in Western culture thus steadily declined until it became the most reactionary. . . . As religion the Protestant Reformation has sadly turned out to be a long-term failure.[19]

This is, alas, a sadly familiar pattern - it could be labeled the religion syndrome. A religion invariably starts out by making a stimulating and uplifting impact upon a given society. With the passage of time, however, it does far worse than die - it reverses itself, becoming in effect an engine attached to the caboose of the train of life, trying with all possible might to drag its followers back into the bicameral era, the vestiges of which remain in and with us. It happened to Christianity with the rot starting shortly after Nicea. The reform movements didn't take long to follow suit, the pattern repeating itself in Christendom in the last two centuries.

Sadly, Irish Christianity would follow a similar path. The vitality-draining rigidity that came to define Christianity on the Continent seeped into Ireland, making its brand, if anything, worse. The sexual abuse of children by priests and the cover-up initiated by church leaders has been as bad as any country where Roman Catholicism has long held sway. The treatment of illegitimate children seems to have been unique to Ireland. They were removed from their mothers and warehoused in orphanages where they were usually treated as if they were to blame for their situation. There were fortunate children who were sent to America in adoption programs.

We are currently witnessing Islam, as an edifying force, in full retreat.

If the Sages, including Jesus, Muhammad, and even Karl Marx (whose teachings impacted populations in the same way), walked among us today, most of their followers would clamor after them proclaiming, "We are your children!" They, in turn, would all recoil in horror as they say, "No, you are not, you are all bastards."

The Renaissance and the Reformation combined to bring poets, artists, theologians, and philosophers to the fore, setting the stage for what Karen Armstrong has called "the Great Western Transformation." Some refer to it as the Second Axial Age.

12

THE GREAT WESTERN TRANSFORMATION

From earliest times science has played a vital role in the search for meaning and an understanding of one's place in the world. D. C. Dennett believes that astronomers and mathematicians collaborated with priests at the outset as they helped each other with difficult and crucial questions: "How many days 'til we have our winter solstice ritual? When will the stars be in the right position for the most effective and proper sacrificial ceremony?"[1]

The breakdown of the bicameral mind in the second millennium BCE gave great impetus to such scientific endeavor. This breakdown was accompanied by the fading away of the voices of the gods. In the next millennium those who still heard the voices, the prophets and oracles, gradually disappeared. The development of writing made possible the preservation of their utterances in sacred texts. They would command our attention for the first 1500 years of the Common Era as we sought to follow our lost divinities. In the next 500 years these writings would steadily lose their authority as the Scientific Revolution helped us to discover our lost contact with the divine in Nature itself.

This search for the divine would have unforeseen consequences:

> It is the Great Human Irony of our noblest and
> greatest endeavor on this planet that in the quest for

207

authorization, in our reading of the language of God
in nature, we should read there so clearly that we have
been so mistaken."[2]

The exposure of our endeavors and focus as being mistaken, instead of being a disillusionment-filled anticlimax, has left us amazed, if not awed, at what has been learned. And deservedly so - those who have led the way in penetrating the darkness have been the most moved by their findings.

Pythagoras of ancient Greece (580-500 BCE) is a good early example. He sought for the lost gods in a theology of divine numbers and their relationships, thus beginning the science of mathematics. In so doing he discovered the numerical ratios of intervals in the musical scale. Two millennia later Copernicus (1473-1543) would see his scientific investigations as a spiritual activity that filled him with awe. Francis Bacon (1561-1626), regarded as the father of modern science, argued in 1605 that reason properly reveals God. Humankind cannot "search too far or be too well studied in the book of God's word, or in the book of God's works, divinity or philosophy, but rather let men endeavor an endless progress of proficience in both."[3] In similar vein Galileo (1564-1642) argued in 1615 that spiritual truth is to be found in the Bible and nature alike: "For the Bible is not chained in every expression to conditions as strict as those which govern all physical effects, nor is God any less excellently revealed in Nature's actions than in the sacred statements of the Bible. . . . Nature is the observant executive of God's commands."[4] Galileo called mathematics the speech of God, and was echoed by Blaise Pascal (1623-1662) and Gotfried Leibzig (1646-1716) who claimed that they heard God in the "awesome rectitudes of mathematics."[5] Pascal is best known for his Christian apologetics, but also made contributions to pure geometry, as well as laying the foundations of the theory of probability. Leibniz developed the theory of differential calculus together with Isaac Newton (1642-1727), whose main motivation in his scientific endeavors was to enhance his understanding of God. He was in fact a closet Unitarian and needed to so remain in order to keep his chair at Cambridge University.

At the end of the eighteenth century Thomas Paine (1737-1809), a committed deist, wrote,

> The Bible of the creation is inexhaustible in texts. Every
> part of science, whether connected with the geometry of
> the universe, with the systems of animal and vegetable
> life, or with the properties of inanimate matter, is a text
> as well for devotion as for philosophy, for gratitude, as
> for human improvement.[6]

Before the Scientific Revolution impacted life in the West, all knowledge that people had was inherited, and this knowledge was proclaimed by the Church to be *the truth*. Francis Bacon (1561-1626) was instrumental in making a break with medieval scholastic thinking: He laid out a classification of the natural sciences and introduced the inductive method of research. It is the process of assuming a theory which is then tested by experiments, precise observation, and measurements. This method has only been applied in the last 400 years and remains unsurpassed as a tool of enquiry. Empirical science has proved itself to be the most reliable way to investigate the physical universe--rigorous yet open to revision, verifiable and self-correcting. The reliable knowledge that has thus been gained has grown exponentially and, in so doing, has come to challenge many central inherited beliefs.

The Church and science would take increasingly divergent paths in their endeavors as the former would become increasingly hostile to findings that undermined ecclesiastical positions held to be absolute.

The issue was whether we are to find our lost authorization through an apostolic succession from ancient

> prophets who heard divine voices, or through search-
> ing the heavens of our own experience right now in the
> objective world without any priestly intercession.[7]

Nietszche would later define knowledge in this context as "the emancipation from the priest."[8] As Geering has pointed out

> In one area of human experience after another what was
> once believed to be supernatural has come to be seen as
> belonging to the natural world; what was thought to be
> of divine origin has been found to be of human origin;
> what was treated as absolute has come to be recognized
> as relative.[9]

This progression would cause humanity's place in the grand scheme of things to become drastically changed, if not reduced. The three most crucial beliefs to be challenged would be 1) our place in the universe, 2) the antiquity of the earth, and 3) our understanding of the origin of life. Conservative Christianity, in particular, is still trying to come to terms with the implications of this well tested knowledge.

A geocentric construct of the universe had always been central to the worldview of people. They had seen themselves to be at the center of the universe. For the Church in the Middle Ages

> the geocentric view was no mere matter of science.
> Rather it was the cornerstone evidence that the entire
> universe revolved around us. With God, angels, man,
> the beasts, and fertile plants made for our benefit, with
> the sun and stars wheeling overhead, we knew our place:
> at the center of God's creation.[10]

The completely unforeseen findings of modern science forever shattered the geocentric universe. It did not happen overnight. In the fifteenth century Nicholas of Cusa (1401-1464) taught that the earth was not the center of the universe. Nearly a century later Nicholas

Copernicus (1473-1543), a Polish astronomer, who was also a monk, published just prior to his death, after 40 years of work, *On the Revolutions of Celestial Orbs.* He placed the sun at the center, circled by attendant planets. His explication viewed by historians of science as one of the driest books ever written was suffocatingly abstruse. His system fits within the framework of Renaissance aesthetics where questions of science, philosophy, and theology were inextricably entwined.

It is called the Copernican Revolution but it really didn't start until some seventy years later when Galileo Galilei (1564-1642) published *Siderus Nuncius* (The Starry Messenger) in 1610. He is considered to be the father of modern science, being the first to combine rational theory with accurate observation and experimentation. He made the first practical use of the telescope in so doing. *A Dialogue on the Two Principal Systems of the World,* published in 1632, was the last straw for the Church. The Inquisition, under Pope Urban VIII, censored this book together with the one written by Copernicus. Previously the Pope while still a cardinal had been very interested in, and encouraging towards, science but he refused to even look through the telescope when urged so to do by Galileo. The latter was forced to acknowledge his "sins" and recant his writings. It is said that while formally so doing he murmured, "Eppir si muove" (But it does move).

Don Cupitt believes that the "greatest and most important quantum leap forward in the entire history of human knowledge was initiated by Galileo and René Descartes (1596-1650), a contemporary French philosopher--the first of such to contribute to the Great Western Transformation. Why-questions (the search for purpose) came to be replaced by the critical thinking stemming from how-questions. The latter play a vital role, whereas the former keep one looking for a ready-made and built-in purposiveness that just isn't there.[11]

The new cosmology shattered Europe's understanding of how the world at large functioned, together with humanity's place and role in it all. The English metaphysical poet John Donne, a contemporary of Galileo's, lamented:

> The new Philosophy calls all in doubt,
>
> The element of fire is quite put out;
>
> The Sun is lost, and th' Earth, and no man's wit
>
> Can well direct him where to look for it. . . .
>
> 'Tis all in peeces, all cohaerence gone;
>
> All just supply, and all Relation.

In the next three centuries Western Europeans would move from seeing themselves enshrined, as God's special creation, at the center of a fixed and finite angel-filled universe, in which everything connects to God, to being located on the third of nine planets, orbiting a common star on the edge of the unremarkable Milky Way galaxy - itself a small part of a vast materialist void. It remains the epochal shift of the modern era, paralleling that of the Axial Age, impacting philosophy, religion, and the collective psyche so forcefully that we are still wrestling with its consequences.[12]

With the passage of time the Inquisition's actions against Galileo became an ever increasing embarrassment for the Catholic Church. It took his and Copernicus's writings off the forbidden list in the nineteenth century. The case was not formally closed until 1992, 350 years after the death of Galileo. Thirteen years earlier Pope John-Paul II had established a commission to study the Church's treatment of Galileo. In a speech to the Pontifical Academy of Sciences (a seeming contradiction in terms), the Pope stated that the condemnation of Galileo resulted from a "tragic mutual incomprehension" and that it had become a symbol of the Church's "supposed rejection of scientific progress." There was no "incomprehension" on the part of Galileo.

The truth eventually proved to be more powerful than ecclesiastical authority.

Galileo was part of a trio of geniuses, whose discoveries and analyses had the effect of desacralizing the heavens. Johannes Kepler (1571-1631), a German astronomer and contemporary of Galileo, formulated the three laws of planetary motion that form the basis of all modern planetary astronomy.

The third intellectual giant was Sir Isaac Newton, an Englishman, who was born the year that Galileo died (1642) and lived for 85 years. Among his many findings was the discovery of the gravitational law. Aristotle's explanation of gravity had been the accepted understanding until then. He had taught that any object must have within it an inherent or natural tendency to try and reach the ground. Somewhat similarly the Church had believed that all nature and history were underpinned by the power of a purposeful God, into whose coherent divine plan they all fitted. Newton was the first to grasp that the heavens and the earth were a single system governed by the same laws.

The research of these three scientists brought within the empirical reach of humans that which had previously been associated only with the divine. When Napoleon Bonaparte asked Pierre Laplace (1747-1827), a French astronomer, why, in his book on the system of the universe, he had made no mention of its Creator, he famously replied, "I had no need of that hypothesis." Suzuki observes, "Copernicus pushed us out of the center, and we've been trying to get back there ever since - claiming power not as part of the web of creation, not even as caretakers, but as masters of a cosmic machine."[13]

Undoubtedly influenced by the eighteenth century Enlightenment, the study of the physical universe would steadily increase the secularization of science until four German physiologists resolved in 1842 that no forces other than physicochemical ones would be considered in their research. Five years later one of them, viz. Hermann von Helmholtz, proclaimed the Principle of the Conservation of Energy. There are no outside forces in our closed world of energy transformations. James Joule, a contemporary English physicist, reached a similar conclusion, proclaiming that "the Great Agents of Nature are indestructible. . . . There is no corner in the stars for any god, no crack in this closed universe of matter for any divine influence to seep through, none whatever."[14]

Another field of study was to mature in the late eighteenth and early nineteenth centuries that would contribute to the tension between science and Christianity. It became known as geology, which would, in effect, add a fourth dimension--that of geological time. During the Renaissance a physician from Saxony published a book on fossils, but it was Scottish geologists that made the most significant breakthroughs in the field.

In the seventeenth century Bishop Usher had calculated the date of creation and beginning of time to be 4004 BCE. In Jewish tradition the earth was believed to come into existence 3760 years before the start of the Christian era. The age of the earth could not be accurately dated until 1907 with the discovery of radioactivity. Geologists concluded at that time that this planet has been in existence for six billion rather than 6,000 years. This new understanding led to the theory of the slow evolution of all forms of life.

The study of what was called "natural history" had been growing in England from the seventeenth century. The dominant motive was the comforting joy of finding the Creator's hand, if not the Creator himself, in nature. The blow was therefore all the more devastating that the announcement should come from two of their own that it was evolution, and not a divine intelligence, that was the cause of all nature. Charles Darwin (1809-1892) and Alfred Wallace (1823-1913), both amateur naturalists, developed the theory independently of each other.

This was not the first time that scientists made the same discovery in this manner, nor would it be the last. Such events have only added more weight to the findings. Wallace called the evolutionary process "the struggle for existence"; Darwin's term is reflected in his watershed book, published in 1859, *On the Origin of Species by Means of Natural Selection*. The book would cause him to become the main target of attack and condemnation.

The theory of evolution by natural selection postulates that human life, starting four billion years ago, has emerged from single cells in the sea. All living things have evolved and changed in response to environmental conditions by means of the natural selection of randomly recurring mutations, developing from the simplest forms to ever more complex ones.

Darwin had not anticipated that his book would find an audience beyond his peers, but the first printing was sold out at the prepublication sale, one third being bought by a chain of libraries--an endorsement equivalent to a recommendation today by Oprah Winfrey. The position of man as the image of God on earth had been left unchanged by the revisions made in cosmology. Even though Darwin made only one cryptic remark in his book--"Much light will be thrown on the origin of man and his history"--his readers were under no illusion as to the consequences of accepting the evolutionary argument for human origins. Cold uncalculating chance had carved the human species out of mere matter.

Perhaps the most disconcerting realization to come from this understanding is that there is no divine hand at the helm - we ourselves are fully responsible for ourselves and the effect of our actions. Equally momentous, Christianity's worldview was no longer sustainable. The human species had been shoved off of its pedestal. There had been no creation of perfect human beings who soon had fallen into a state of sin. This being the case, Jesus was not obliged to pay the ultimate price to redeem a lost and damned humanity. The traditional explanations of, and need for, salvation die, "not because the truth they sought to convey is wrong, but rather because that truth was conveyed in a way that our expanded knowledge has shown to be unbelievable."[15]

A further undermining of traditional Christian understanding was brought about by the development of the scientific tools of historical and literary criticism, which developed simultaneously with what came to be known as Darwinism. These disciplines were used to study the Bible itself and brought to light the human as opposed to the divine origins of the book. The challenge now was to distinguish between history, legend, and myth.

This study has proved to be a much greater cause for alarm within Christianity than the theory of evolution by natural selection, as it has been promoted by the Church's own scholars. Protestants were heavily involved in this field in the latter half of the nineteenth century. It had diminished somewhat by the middle of the next century, only to be revived by the Jesus Seminar/Westar Institute. Catholic scholars became active in the second half of the last century, only to be silenced by Pope John-Paul II.

The Bible, the major means of receiving messages from a long withdrawn God, was found to be no such channel. It had instead been shown to be a very human collection of writings. Not a few Christians have been unable to come to terms with this finding. They continue to close their eyes and seal their ears as they cling to the most tactile vestige of the bicameral era.

Karen Armstrong calls these scientific advances and the technologies to which they gave birth as the Second Promethean Revolution, the first being the discovery of fire. A. A. Michelson, America's first Nobel science laureate (awarded in 1894), summed up the consensus of the world's physicists by stating, "The more important fundamental laws and facts of physical science have all been discovered, and . . . the possibility of their ever being supplanted in consequence of new discoveries is exceedingly remote."[16]

This was said six years before the birth of quantum theory and eleven years before the special theory of relativity was formulated. String theory followed, and the challenge that occupied Albert Einstein in his last years, the unified field theory, is still out there.

There are still things that remain unknown as there are questions that science, as yet, has been unable to answer. Patricia Williams refers to them as black boxes. The theory of evolution raised far more questions than it initially could answer. Yet one by one these black boxes continue to be opened. Darwin, for example, did not know how characteristics are inherited. Not until 1900 did science recognize genes, discrete factors that carry inheritance and that can be mathematically manipulated. This in turn exposed yet another black box: genes were still invisible to then available technology. Some thus thought that living organisms contain a vital force beyond the scope of science, a supernatural power that imparted life. Science illuminated that black box in 1953 with the discovery of the double helix of DNA and the chemical nature of genes. The force turned out to be a chemical bonding, a natural force.[17]

The twentieth century witnessed a gradual rapprochement between science and religion. By 1900 the various scientific disciplines had matured and begun to engage in dialogue with religion. More and more scientific research has come to be appreciated as spiritual speculation, contributing as it does to a sense of awe at what has been learned. The Gifford lectures, established in 1887 by Adam Lord Gifford, are given in the course of an academic year at each of the four Scottish universities in turn. The late Carl Sagan (1935-1996) had the honor in 1985. He was a prominent American scientist known for his research on the possibility of extraterrestrial life. He entitled his lectures "The Varieties of Scientific Experience--a Personal View of the Search for God.

Sagan's emphasis was more the search for natural truth than on "a search for God." At the outset he informed his listeners that "the word 'religion' comes from the Latin for 'binding together,' to connect that which has been sundered apart. . . . And in this sense of seeking the deepest interrelations among things that superficially appear to be sundered, the objectives of religion and science, I believe, are identical or very nearly so." Sagan came to see science as "informed worship" and as a "two-pronged investigation into the nature of the world and the nature of ourselves."

Part of this second prong, our human nature, took the form of the study of the organization of human society and the relationship of individuals to it. This endeavor could have become a major part of the Church's work had it not been almost totally preoccupied with preparing its adherents for the afterlife.

France played a major role in pioneering the study and improvement of human society. The French Revolution marked the birth pangs of a new social awareness, which led to an unstoppable determination to foster life with the new values of Liberty, Equality, and Fraternity. This would come at the expense of Christianity because it was in France, more than anywhere else in Europe, that almost total rejection of traditional Christianity took place.

A swing from supernaturalism to naturalism was central to this development--from God to humankind. This was accompanied by the growth of materialism and socialism. Baron D'Holbach (1723-1789), a French philosopher, was the first to openly declare himself an atheist. He was militantly anti-clerical and desired the destruction of all religion--

and this in the interest of truth and morality. He believed that religion was deliberately perpetuated by the priesthood because of the power which it placed in their hands.[18]

August Comte (1798-1857), a French philosopher and preacher of a religion of humanity, coined the term 'sociology' in 1839. He meant the concept to be a comprehensive discipline which would link history, morals, and politics. Comte founded the Positivist Society of Paris in 1848 to promote and expound the new religion of Humanity. It's guiding principle was "Live for Others." He also coined the term "altruism" - consideration for others without any thought of self as a principle of conduct.[19]

This focus on communal life and its needs was not in fact new thinking. It was a return to the heart of the teaching of the Axial Sages that people should look out for one another. An amazing aspect of this development, and sad, is that it happened outside the purview of established Christian religion, if not in spite of it.

Not only did the human being in his societal setting come under study, but also that which is within himself which enables him and affects his conduct as an individual.

Ever since people began to reflect on their makeup and nature they have used such concepts as spirit, soul, and mind to refer to one's inner non-physical workings; that which refers to one's ability to think and reason, and to participate in that level of consciousness which seems to distinguish the human species from all other creatures. Investigation of this inner life would, not surprisingly, lead to a revolutionary understanding of it, resulting in the birth of a new science that would be called psychology.[20]

The significance of this for religion can hardly be overestimated, because the inner, or spiritual, life has always been the dominant concern of the various religions. If it is true that "Modern psychology provides a totally new understanding and judgment of the sexual, emotional, ethical, moral and religious existence of man," then a radical change in religion and understanding of the foundation of ethics and morals becomes inevitable.[21]

The perennial problem has always been how the inner life is to be related to the physical life of a person: Are they two independent entities or interdependent or ultimately one? Plato believed a person to be composed of a mortal body which temporarily housed an immortal soul. Both the Christian and the Jewish view have been greatly influenced by him.

A long succession of philosophers has wrestled with this issue. It was the empirical science of physiology which was instrumental in bringing new understanding to the mind/soul--body problem, serving as a midwife to the birth of the new science of psychology. Wilhelm Wundt (1832-1920), the acknowledged father of psychology, and the equally famous William James (1842-1910) started out as professors of physiology.

Psychology looks for the ways in which human feelings, emotions, and thoughts arise from tangible and this-worldly origins and, to the extent that it has been successful, it has provided alternative explanations to those inherited from traditional supernaturalism, explanations which modern people find much more convincing. At a very early stage, a further development took place which was destined to be more threatening to traditional religion than all the other discoveries of psychology.

Sigmund Freud (1856-1939) called it psycho-analysis. Its impact has been compared with those made by Copernicus and Darwin.

> As Copernicus destroyed the illusion of the earth's and
> man's central position in the universe, and Darwin
> destroyed the illusion of man's uniqueness in living

nature, Freud dealt a lethal blow to man's perhaps greatest illusion - that of being master of his thoughts and actions.[22]

It was Freud's great contribution to produce the clinical evidence to support the concept of the unconscious and to show some of the ways in which it operates.

We can also now appreciate that the unconscious is rooted in the bicameral mind. Thus, the source of the human urge to hear from the gods, together with other psychic activity, goes way back to the distant past. Furthermore, modern psychology has supplied natural explanations of experiences which have traditionally been attributed to divine sources. Conservative Christianity has not yet come to terms with these implications.

There is, however, a great benefit to be gained from the ambivalent effect of psychology on the understanding of religion, for it applies to *all* religious traditions. It had always seemed to be necessary to conclude that if one religion was totally true (because it had been divinely revealed), then all the others must be suspect if not false. "The human sciences of psychology and sociology opened up a way by which the relative value of each of the great religious traditions can be adequately acknowledged."[23]

The Scientific Revolution may have drastically changed our understanding of the divine, but it has not diminished our potential for being thrilled and awed by a better understanding of ourselves and various aspects of the world at large. Science can hold its own with the creative arts even when it is reduced to a language of symbols and numbers. There is nothing more elegant or profound than $E = mc^2$. These five symbols tell us how the Big Bang started, and with it the whole process that creates life itself.

Spirituality and science are inextricably linked. As a preacher asked,

"If the world were not wondrous and captivating, mysterious and powerful, do you think there would be any science?"[24]

There were two distinct developments that brought about the Great Western Transformation, the second being in the field of philosophy and metaphysics. Following a parallel path to that of scientists, philosophers, as they emerged, soon found themselves functioning outside of the Church or without its blessing and approval. All higher education in the West, until fairly recently, took place in Church-owned institutions, which over time have become true universities. Not a few of the first philosophers had thus studied to be clerics but found themselves informed and challenged by the enormous growth in knowledge and understanding gained through scientific endeavor.

The roots of philosophy go back to the heart of the Axial Age in classical Greece, the sages Socrates and Plato being the most prominent exemplars that spring readily to mind. From the very beginning philosophy contributed to the growth of the consciousness that emerged with the breakdown of the bicameral mind in the second millennium BCE. Ancient Greece, like all populations of that era, had been in the grip of myths. Greek philosophy was characterized in its beginnings by a merging of mythos with logos.

In his book *The Masks of God* Joseph Campbell lists four functions of mythology. The fourth one parallels the conception of philosophy as a guide: "to initiate the individual into the orders of his own psyche, guiding him towards his own spiritual enrichment and realization."[25] Mythology and philosophy are thus related: both are symbolic, and the characters and episodes of the former refer to metaphysical and psychological mysteries.

There is a philosophical--theological spectrum in the movements spawned by the Axial Sages. The monotheistic religions are almost purely based in and on theology, while Hinduism, Buddhism, and Confucianism are a varying mixture. The Greek product, however, is the essence of philosophy, which in turn has impacted Judaism and Christianity. In the Bible God is represented as the creator of everything that exists, holding a position of unchallengeable authority. The ultimate loyalty of thought and life is to God rather than humankind. By comparison, the sympathy and respect of the Greeks was for humanity and human reasoning.[26] Thus, people would come to see theology as claiming to be in possession of the truth, in contrast to philosophy, which is in quest of the truth. An anonymous definition states, "Philosophy is questions that may never be answered. Religion is answers that may never be questioned."[27]

The major characteristic that separates philosophy from theology is that the former does not accept the concept of revelation as being a special preserve of any people. One has to rely on reason in "finding the ground of being and the fundamental structuring of order of the universe."[28] A commonality of both disciplines is the striving of their practitioners to feel at home and secure in the universe. Philosophy's major dynamic is that of asking questions about the "truth," which is the easy part when compared with finding the answers. To philosophers, "truth" is not an absolute concept; it cannot be captured for all, yet alone for all time.

Maimonedes came to grips with philosophy a century before the influence of the Renaissance. He did it in the context of reconciling it with the Law. This was the thrust of his renowned book entitled *The Guide of the Perplexed*. Maimonedes wanted to move his readers to a deeper appreciation of religion, that which would be in harmony with reason. He saw the writings of Plato, Socrates, and the Stoics as being transformative of life, rather than merely intellectual, that they sought to "form more than inform," "to form people and to transform souls." As Maimonedes understood Socrates: knowledge was not a set of propositions, but rather a way of being, conveyed through dialogue.[29]

The ethos of Greek philosophy was portrayed in the Parthenon, completed in 432 BCE. It embodied the values of Athens, especially democracy - two Greek words that mean people power. The Parthenon remains an icon of Western civilization - the most copied building in the world. The Elgin marbles that once lined the walls depict both human and mythological figures, making the structure as much a temple to themselves as to their gods.

The Renaissance was instrumental in the revival of philosophy in the West as it became reacquainted with the Greek and Roman classical thinkers. Justinian I (483-565) had abolished the Greek schools of philosophy in the interest of promoting Christianity. Later the Church and its scholastic forces would succeed in dampening the thinking and imagination of the populace at large as it turned mythical concepts into supposed factual truths. Philosophy had always had a mythical element and function, but this too had died. Martin Heidegger (1889-1976) would say late in the age of modernity that the vocation of contemporary philosophy was to move from logos back to mythos, to restore humanity to the fullness of its being, and a realization of the human relationship with Being. Philosophy must always have a mythical element.[30]

The restoration of humanity to the fullness of its being would, among other things, require a movement from heteronomy to autonomy. Heteronomy is in play when one is under an authority outside of oneself. The degree to which one slavishly follows the dictates of a religion, for example, to that degree one is heteronomous. Autonomy, on the other hand, is the state in which final authority is believed to be seated in the inner self.[31]

> The voice which speaks with authority to autonomous
> human beings is heard from within rather than from

without. However much people may continue to value the voices which speak to them from without, it will be the inherent value of what is spoken, rather than because of the status of the speaker.[32]

This movement from heteronomy to autonomy would mean that all traditional sources of authority - the Church, priests, the Bible, royalty, the aristocracy, and the civil institutions would come to suffer a slow but sure erosion. This process is still at work and is by no means near completion.

René Descartes (1596-1650), as mentioned earlier, was a pioneer philosopher with respect to the Great Western Transformation. He was, obviously, a product of the Roman Catholic Church and remained in good standing with it, even though he rejected scholasticism. Although he is best known for the phrase *Cogito ergo sum* (I think, therefore I am), he also exclaimed "Doubt!"--a word that would reverberate ever more loudly through the next four centuries. This word was the gauntlet thrown down, not only by science but by philosophy as well.

As modernity has continued to make ever more knowledge and experiences available to one and all, diversity has been encouraged. Diversity in turn has created choices, which in turn create doubt. And too much doubt can lead to desperation, which leads, in turn, to the search for certainty, a characteristic of the bicameral mind.[33] In those times there was no such thing as doubt; one just obeyed the voices of the gods. This embracing of certainty is the cornerstone of fundamentalism, which has paralleled the growth of doubt.

Descartes came to realize the extent to which one's beliefs are intimately linked with one's environment. He wondered how religious certainty could be a mere accident of birth, and he came to conclude, "The chief cause of our errors is to be found in the prejudices of our childhood."[34]

Descartes was in many ways a pivotal figure, because he also began the Age of Reason. It is also referred to as The Enlightenment or the Age of Rationalism. It lasted until the late eighteenth century. Reason, observation, and experiment was the Enlightenment's trinity. The movement both contributed to scientific discoveries and was in turn greatly influenced by the physical sciences, which resulted in knowledge being organized in encyclopedias and the founding of scientific institutes.

Philosophers also began to challenge the temporal, civil authority of the established churches as they appealed for, and then struggled over, rules for negotiating the newly emerging civil society. They critiqued the supernatural dogmas that Christianity claimed as its authority and, therefore, its right to control public affairs. This in turn contributed directly to the American and French Revolutions.

Christian establishments would lose ground throughout the West as they suffered a permanent loss of temporal power. While at the beginning of the eighteenth century Christian establishments were fully in control of civil society throughout Europe, by the nineteenth century the situation had begun to turn, and by the beginning of the twentieth century the battle had been completely lost. Unable now to set the rules for public discourse, Christian leaders withdrew from the public arena, retiring to be leaders of the faith community only. In the second half of the nineteenth century, in a reaction to this trend, the Vatican came to sharpen its arguments about Papal infallibility while some Protestants shaped arguments for a fundamentalist Christianity.

The Enlightenment's reach went even further as it undermined the Western metaphysical tradition. Metaphysics, in dealing with the first principles of things, overlaps a vital area of religious concern, as it works at understanding the inner life of a person. The understanding of God's nature and existence was greatly affected in all this as the need to harmonize science and free will with the existence of God grew. The school of theological reasoning known as deism emerged. It asserts that God exists and that he created the world but has no present relation to it. He so organized nature that it proceeds mechanically, like a perfect clock.

An impressive procession of philosophers followed in Descartes' train. David Hume (1711-1776), a Scot, was considered to be the greatest British philosopher. He undermined the attempt by some enlightenment thinkers to construct a rational religion which would preserve Christian ideals and yet remain intellectually respectable. Hume effectively brought to an end the marriage of faith and reason, which had characterized Western Christian thought since the age of the second century apologists. He was an agnostic a century before the term was coined, arguing that the existence of God could neither be proved nor disproved.

Voltaire (1694-1778), a contemporary of Hume, used the pen name Francois Marie Arouet. He was the chief example of French deism, and his philosophical work influenced European thought for generations. He changed the way that the world thought and has been embraced as one of the world's great men. Voltaire became the foremost apologist for the leading ideas of the eighteenth century - free inquiry, human dignity, equality, and freedom of conscience.

The steadily growing variety of ideas and topics under discussion and the increasing zeal for observing and measuring the cycles of nature kept strengthening deism and atheism, while weakening the credibility of Providence. The Lisbon earthquake of 1755 "supplied a brutal confirmation of disbelief."[35] It happened on the eve of All Saints Day while the faithful were in church, where many perished. A tsunami in the Tagus River together with raging fires completed its destruction. It is estimated that 100,000 were killed. In a long poem Voltaire asked:

How could a personal God endowed with power and justice ordain such a holocaust? For what conceivable reason kill worshipping men, women and children in a peculiarly horrible manner? That they were worse sinners than the same number of Parisians or Londoners was a contemptible answer. There *was* no answer, except that the forces of nature acted independently of their creator.[36]

Immanuel Kant (1724-1804) was a German philosopher whose work was epoch making in that he established the main lines for philosophical developments since his time. He summed up the fundamental thrust of his philosophy with four questions: 1) What can I know? 2) What ought I to do? 3) What may I hope? The fourth question was the sum and substance of the other three--What is man?

Kant lived through the end of the Age of Enlightenment, and he noted that its effect had been to free philosophy from subservience to theology. Rather than bearing the latter's train, it would carry the torch ahead. They had finally become divorced from one another.[36] He said that "Enlightenment is man's exodus from his self-incurred tutelage. Tutelage is the inability to use one's understanding without the guidance of another person. . . . 'Dare to Know' [*sapere aude*]. Have the courage to use your understanding; this is the motto of the Enlightenment."[37] This exodus was part of the transition from heteronomy to autonomy.

An important consequence of the Enlightenment was the increasing attention given to the study of history, leading to the development of historical scholarship. Traditions and writings of and about the past, which had long been accepted without question, became more and more subject to doubt and critical investigation. The Bible came to be radically reassessed in this process. The desire to find out "just exactly what happened" continues to be an important characteristic of scholarship. Scientific tools of historical and literary criticism, having been developed over time, now make it possible for historians to aim for producing a reliable picture of the past as they try to distinguish between reliable evidence, myth, and legend.

As the Cartesian view of the world became more pervasive, a change in outlook began to occur. The undermining of what was at one time embraced as eternal truth led to spiritual uncertainty. Not only philosophers but poets and writers as well began to counterattack. Jean-Jacques Rousseau (1712-1778) prefigured the changes that would take place. Rousseau rebelled against the dominant values of his time, such as rationalism and the rigidity of classicism. He, along with William Wordsworth (1770-1850) talked about the "feeling intellect" as demonstrated by the urge to sympathize with all living things, which was beyond the scope of reason alone. European thinkers came to prefer passion and spontaneity over discipline, order, and control. This change introduced the Romantic Movement, which would come at the expense of the Age of Reason. It began in the last decade of the eighteenth century and lasted for about 60 years.

The Romantic Movement was not so much a revolt against reason as making a case "for the work of mind-and-heart." Feeling was seen as coming first, with reason then giving it form and direction.[38] Spirituality was validated anew and religion, with a modified orthodoxy, enjoyed a renaissance as one of the indispensable works of mind-and-heart. The teachings of the ancient creeds came to replace the abstract propositions of Deism. For the Romanticists, the vastness of the universe created awe.

The movement is noted for the remarkable poetry it produced. It has often been discounted as being sentimental because of its irrational character. The best of the Romantic poetry was, however, deeply subversive as it attacked (and still does) conventional wisdom. The writers of such work trusted deeply in the human capacity for perception and the crucial insight that it brings. David Suzuki observes, "Artists of all kinds tend to see their work as similar to, even identical with, the work of the natural world and its continual process of creation. 'Great works of art,' according to Goethe, 'are works of nature just as truly as mountains, streams and plains.' "[39]

Romanticism, while having its own shortcomings, corrected the Enlightenment's errors and succeeded in deepening and amplifying all the categories of art and thought.[40]

Friedrich Schleiermacher (1768-1834) was a product of the Romantic Movement. He was a mystical theologian who rejected dogma, defining religion in terms of feeling and intuition. He aided and abetted what would become a twentieth century characterization, the privatization of spirituality. Schleiermacher based his call for faith on "the autonomy of religious feeling" which he saw as a human given.

Georg W. F. Hegel (1770-1831), a contemporary of Schleiermacher, started out as a theological student but moved into the philosophical field, believing that philosophy had to assume the role previously played by religion. He argued that science and religion are both essential and that they must be reconciled. He used his famous construct of Thesis and Antithesis leading to Synthesis. Science and religion, the temporal and the eternal, should become a new form of religion that would supersede the old. His complicated new form of religion did not draw a large following, but in the latter part of the twentieth century both theologians and philosophers studied Hegel with renewed interest.

Ludwig Feuerbach (1804-1872) was a key interpreter of post-Enlightenment religion. He also began his career as a theological student but came under the spell of Hegel and devoted himself to philosophy. Feuerbach came to believe that, "Man is not only a spiritual being, he is also an earthly being, inseparable from the earth."[41] Feuerbach furthermore believed that God was a projection of the true nature of human beings: "Thus, God is derived only from man, but not conversely man from God. . . . God is what human beings would like to be; God is man's own essence and goal, conceived as a real being."[42] He was presaging Nietzsche's "Übermensch" while contending for the opposite of Hegel's philosophy--the humanization of God rather than the deification of humanity. A study of God would turn out to be an exercise in human self-understanding.

Feuerbach was also prophetic in stressing where society's focus should be. He argued that in true religion human beings would recognize their dependence on nature and the necessity to live in harmony with it. While the primal religions had made too much of nature, the theistic religions had done the opposite.[43] A consequence of this tendency was the paralyzing of human effort to improve the world. People, at the beginning of the third millennium CE, have become increasingly aware of this need.

David Strauss (1801-1874) was a contemporary of Feuerbach and followed a similar career path. He was also strongly influenced by Darwin's writings. Towards the end of his life he wrote *The Old Faith and the New,* which illustrated how his worldview was changing. He believed that the world had crossed a threshold of change which, while not making religion obsolete, demanded a radically new form of faith.[44]

Søren Kierkegaard (1813-1855), a Danish philosopher and another Feuerbach contemporary, was a quintessential Romantic thinker, defending Christianity against science and rationality. He insisted that religion demanded a commitment that could not be justified by any logical process, because it called for a "leap of faith."

Kierkegaard ridiculed Hegelian philosophers for leaving out the role of the individual in their worldview. He wanted his gravestone to read

"Here lies Kierkegaard--that individual." He encouraged the movement from heteronomy to autonomy.

Karl Marx (1818-1883) was born into a Jewish family that had converted to Protestantism. He was a contemporary of Strauss but studied law, philosophy, and history. He was greatly influenced by Feuerbach and Hegel but became much more widely known than both of them in becoming the founder of a new religion.

Marx will forever be linked to the statement "religion is the opium of the masses." He was, however, somewhat sympathetic to religion, seeing it as a source of solace that should be set aside until an unfair economic system--the source of people's pain--had been eradicated. The famous line, placed in its context, bears this out. He wrote in 1844,

> Religious suffering is, at one and the same time, the expression of real suffering, and a protest against real suffering. Religion is the sigh of the oppressed creature, the heart of a heartless world, and the soul of soulless conditions. It is the opium of the people.

> The abolition of religion as the illusory happiness of the people is the demand for their real happiness. To call on them to give up their illusions about their condition is to call on them to give up a condition that requires illusions. The criticism of religion is, therefore, in em-bryo, the criticism of that vale of tears of which religion is the halo.[45]

Marx was interested in faith because of what it told him about human suffering.

The abolishment of religion came to be a key component in the establishment of Marx's teachings. It is, however, more than a little ironic that Marxism itself became a religion. It is replete with its own eschatology, believing that a revolution carried out by the proletariat would bring about a new social order. His writings, especially *Das Kapital* and *The Communist Manifesto*, would come to be regarded as the new sacred canon.

Communism became fully developed as a religion in the cult of personality that was erected around Stalin. This is true of all personality cults. They adopt the worst characteristics in that they rob their followers of their autonomy and freedom. They are, in truth, transported back to bicameral conditions. Stalinism evidenced the full profile of true religious belief. One of the wrongdoings defendants were charged with in the Moscow show trials was the crime of "sacrilege." Leon Trotsky, a prominent Communist until his exile by Stalin, said, "None of us desires or is able to dispute the will of the Party. Clearly the Party is always right." Some defendants were so committed that they were willing to confess to crimes that they did not commit in the deluded hope that their own disgrace and death would serve some higher purpose.

Marx came to be regarded as a prophet in the full sense of the word and can be numbered with the Sages as one of the great religious founders. Yet his religion was completely different in that his teachings caught the imagination and won the allegiance of modern people, particularly in those geographical areas where people felt themselves to be oppressed, viz. Russia, China, South America, and sub-Saharan Africa.

Yet Communism, as a religion, is distinctly different. It is without supernatural aspects, being non-theistic and humanistic. Marxism is unique in another way: it has evolved, flourished, and entered into sudden decline, all within a century. The rapidity of social and cultural change in modern times partly explains such brevity.[46]

Friedrich Nietzsche (1844-1900) was one of the major influences of twentieth century thought and a prophet for the twenty-first century.

Because his mind was afflicted (possibly by the ravages of syphilis) for the last decade of his life, conservative Christianity, in an attempt to ignore the significance of his writings, has tried to convince itself that all his writings are the ravings of a madman.

> R. J. Hollingdale, a translator of some of Nietzsche's work, said,
>
> > The twentieth century came to birth in the mind of Friedrich Nietzsche during the 1880's; and it is his particular and undying distinction that when he saw the blood-red dawn of our day he did not turn from it in distress and leave the future to fend for itself, but wearied himself to find a means whereby this new and more terrible day could be endured, welcomed, and enjoyed.[47]

Martin Buber, a twentieth century philosopher, referred to Nietzsche as "the first pathfinder of the new culture, the awakener and creator of new life-values and a new world-feeling."[48]

As a contemporary of Darwin, he was the first to meet squarely the challenge of modern natural science which, in showing man as being part of nature instead of God's providential plan, had fundamentally changed history. His greatness was to perceive the radical nature of the cultural and religious changes that would take place--that he was living between two ages, one already dying and the other waiting to be born. Western Christendom had come to an end, and thus concepts of ultimate reality itself were in a state of change and flux. With his dictum "God is dead, and we have killed him," Nietzsche was the messenger, not the cause. The God who presided over Christianity was no longer believable. He suggested that if this religion were voluntarily to bring about its own demise, it would be its finest hour.

In playing the role of the canary in the mineshaft, he sought to warn others of the challenges that would flow from these developments. Chief among them would be morality itself. Nietzsche was the first important philosopher to talk about values. The death of God would mean an end to the absoluteness of all values and truths. Religion could no longer serve as the foundation for moral values. He believed that people themselves are the creators of values: "There are no moral phenomena at all, only a moral interpretation of phenomena."[49] The former "eternal values" has fostered a slave morality - that which functions on the basis of what all people have in common--and takes no cognizance of values peculiar to each individual. This need to seek approval by conforming to a widely accepted norm not only stunted moral growth, it also smothered initiative and creativity and crushed the freedom of the human spirit. It is now widely recognized that the person of genius, of creative spirit, must often break out of the accepted morality of his time in order to be creative. It is this creativity which saves humankind and not religion. The artist is of supreme importance.

Nietzsche's answer to the death of God is the "Übermensch"--a word that defies translation. "Superman" has been used up by the science-fiction character and thus does not help to enlighten. "Exceptional" and the Yiddish word "mensch" speak to aspects of its meaning. Barzun sees it as referring to the self-development of an individual into a creature, a state above and beyond what he/she is now.[50] Geering says, "The Übermensch is the one who has overcome the HUMAN (mensch) in himself--the one who has overcome the animal nature in humankind."[51] Maimonides was one of the earliest philosophers to describe some of the qualities implied in "übermensch." In explicating prophecy he wrote it "rests only upon a sage great in wisdom, heroic in character, whose reason overcomes his passion, and who has a broad and sound mind."[52]

The Übermensch is the person who has come to terms with the fact that there is no ultimate power that one can fall back on in order to "get it right," but that instead, if there is any contribution that can be made

235

towards the good, it has to come from us alone. Like other important German concepts it is best to embrace the word that Nietzsche coined. The Übermensch is one who has made the transition from heteronomy to autonomy.

James Joyce (1882-1941), an exceptional Irish novelist, wrote, among other works, *A Portrait of the Artist as a Young Man*. It is an autobiographical novel which describes the waning of his attachment to the security offered by Catholicism, opting instead for freedom as an unfettered artist. In Nietzschian fashion he realizes that he must become "a priest of art," which is an individualistic endeavor as opposed to a social or communal state.

Alfred North Whitehead (1861-1947), a British philosopher and mathematician, did much to narrow the gap between philosophy and science as well as between science and religion. He insisted that scientific knowledge, though precise, is incomplete. It must be supplemented by philosophical principles and by the insights of poets.

Whitehead developed process philosophy which expresses the pervasive twentieth century dissatisfaction with the concept of an unchanging God. His god does not stand outside the flow of history in an eternal present, knowing and determining everything that happens, but rather makes new things possible that he does not control, such as the actions of our free will.

After World War I a new spiritual consciousness, as opposed to a movement, developed. There was no founder, philosopher, or prophet, but rather a coalescing of the elements of the Great Western Transformation. Human capabilities, such as the capacity for reason, are emphasized. The right of all people to develop to their full potential is promoted. The focus of faith is on humanity rather than divinity. The blessings of life are available to all, as opposed to the chosen or saved, and they appear in the simple dress of the everyday. This humanism has a courageous worldview, believing that the world's future is in our hands alone, that history is open ended, and that people can make this world a better place in which to live.[53]

If indeed history is open ended and there is no such concept as revealed and absolute truth, then it follows that there are no absolutes with respect to ethics and morality. What, therefore, is the relationship, if any, between ethics and religion?

13

RELIGION AND ETHICS

Ethics, which is concerned with an accepted standard of good behavior, was at the heart of the teaching of the sages, as evidenced in their varied articulations of the Golden Rule. Epicurus (340-270 BCE), for example, was a Greek philosopher who developed a system of ethics. His followers were known as Epicureans. He believed that there is "no one who governs and orders being," and thus all things are due to chance. Epicurus believed pleasure "to be the beginning and end of the blessed life, but pleasure to him was not so much active enjoyment as the absence of pain, and thus not all pleasures were to be chosen.

Western religion, viz. Christianity, ended up denying responsible choice. One was expected to unquestioningly follow what was promoted as God's directives, regardless of the consequences. This "right action" was what God required, and it was given once and for all time. The value of a people, of an individual, was to be measured by the degree of obedience to God's will, and one's punishment or reward depended directly upon the degree of such obedience.

Pierre Bayle (1647-1706) was the first modern to argue that morality is not necessarily dependent upon religious belief, and that, equally important, religious belief does not guarantee a high moral life. The sad fact is that monotheistic practitioners, in particular, use religion to justify harmful deeds and acts. Christianity is replete with carnage committed in the name of God. Muslims, on an ever increasing scale, are blowing up and maiming innocent people in praise of Allah. And in Israel it is the most religious Jews who are causing injustices and indignities to be heaped upon the Palestinians.

There is a peculiar and persistent pattern that in countries where one particular religion dominates, corruption and wrongdoing are rampant. The more religious a country claims itself to be, the greater the evil that is committed. Italy, for example, which has been dominated by Roman Catholicism for the better part of two millennia, is the birthplace and nourisher of organized crime. It was in South Africa, which long and loudly proclaimed itself to be a Christian nation, that apartheid was developed and enhanced. And it was in the Bible Belt, the southern states of America, that slavery, Jim Crow, and barbaric lynchings were mainly implemented. It is sadly and painfully obvious that the moral influence of Christianity in these situations has been made conspicuous by its total absence.

Another variation of the abusive use of religion is as a cover for, or to distract from, wrongdoing. On a seemingly more benign level there is the use of the sanctuary as a divine prison. In this situation people do not want the ethics and precepts of Jesus to "cramp their style" during the week. This most often involves the pursuit of what the New Testament referred to as "filthy lucre." It is somewhat ironic that some of the dynamics of accumulating wealth run parallel to those of Christianity.

> Nothing resembles monotheism as much as moneythe-
> ism. Because they are so closely joined, moneytheism
> and monotheism have had a tempestuous relationship
> throughout Western history. Interrupted by periods of
> intense conflict, alphabet (literate) cultures have usually

found a way to accommodate the twin aspirations of wanting to be nearer to both *Gott* and *Gelt.* The Puritan ethic encouraged guiltless devotion to both. Profits and prophets coexist.[1]

There is also, sadly, a more blatant misuse of religion. Movies often are a mirror of life's activities. One example is found in *The Godfather.* The storyline has one of the main characters attending the baptism of his sister's baby, which will sanction his role as its godfather. This is the time that is chosen for his thugs to go out and liquidate the competition. A second, real-life example concerns a gay man who was touring Europe with a straight friend. He had a partner back home but while touring made heavy use of a guide that shows where one can encounter gay lovers in each European city. While touring the Vatican he went to confession for the first time in twenty years. He proudly showed people the note written on a Vatican letterhead describing the penance that he needed to do. That night, with the guide tucked under his arm, he went out in search of new lovers. The use of religion as a slate cleaner is a widespread practice.

The saying that patriotism is the last refuge of a scoundrel is not true; it is religion. Whenever wrongdoers claim to be covered by the blood of Christ they are more often than not given a free pass by the Christian public. It is as if scales come over their eyes, or they become sidetracked from the wrongs committed by the "born again" miscreant.

It has long been painfully obvious that the standards, considered to be divinely sourced, were not effective in improving the lot of humankind. The Revolutions that took place in the New World and France at the end of the eighteenth century flowed from the recognition that all people, because they were people, had certain rights. These were seen as self-evident truths. No divine source was invoked to add weight to these concepts.

It was science, natural science in particular, that would radically change the long-standing view of the Divine ruling over all humanity. Friedrich Nietzsche (1844-1900) was the first philosopher to realize that the newly gained understanding of human origins would end the absoluteness of all values and that religion (Christianity in the European context) could no longer serve as the foundation for moral values or right action. As already mentioned, he believed that "there are no moral phenomena at all, only a moral interpretation of phenomena."[2]

Actually, human awareness of the need for "a moral interpretation of phenomena" started much earlier than the understanding gained in the Great Western Transformation. The rise of consciousness made it necessary to find substitutes for our previous divine-sourced volition which had obliged people to obey the hallucinated voices they heard. The earliest mythology reflected this blind obligation. Hebrew and Hindu myths showed that the moral and natural order was fixed for all time - humanity was not free to establish for itself the social norms and aims of life and to work towards them by means of developing its own institutions. To live according to those ancient laws and believe according to ancient faith have become equally impossible.[3]

Humanity has gradually come to realize that behavior must be guided from within one's consciousness rather than by Mosaic Laws or the Hammurabic Code, carved in stone and controlling human behavior from without. This change in the source of one's volition was acknowledged by the Hebrew prophet Jeremiah who, when referring to a new covenant, wrote:

> I will put my law in their minds and write it on their
> hearts. Jeremiah 31:33.

On an academic level ethics is that branch of philosophy which studies the principles of right and wrong in human conduct. Morality is a synonym of ethics. As it has been simply put, "something that is moral is beneficial to society, and something that is immoral causes society harm.[4] This speaks to Nietzsche's definition of morality as being an interpretation of acts of behavior. Interpretation, in turn, is always influenced by the observer's perspective and values. And it's the latter that play a decisive role in all human behavior. Values are things or acts which are chosen by, and desirable to, an individual and/or that person's culture. This, among other things, makes it very clear that universal absolutes cannot be applied to morality. Values can, and do, differ markedly; gold, for example, had minimal value to the Aztecs and Incas and extreme value to the Conquistadors and their society.

One of the many things learned through scientific endeavor is that ethics was part of the evolutionary process. Patricia Williams, a philosopher of science and a philosophical theologian, has described this development. By the 1970's sociobiology could offer an evolutionary explanation of animal social behavior that was genetically based. It was in turn extrapolated to humanity resulting in the discipline of evolutionary psychology. Observers have learned, for example, that among creatures of like species, the amount of cooperation between them correlates with the degree to which they are related. Cooperation with relatives and mutual sharing among non-relatives, a common human trait, form the basis of evolutionary psychology. Appendix C provides a summarized explanation of four terms, the Four Rs, which capture the fundamentals of the evolution of human dispositions, viz. resources, reproduction, relatives (from kin selection), and reciprocity.

These discoveries of the last thirty years have made it increasingly obvious that there is a deep commonality throughout humanity, despite the differing values of the many varied cultures:

> Cross-cultural analysis reveals that there really are some
> basic mental traits that are universal - in the sense that
> they are normal everywhere. . . . It is hard . . . to resist

the evidence that, starting with our common biology and the shared problems of the human situation, . . . human societies have ended up having many deep things in common. Among them are practices like values resembling courtesy, hospitality, reciprocity, the resolution of social conflict, and concepts such as good and evil, [and] right and wrong.[5]

These values have made it possible for humanity to not only survive, but to thrive, which one can safely conclude is both desirable and good. The enabling dispositions of the Four Rs, in particular, are thus essential--their fulfillment cannot be "evil." And yet an inordinate use of these human dispositions can lead to activities that harm not only the participant, but others as well. Undue pursuit of resources, for example, results in greed and miserliness. In the case of reproduction, lust, jealousy, and murder can take place. With regard to relatives, nepotism, ethnic wars, and genocide can, and do, develop. And where reciprocity is in play, pursuing justice exclusively for oneself or one's ethnic group distorts fairness toward others, causing justice to be circumvented. That which is necessary can also be the source for evil.

This evolutionary process can be clearly seen to be in conflict with certain cardinal beliefs. The doctrine of original sin can now be seen to have no foundation. Neither can predestination, foreordination, nor economic or any other type of determinism be a factor in human conduct.

The consequences of chosen actions even apply to animals other than human. People have some capacities that have greater potential than those found in other animals. It seems that chimpanzees have a conscious concept of self, whereas humans are not only aware, but we are aware that we are aware. We have been uniquely conscious since the breakdown of the bicameral mind. We are neither guided nor driven by these special capacities as are other animals. But we can (and do) abuse the Four Rs in far greater degree than all other creatures. Yet we are equally capable of taking steps to reform our abuses and thus provide hope for a better world. We are capable of reevaluating and adjusting our ethics to this end.[6]

It is in this context that Edward O. Wilson writes that the new drive to save the world's

> fauna and flora begins, as in all human affairs, with ethics. Moral reasoning is not a cultural artifact invented for convenience. It is and always has been the vital glue of society, the means by which transactions are made and honored to ensure survival. Every society is guided by ethical precepts, and every one of its members is expected to follow moral leadership and ethics-based tribal law. The propensity does not have to be beaten into us. Evidence exists instead of an instinct to behave ethically, or at least to insist on ethical behavior in others.[7]

Nietzsche not only drew attention to the ethical implications of our new understanding of humanity, he wrote at length of morality. Appendix D summarizes some of his philosophy on humanity's relation to ethics. He saw an evolution of morality from early humans as being pre-moral before passing through a moral era and now arriving at the beginning of the extra-moral era.

The ethics that evolved in meeting the demands of the Four Rs did not go far enough. Crucial to the survival and thriving of humanity was its social orientation as evidenced in conduct that was characterized by voluntary compassion. All actions, whether relating to morality or not, are initiated voluntarily. Homo sapiens has not been programmed to "do the right thing." Ethics and values have to be applied by personal choice and initiative.

The reach and scope of ethics were greatly enlarged when the sages of the Axial Age introduced their various versions of the Golden Rule. They taught their followers that a life that ignores the suffering of others was inauthentic. The arrival of consciousness resulted in, among other things, a sense of personal responsibility. Morality per se is not a product of religious traditions. Pre-conscious mythology was based on the dichotomy of good and evil. It can also be clearly seen that it was integral to the evolution of the Four Rs. It is because of this pre-religious duality, together with the propagation of the Golden Rule in its varied forms by the Axial Sages, that religions are ethically inclined.

Religious leaders are either not aware of these sources or they reject them as the foundation of ethical behavior. They thus maintain that without a belief in God and/or absolute standards, there can be no genuine moral conduct and that the current moral confusions in Western society are directly related to the erosion of religion.

Because ethical guidelines have always been part of the human scene, some moral practices are truly ancient. Furthermore, they have come to be viewed as holy with the passage of time and thus worthy of great reverence. Nietzsche referred to this as "the morality of pious regard for the old." The Ten Commandments is a prime example. They were derived in part from earlier law systems such as that of Lipit-Ishtar and the Code of Hammurabi - so-called "pagan" codes. The very age of these codes caused them to become increasingly removed from their origins, which, in turn, have long been forgotten. Seven and a half of the Ten Commandments are either not legally enforceable or are no longer part of American law. Prohibitions against murder and stealing still apply, while lying is an offense only if it occurs while under oath. Furthermore, some implications of other commandments have been anathema for the last couple of centuries. In biblical times slavery was accepted - it was only forbidden to covet a neighbor's slave and/or his wife. A wife was regarded as property. To this day the wife becomes the property of the husband in Jewish Orthodox marriages.

One law that has not weakened with time is the highest and most universal of values and stems from the genetic drive to survive--the preservation of life. "Thou shalt do no murder" is a moral imperative in any and all societies for obvious reasons.

> We hold the principle on moral, not theological grounds. We justify it by reference to the way in which violating it would cause harm to persons or their interests, or violate their rights or cause injustice. The argument from divine sanction, by itself, does none of these things. We obey the commandment against killing because murder obviously violates the important moral principle that we should not harm persons, not because of its divine command.[8]

If there is one moral imperative, more than any other, that Christianity and Islam, in particular, have violated, it has been the taking of human life. Not just the killing of those outside "the faith" has occurred but widespread religious fratricide as well. The obliteration of the Albigenses in southern France and the countless drownings and incinerations of fellow Christians are the most horrific examples. The Reformation resulted in innumerable religious civil wars between Catholics and Protestants.

Then there are, of course, the Crusades in which Christian Europe sought to conquer, if not eliminate, Islam. It was not just Muslims who were viewed as being the enemy, but Jews as well. Christian inspired, if not always led, attacks on Jews took place throughout Europe for 2,000 years, culminating in the Holocaust. The German churches, both Catholic and Protestant, for the most part looked the other way during this period. There were some glorious exceptions, Dietrich Bonhoeffer, among church leaders, being the most prominent. There were many people throughout Europe who risked their lives to shelter and rescue Jews. Invariably these were people who had not allowed themselves to be shaped by the prevailing religious mindset, being seen as eccentric by the robotomorphic culture.

The Vatican itself turned a blind eye to Nazi Germany's treatment of Jews and indicated in 1943 that it wanted to keep Jews out of the Holy Land, stating that, "If the greater part of Palestine is given to the Jewish people, this would be a severe blow to the religious attachments of Catholics to this land. To have the Jewish people in the majority would interfere with the peaceful exercise of these rights in the Holy Land already vested in Catholics." Even after Israel was founded in 1948, the Vatican's official newspaper insisted: "Modern Israel is not the true heir of biblical Israel. . . . Therefore, the Holy Land and its sacred sites belong to Christianity, the true Israel."

Only in the 1960s, under Pope John XXIII, did Vatican attitudes begin to change, with Pope John Paul II declaring towards the end of the twentieth century that "Judaism is a sister religion with intrinsic and eternal values."[9]

Islam's rapid spread was largely due to military conquest. The choice was to convert or be slaughtered. Fratricide emerged soon after the death of Muhammad as Sunnis and Shi'ites have sought to dominate each other ever since. It is sadly ironic that currently, on an ever increasing scale, Muslims are copying the now moribund Christian practices. Muslim is shooting and blasting into pieces Muslim for being the wrong kind of Muslim. Shakespeare had it right when he wrote, "It is a heretic that makes the fire, not she which burns in it." (*The Winter's Tale*, Act II, Scene 3.)

The violation of the highest value, preservation of life, has taken place throughout the New World. First the Conquistadors and then the English saw themselves as Christians bringing enlightenment to primitive savages. And yet the Europeans raped, pillaged, and massacred on a massive scale. Had they been honest, a supposedly Christian precept, they would have had to say, "We have found the savages, and they are us."

The tragedy, for Christianity in particular, is that fulfillment of the Golden Rule has through the centuries "been more honoured in the breach than the performance." In a newspaper column published in 2005, Rosa Brooks spoke to this trend and opened with the statement, "It's official: too much religion may be a dangerous thing." This conclusion stems from a study of the correlation between levels of "popular religiosity" and various "quantifiable societal health" indicators in 18 prosperous democracies, including the United States. The religious markers were claims of absolute belief in God, frequency of praying, and attendance at religious services. The indicators of social health were data on rates of homicide, sexually transmitted disease, teen pregnancy, abortion, and child mortality.

Most religious democracies exhibited substantially higher degrees of social dysfunction than societies with larger percentages of atheists and agnostics. America, with by far the largest percentage of people who take the Bible literally and express absolute belief in God, and having the lowest proportion of atheists and agnostics, has by far the highest levels of homicide, abortion, teen pregnancy, and sexually transmitted diseases. A similar lack of moral influence can be seen in the practice of music piracy. Born-again Christian teens engage in this practice (both with secular productions and contemporary Christian music) to almost the same degree as non-Christian teens (76 percent versus 81 percent). Within America itself, where values are concerned, the substantially more secular states routinely leave the Bible Belt states in the dust. These findings suggest that, contrary to popular belief, lack of religiosity does societies no particular harm.

Another columnist, Niall Ferguson, argued that "if nothing else, a weekly dose of Christian doctrine helps to provide an ethical framework for life." He believes that the "de-Christianization" of Europe has created a "moral vacuum." Ferguson blithely ignores the fact that it was not atheists blowing up people in Madrid and London, but rather religious fanatics. He laments that in "morally adrift" Britain, fewer than one in ten people would be willing to die for their religious beliefs. The atrocities committed in London were, alas, done by people who did die for these reasons. One must conclude that one of the most serious threats humanity faces today is religious extremism. It would seem that in many Muslim lands high levels of social dysfunction have fueled this extremism.

It should be noted that within established religions there have always been those who opposed doing harm to others. In what would become the United States of America, slavery was widely practiced in the southern colonies, primarily to meet the challenges of labor intensive cotton farming. Justification of the practice came to be intensely debated in the Protestant denominations, causing some, such as the Baptists, to split into two totally separate associations. The South could of course use Scripture to justify the practice of slavery.

The issue of slavery led to the Civil War, a major outcome of which was the granting of full citizen rights to the former slaves in a program called Reconstruction. Because of being a greater proportion of the population in some states such as South Carolina, Mississippi, and Louisiana, the former slaves soon obtained political power. This situation was anathema to southern whites, and within a decade they had reasserted their primacy by means of intimidation and slaughter. The bloodiest event took place in Colfax, Louisiana, where hundreds were slaughtered, many bodies showing several marks of violence.

As early as 1868 terrorist organizations such as the Ku Klux Klan, the

White League, and the White Line had begun indiscriminately slaying black people. Members of the Ku Klux Klan, which is still active today, saw it as their Christian duty to keep "inferior" people form having authority over whites. The defeat of Reconstruction, "idealized in the South as courageous whites facing down black hordes, is enshrined in Southern memory as the time of 'redemption.' "[10] Blacks in the South were betrayed by the North. A Civil Rights bill, passed in 1873, was declared to be unconstitutional by the Supreme Court. Reconstruction died in 1877 in a closed room deal. The Plessy vs. Ferguson decision made by the Supreme Court in 1896 confirmed that segregation was legal. By the late nineteenth century blacks in the South were treated worse than slaves. Many were just rounded up and forced into labor gangs. As nobody owned them, there was no monetary loss caused by beating or working them to death. Others could be literally roped in to take their place. By 1913 most of the rights won by blacks were taken away. William Jennings Bryan, an unabashed Christian fundamentalist from the North, who ran for president three times in the early twentieth century, refused to disavow the Ku Klux Klan for rear of losing votes in the Bible Belt.

The worst race riot in American history occurred in Tulsa, Oklahoma in 1923. Thirty-five blocks of Greenwood, a black suburb, were burned to the ground. Three hundred blacks were killed. Not even one white was prosecuted. This was not the worst of the horrors. Lynching took place on a mind-numbing scale.

About 5,000 Americans were lynched between 1882 and 1968, with the practice most prevalent in the late nineteenth and early twentieth centuries. Lynchings occurred in all but four states, and victims included whites, Asians, and Jews. But the practice was most common in the South and most often aimed at blacks. Seventy percent were the descendents of slaves. It came to have religious and patriotic connotations. Black veterans from both world wars were lynched, sometimes while wearing their military uniforms. For a while after World War I a lynching took place, on average, every four days. A black farmer was lynched in South Carolina in 1916 for arguing with a white farmer over the price of cottonseed. Black leaders and businessmen were often lynched for overshadowing white people.

These were not crimes committed in secret--they were often community events. The last lynching as a spectacle occurred in 1934. It was advertised on the radio. Photographs of these events show crowds milling about the mutilated, dangling bodies. They often included laughing, smiling women and children dressed in their Sunday best. It was common practice to cut up the ropes used for lynching and sell the pieces as souvenirs. One lynching that took place in Waco, Texas was attended by 15,000 people, which was half of the city. The police chief and mayor were there. While alive, the victim was castrated and his ears and toes cut off before being dangled over a fire. When he tried to climb up the chain from which he was suspended, they cut off his fingers. He was raised above the flames from time to time to prolong the process. All of this was accompanied by cheers from the throng. It took 30 minutes for him to die.

Ida B. Wells-Barnett was an anti-lynching crusader. Born into slavery in 1862, she became the nation's leading agitator. Nothing seems more obvious today than to say that lynching is wrong, but that was a less-than-mainstream notion in the 1890s. Editorials appeared in the *Washington Post* and *New York Times* condemning Wells-Barnett for her "exaggerations" and for her "shameful failure" to highlight black crimes against whites. Historians have estimated that less than one percent of the lynchers were ever convicted.

There were 216 attempts in Congress to stop lynchings. All of the attempts were thwarted. Seven U.S. Presidents lobbied for such laws. Three of them passed the House of Representatives, but Senators from the Bible Belt blocked the legislation by the use of filibusters - once in a monumental battle carried out on the Senate floor for six weeks in the late 1930s. A non-enforceable resolution was passed by the Senate in June of 2005, in which it apologized for its failure to act. The resolution expressed "the deepest sympathies and most solemn regrets of the Senate to the descendents of victims of lynching, the ancestors of whom were deprived of life, human dignity and the constitutional protections accorded to all citizens." No voice vote was taken so there was no way of knowing who was for or against it.

Civil rights legislation was passed in 1964 guaranteeing, among other things, the right of all African Americans to vote free of any race-related restrictions. Four years later, when Richard Nixon was running for President on the Republican ticket, he went throughout the South talking about states' rights. This was code for, "We will keep the nigger in his place." By the end of the century all the Bible Belt states became Republican. Southerners until then had never forgiven the Republicans for leading and winning the Civil War. They have finally acknowledged that they are fellow travelers with conservative Christian Republicans. Ironically, they also fervently embrace preserving fetuses and the lives of people in a permanent vegetative state.

It finally took the secular government to impose ethical imperatives in the Bible Belt. The Christianity that dominated the South, and still does, did not address the racial inequities - not to mention iniquities - that were at large. Ethical conduct and religion were at odds with each other. This had long been true on a vast scale. Christianity caused war, ill treatment, and loss of life throughout Europe. If anything, people have been moral in spite of religious influence. August Comte initiated a new religion of Humanity in secular Paris in the middle of the nineteenth century.

In an editorial in *The Fourth R,* Robert W. Funk, the founder of the

Westar Institute, quoted a letter that expressed what countless others have discovered:

> 'George' is now convinced that God does not exist, at least not as is commonly understood, and he is certain that consciousness does not continue after death. . . . For him the whole incredible façade of traditional religious beliefs suddenly collapsed under its own weight. Initially, he confessed that he felt betrayal, anxiety, fear, even terror as he became aware of the immense loss. But then, when the dust had settled, he began to feel serenity, exhilaration, happiness, and complete freedom. His confession he thought of as a declaration of independence from the tyranny of the old concepts, rituals, narratives, agencies, and institutions. At the same time, he discovered to his utter surprise that he still cared about the same things as before. That was also a revelation. That he was still devoted to the same standards of behavior and the same causes meant that the old dogmas were not the foundation or the inspiration of his deep convictions.[11]

In similar vein Holloway writes, "What many people have clearly departed from is any sense that the moral life, lived intentionally, and consciously, is consistent with blind obedience to any authority, including what is alleged to be divine authority."[12] Furthermore, it has become clear to many that it is not sufficient for some holy scripture or other to label an act as being good or bad - it needs to be justified on moral grounds. An act is considered to be harmful because one is able to give proof of the harm. Morality can thus be based on observed consequences rather than religious beliefs or superstitions. A wrong act is one that manifestly does harm to others. Yet there can be ambivalence, even in these circumstances. Campbell points out that "whatever you do is evil for somebody. This is one of the ironies of the whole creation. . . . In [many] traditions good and evil are relative to the position in which you are standing. What is good for one is evil for the other."[13] This is probably what Shakespeare was referring to when he wrote, "There is nothing either good or bad, but thinking makes it so."

There is no one source of ethics, no fixed foundation on which moral principles can be based. Therefore no entity can own all moral truth. And because we find ourselves constantly facing new moral challenges, there are times, because of opposing goods, when more than one ethical position is found. We sometimes have to learn to live with contradictions.

Furthermore, not only can and do moral values exist apart from religion, they can and do change over time. The "Sabbath" is an obvious example. This day of rest was spelled out in the Ten Commandments. Europe came to maintain Sunday as the day to be set apart from the activities of the rest of the week. This custom was continued in the new world. The various states established so-called blue laws to preserve the practice. In the course of the twentieth century these laws steadily came to be ignored or removed from the books. It seems that in America the movement of goods, and thus the promotion of wealth, came to trump the keeping of the fourth commandment.

A further example concerns marriage and parenthood. On an ever increasing scale couples now live together without the sanction of a state-authorized marriage license. Traditionally, children born in such circumstances were classified as bastards. Under common law, a child born outside marriage used to be *fillius nullius,* the child of no one. In the Middle Ages it was even a lesser crime to kill a person who had been born to an unmarried woman. In America, well into the 1960s, such a child's birth certificate might be stamped 'bastard." In 1968 a

Supreme Court ruling repudiated centuries of settled law by granting constitutional recognition and protection to both children born outside of marriage and their parents. This position was reinforced over the next several years, requiring every state in the country to overhaul their statutes. As Campbell states,

> Our time has changed so fast that what was proper 50 years ago is not proper today. The virtues of the past are the vices of today. And many of what were thought to be the vices of the past are the necessities of today. The moral order has to catch up with the moral necessities of actual life in time here and now. . . . The old time religion belongs to another age, another people, another set of human values, another universe.[14]

Holloway sees two factors in play that are causing moral confusion and change. One is erosion of tradition and the other is the crisis of authority. Moral traditions are more and more being seen as human creations, usually in response to the challenge of specific circumstances. And "today authority has to earn respect by the intrinsic value of what it says, not by the force of its imposition. . . . We no longer live in command societies in which we instinctively obey orders from above, wherever above is thought to be."[15] The bicameral era was the very essence of a command society. The attainment of consciousness prepared the way for us to be fully responsible for our decisions and actions.

What is not surprising, but nevertheless lamentable, is that religion in general, and Christianity and Islam in particular, have been anything but leaders in coming to terms with these changes. As Wilson observes in the context of ecological challenges,

> In modern times, as knowledge of the material world and the human predicament has soared, the leaders have followed rather than led the evolution of ethics.

> First into the new terrain venture saints and radical
> theologians. They are followed by growing numbers of
> the faithful and then, warily, by the bishops, patriarchs
> and imams.[16]

In the train of life, religion is not even in the caboose. It tends rather
to be an engine backed on to the caboose, tugging mightily in the
opposite direction. Religion is invariably the last aspect of culture to be
dragged kicking and screaming into the light of new knowledge and
understandings.

A third factor causing moral confusion stems from the challenges
raised by technology. Our ability to do things has been increased a
thousand-fold, but our moral understanding about what ought to
be done has not kept pace. Institutions such as hospitals have ethics
committees that meet on a regular basis to wrestle with new issues and
circumstances that require ethical evaluation. The ever growing evidence
of the ecological damage being done to the earth's environment has
become an ethical dilemma that the nations of our planet can no longer
ignore. Values that are universal in scope are urgently needed, as our
very survival seems to be under threat.

> Life, in both its knowing and its doing, has become
> today a 'free fall,' so to say, into the next minute, into
> the future. So that, whereas formerly those not wish-
> ing to hazard the adventure of an individual life could
> rest within the pale of a comfortably guaranteed social
> order, today, all the walls have burst. It is not left to us
> to *choose* to hazard the adventure of an unprecedented
> life: adventure is upon us like a tidal wave.[17]

The abandoning of previous moral traditions as new ones are created
is one of the activities that only humans can do. We can and do play
a decisive role in shaping our own destiny. We ourselves cultivate our

human values and are thus in the healthy position of being able to live with, instead of for them. This voluntary acceptance of ethical guidelines spells a major difference between humans and insects. People in Nazi Germany lived *for* its system of values. At the Nuremberg trials many of those brought before the court offered the defense that they were just following orders and therefore not liable for the death and torment their actions engendered. The ultimate justice in the verdicts at Nuremberg lies in the rejection of this defense and in the affirmation of the concept that we all, individually, are accountable as human beings.

When people emerged as conscious beings it became possible for us to play an active role in determining our actions, such as choosing to live a moral life. We attained freedom, without which there can be no moral life as such, nor the ability to reflect upon the consequences of our actions. This freedom even extends to the ability to resist a fundamental imperative of our genetic heritage, one of the four Rs, reproduction. For more than 99.99 percent of our evolutionary history humans have not had the luxury of deciding whether to reproduce: simply engaging in sex took care of that. But now, 30 percent of the women in northern Europe, the highest proportion anywhere on earth, are intentionally childless. It rises to 40 percent among college graduates.[18] Part of the rationale for such a choice must be the realization that our planet is becoming overpopulated and thus more at risk.

Consciousness also gave rise to creativity, another ability that is unique to humanity. Artists have a vital role to play in maintaining a dynamic morality. And it is they who encounter the most condemnation when they address morality. Humankind still has many strong ties to the bicameral era, and thus not a few feel compelled to resist all change. Nietzsche has Zarathustra say: "Whom do they hate most? The *creator* they hate most: he breaks the tablets and old values. He is a breaker, they call him lawbreaker. . . . The good are unable to create; . . . [instead] they crucify him who writes new values on new tablets."[19]

Henrik Ibsen did exactly that in his plays and was rejected at first by the public. His writings supported the then new thesis that the most admired virtues and revered institutions were obstacles to the good life: marriage, always telling the truth, respect for authority, and propriety at all costs. All these actions were seen to be the causes of disaster for the individual and ultimately for society at large. He and other contemporaries, such as Oscar Wilde and George Bernard Shaw, denounced the old morality as no longer serving moral ends.

As part of his analysis of the last 500 years of life in the West, Barzun wrote,

> What then did the new code command? The answer was not simple. Art itself, not this or that message, was to be the guide to conduct - ` art by its truth, harmony and grace molded the spirit; aesthetics was a form of ethics. In other words evil is ugly and detestable.
>
> Such a rule means that rules carved in stone for the whole world are as inadequate and misleading as local conventions. Life's complexities must be artfully, not mechanically, handled. As Shaw pointed out: 'Do not do unto others as you want them to do unto you; they may not have the same tastes.' What art teaches at this point is fitness. Time, place, persons, create a unique situation that the moral being deals with as one seeking the most harmonious result.[20]

Living a moral life demands constant attention. It is, however, very rewarding, for in sustaining social awareness we live an ever more meaningful life as we pursue our spiritual journeys.

14

RELIGION AND THE NEW REALITY

The essence of the rise of consciousness and its climaxing with the Axial age was the dawning of human reason. No longer was humankind to be guided by the courses of the planets and the analogies observed in plant life. Nor was it to be informed anymore by bicameral voices. All this would be replaced by reason. Furthermore, the Axial Sages would urge people to be individuals, to think and take responsibility for themselves in thought and deed - in a word - to be free.

Not only has the emergence of consciousness made human beings capable of reason, they can also, individually, come to an understanding of life. Campbell made a crucial observation: "Because somebody's mind is capable of true knowledge you don't have to have a special authority, or a special revelation telling you that this is the way things should be."[1]

Before the Age of Reason there was only one brief and glorious moment of freedom of enquiry, and it was confined to one European country. King John II of Transylvania, which stood between the Ottoman Empire under Suleiman the Great and the Hapsburg Austrian Empire, issued the Act of Religious Tolerance and Freedom of Conscience in 1568. It "was astonishing for its perspicacity, intelligence, and sophistication."[2] The act was effective for only three years, until the death of the king.

John II's successor invited in the Jesuits, who, in mutual agreement with the Calvinists, saw liberal religion as an enemy. "Heresy aside, a movement that placed moral responsibility with the individual was an overwhelming threat to centralized power."[3] The need for absolute control was common to both the Catholics and the Reformers.

More than two centuries would pass before such freedoms would be spelled out in another nation's laws. They were first developed in the colony of Virginia at the instigation of Thomas Jefferson, who succeeded in reversing 200 years of Anglican dominance by getting the Statute for Establishing Religious Freedom in Virginia to become law. The Jefferson Memorial has inscribed on it a prime Jeffersonian guiding principle: "I have sworn on the altar of Liberty eternal hostility against every form of tyranny over the mind of man."

He was by no means the only founding father with such convictions. James Madison argued that religion can only spring from reason and conviction, not force or violence. Beginning in Europe and then throughout the world religious liberty would come to be viewed as an American triumph.[4]

> [Jefferson's] dream proved so lasting that it would never cease to trouble the conscience of a nation. On the eve of the Civil War Abraham Lincoln stated: 'All honor to Jefferson, to the man who, in the concrete pressure of a struggle for national independence by a single people, had the coolness, forecast and capacity to introduce into a merely revolutionary document an abstract truth, applicable to all men and all times, and so to embalm it there, that today, and in all coming days, it shall be a rebuke and stumbling block to the very harbingers of reappearing tyranny and oppression.'[5]

The American Revolution was in effect a second Renaissance, a revival of the teachings of the Axial Sages. They wanted people to not only cope with life and survival but to thrive. They offered a scaffolding that could bring people to a fuller understanding of themselves and their place in the world. The various religions that formed as people followed and applied the sages' teachings, played the role of a tutor. However, a major problem arises when the tutor continues to control his charges once they have become mature. He ends up undermining his own work and harming his protegés. The damage done is far worse when the tutors themselves, not only don't continue to grow, but retrogress instead. The reality of course with all things organic is that either growth continues or decay sets in. There is no such option as staying in place by treading water.

This dynamic was in play in the American Unitarian Church in the 19th century. In 1866 it sought to reaffirm its Christian faith stance. Those who saw this as a retrogressive move argued that Christianity is the faith of the soul's childhood, whereas Free Religion is the faith of the soul's adulthood. In similar vein Robert Ingersoll, in his lecture "The Gods," argued, "We are not endeavoring to chain the future, but to free the present. We are not forging fetters for our children, but we are breaking those our fathers made for us."[6]

Despite the groundwork that was laid by the Axial Sages, the religions that emerged from their teachings all came to show a dismaying predilection towards rigidity, ossification, and atrophy. All of them, in varying degree, over time, have returned their followers to a preconscious mindset. We remain connected in some way to bicameral times. The hardwiring is still there. Succumbing to an authority structure and/or figure can make one feel safe, that one has come home.

A painfully vivid picture of what religion can do to people was made by Fyodor Dostoevsky in his classic novel *The Brothers Karamazov* written in 1880. He used a parable concerning "The Grand Inquisitor."

It has a Roman Catholic setting, Dostoevsky being disposed to put down that institution, the better light in which to place the Russian Orthodox Church. The latter has, however, been just as harmful to its members.

The setting is Seville in the 16th century, at the height of the Spanish Inquisition. Jesus appears a day after almost a hundred heretics have been burned at the stake by the cardinal - the Grand Inquisitor - "in a magnificent *auto da fé,* in the presence of the king, the court, the knights, the cardinals, the most charming ladies of the court, and the whole population of Seville."[7] Advance the scene 400 years and Dostoevsky could have been describing a lynching party in the American Bible Belt. "He came softly, unobserved, and yet strange to say, everyone recognized Him."[8] Jesus repeats many of the compassionate acts of his life on earth and a huge throng is drawn to him. The Grand Inquisitor comes by, almost ninety now, in his coarse, old monk's cassock. He recognizes Jesus and immediately has him imprisoned.

The Grand Inquisitor visits him that night and asks, "Why, then, art Thou come to hinder us. . . . Dost Thou know what will be tomorrow? . . . Tomorrow I shall condemn Thee and burn Thee at the stake as the worst of heretics. And the very people who have today kissed Thy feet, tomorrow at the faintest sign from me will rush to heap up the embers of Thy fire. Knowest Thou that?"[9]

Ivan's brother Alyosha (two of the three brothers), who is himself a monk, does not understand so Ivan interprets for him: The Grand Inquisitor is telling Jesus that He, Jesus, has put everything in the Pope's hands and it is still there--there was no need for Him to come back.

'. . .Thou mayest not add to what has been said of old, and mayest not take from men the freedom which Thou didst exalt when Thou wast on earth. Whatsoever Thou revealest anew will encroach on men's freedom of faith;

for it will be manifest as a miracle, and the freedom of their faith was dearer to Thee than anything in those days fifteen hundred years ago. Didst Thou not often say then, "I will make you free"? But now Thou hast seen these "free" men,' the old man adds suddenly, with a pensive smile. 'Yes, we've paid dearly for it,' he goes on, looking sternly at Him, 'but at last we have completed that work in Thy name. For fifteen centuries we have been wrestling with Thy freedom, but now it is ended and over for good. Dost Thou not believe that it's over for good? Thou lookest meekly at me and deignest not even to be wroth with me. But let me tell Thee that now, today, people are more persuaded than ever that they have perfect freedom, yet they have brought their freedom to us, and laid it humbly at our feet. But that has been our doing. Was this what Thou didst? Was this Thy freedom?' [10]

The Grand Inquisitor then claims their "perfect freedom" as a credit to himself and the Church, because at last "they have vanquished freedom and have done so to make men happy."[11] He later upbraids Jesus for giving people greater freedom than ever instead of taking it away, and reminds him, "Didst Thou forget that man prefers peace, and even death, to freedom of choice in the knowledge of good and evil?"[12]

As evidence that this parable is not just a flight of fancy there is the supporting philosophy of the behaviorist B. F. Skinner. The popularity of his book *Beyond Freedom and Dignity* testifies to the vast number of people who are crying to be told that freedom is an illusion and that they need not worry about it any longer.

Skinner argued the need to develop a technology of behavior, but that man's belief in freedom and dignity stands in the way. He proposed this development for the sake of humankind. The Grand Inquisitor says, "We shall plan the happiness of universal man." Both he and Skinner regarded freedom as the main enemy.

It needs to be acknowledged that belief systems can have a stabilizing effect on society and bring order to otherwise disordered lives. The truth claims of historical religions offer some people the kind of absolute and defining structure they need, if their lives are not to descend into chaos. Holloway calls it addiction to religion, which can save a variety of addicts from chaos and destruction.[13] It may well be the only way to rescue certain people from something worse. Marx no doubt understood this function of religion, seeing it as a necessary drug for the suffering and afflicted masses.

The Great Western Transformation, a three century long process of modernization, brought about a series of profound changes. On the level of just living life the growth in knowledge and the technology it spawned diminished the demands of traditional agriculturally based cultures. Industrialization increased the means and options for survival. Many long-standing societal constraints gave way as political and scientific revolutions reorganized society.

The scientific revolution, initiated by a small group of intellectuals, resulted in a new value-free cosmology that made humanity feel very insignificant and unimportant. The old absolute reassurances, values, and destiny offered by Western religion were no more. Science had raced far ahead of the people's ability to absorb what it revealed. We are still struggling to come to terms with these findings.

This erosion of religious views parallels the breakdown of the bicameral mind. It continues to work "serious changes in every fold and field of life.[14] The Christian associations that have suffered the biggest losses of membership as conscious logic has grown are those maintaining the older orthodox positions, "ritually closer to the long apostolic succession into the bicameral past."[15] Scientific and critical thinking have gradually eroded dogmatic belief, forcing the need for revision upon revision of traditional theological concepts to be made. The metaphoric meaning behind ritual became unsustainable. The historical beliefs that told people who they were and what they should be dissipated. The role of myth, being seen as antithetical to the age of reason, became greatly reduced.

But humanity was, and continues to be, stuck with a great longing for contact with the gods. Nostalgia for the old religious cosmologies and beliefs would only grow, leading to the eighteenth century phenomenon of scientifically enlightened lands experiencing the rise of God-seeking movements that enthralled masses of people. There was Pietism in Germany, Methodism in England, and the Great Awakening in North America. This was accompanied by the totally irrational and baseless idea of witchcraft and the drastic measures taken to eradicate something that did not in fact exist. These deeply emotional and illogical movements characterized the age as much as science did.

A long-term effect of these revivals and awakenings was to move their participants away from becoming autonomous and back towards heteronomy - towards a bicameral mindset. Christianity became even more impervious to change and the new realities. As Don Cupitt notes

> People have been demanding the reform of the Church and the modernization of Christianity at least since the days of John Wycliffe in fourteenth century England. . . . The old Church takes no notice but simply chugs on, always the same. In the end it tends to win, for the Church is an anvil that has worn out many hammers.[16]

The Roman Catholic Church, doubtless because of its longer

tradition, has been the most highly resistant to change. The Reformation by itself was a major shock and challenge to its supremacy. Protestantism more than anything else, caused Catholicism to seal itself off from the influence of emerging modernity.

Pope Pius IX (1792-1878) was hostile toward any scientific challenge to religious authority. He convened what became the *First* Vatican Council (1869-70) in order to stifle rebellious modernizers within the Church by proclaiming papal infallibility. He declared, "Let him be anathema . . . who shall say that human sciences ought to be pursued in such a spirit of freedom that one may be allowed to hold as true their assertions, even when opposed to revealed doctrine."[17] Not until 1950 did the Church under Pope Pius XII arrive at the decision that believers might retain an open mind regarding the evolution of the human *body* as opposed to the soul.

Reconciliation with some of the new understandings that came through science finally had to be made. Besides the "rehabilitation" of Galileo, Pope John Paul II acknowledged in 1999 that "Heaven is not a place but a state of mind." In the mid-twentieth century there were some Catholic theologians who attempted to come to terms with the changes in philosophy and worldview that had developed. Pope John Paul II succeeded in sidelining or silencing all of them in his determination to drag Catholicism back to sixteenth century thinking. His successor, Pope Benedict XVI, wants to keep it there.

There is, however, protest from within. In an unprecedented challenge to the authority of the Catholic Church, a coalition of twenty liberal U.S. Catholic groups attempted to collect one million signatures in 1996 on a referendum calling for sweeping church reform, including the ordination of women and permission for priests to marry. The campaign followed similar efforts in Europe, where nearly two and a half million Catholics, primarily in Austria and Germany, had signed petitions decrying what they view as antiquated, authoritarian, and discriminatory church practices. Organizers of the American referendum drive said they had decided to launch the effort because they believed the U.S. hierarchy was out of step with the views of many rank-and-file Catholics.

The Second Vatican Council has been a factor in these developments. Independent Catholic movements have gained momentum in America over the last decade. The sexual abuse scandal has provided a further spur. Ironically, some have formed in reaction to what was seen as the liberalizing effects of Vatican II, while other groups were open to having married priests and ordained women as leaders.

The Roman Catholic Church, as old as Christianity itself, has not only held its followers in greater thrall than any other denomination, but its leaders, typical of long-standing dictators, have been primarily, if not solely, concerned with the institution's image and welfare.

In the last decade of the twentieth century, the sexual abuses committed by Catholic priests in America finally reached critical mass. (Ireland owned up to the same problem in 2005, being closely followed by much of the continent.) Catholic authorities have had documentation for 1700 years about priests who were sexual predators. In the fourth century CE, St. Basil of Caesarea set up a detailed system of punishment to deal with clerics who molested boys at their monastery.

Pope John-Paul II, who seemed to be more annoyed than conciliatory about the damage done, largely ignored the abuses committed and covered up by church leaders. While leading a huge mass in Canada, as the crisis peaked, he made the astonishingly lame defense that the great majority of priests had not committed sexual abuses. (The argument was repeated by the presiding bishop at a conference of the church's leaders.) Many attending the Pope's mass cheered his pathetic argument as they dutifully fulfilled their role as religious serfs before their feudal lord.

Even at the present time some American apologists for the Catholic Church seethe at what they call the critics' preoccupation with sex.

Perhaps the most dismaying aspect of the sexual abuse scandal is that an institution that is seen to be there for humankind's ultimate good could be responsible for the extreme opposite. William Lobdell was a one-time religion columnist and reporter for the *Los Angeles Times*. He had come to embrace Christianity as an adult. In a column about the abuse, he wrote

> I understand that I was witnessing the failure of humans, not God. But in a way that was the point. I didn't see these institutions drenched in God's spirit. Shouldn't religious organizations, if they were God-inspired and driven, reflect higher standards than government corporations and other groups in society.[18]

The sexual abuse and cover-up mocks the efficacy, if not the very existence of such a being. Nietzsche commented on just such a contradiction: "What differentiates us is not that we find no God - neither in history, nor in nature, nor behind nature - but that we do not feel that what has been revered as God is 'god-like.'"[19] Lobdell decided to leave the Church.

It is not just the pandemic sexual abuse of children that is causing people to leave the Catholic Church. The author Ann Rice, who was raised Catholic, became an atheist, then returned to Catholicism in 1998, declared twelve years later that she was leaving Christianity. She said that she still believed in God, but that

> in the name of Christ, I refuse to be anti-gay, I refuse to be anti-feminist, I refuse to be anti-artificial birth control. I refuse to be anti-Democrat. I refuse to be anti-secular humanism. I refuse to be anti-science. I refuse to be anti-life.[20]

The Reformation, which initially stirred and energized much of Europe, failed miserably to weaken the hold of Christianity upon people. Virtually all of the reform movements and new sects ended up becoming yet another variation of the Church they wanted to reform. They tended to become, if anything, even more oppressive. Barzun observed, in analyzing John Calvin, John Knox, and Puritanism, that

> Revolutions paradoxically begin by promising freedom
> and then turn coercive and 'puritanical' to save them-
> selves from both discredit and reaction. Creating a purer
> life requires that people forget other aims, therefore
> public and private conduct must be regimented. . . .
> Old shackles are thrown off, tossed in the air, but come
> down again as moral duty well enforced.[21]

The best achievement of the Protestant Revolution was that it "destroyed unified Christendom by the emergence of many sects - these challenged and broke authority everywhere."[22]

The Lutheran principle of "the priesthood of all believers" had more impact on the culture at large than in the churches as laymen came to replace clerics in government. "Religious faith as such did not weaken but many saw such ideologies as interfering with governance."[23] This was not a case of the development of separation of church and state. There is still a state church throughout much of Europe today, but it has little if any influence upon the state. Ironically, in America, where there always has been this official separation, conservative Christianity has had a steadily increasing influence on the state in recent years. If a non-Christian were to run for president, he would have something in common with atheists--he wouldn't have a prayer.

This principle--the priesthood of all believers--is still struggling to make headway in Christianity four centuries later. There has, in recent years, been some lessening of the role of the ordained ministry and the increase of responsibility by some individuals for their own spiritual fulfillment.

Whether he so desires it or not, the role of the priest has changed. It is challenged by psychiatry for one. Geering notes

> Whereas people formerly went to the priest for spiritual healing, they now turn to the psychiatrist for mental health. . . . It is not surprising that in recent years there has been an identity crisis in the priesthood and the ordained ministry of the Churches. It is no longer clear, as it used to be, just what the role of the professional clergy really is.[24]

The churches (both liberal and conservative) have not been of much help as they seek to maintain the traditional forms of their faith, acting as if nothing much has happened or changed. Roy Harris calls this holy narcolepsy, which has brought about a crisis of credibility for the churches. Those who

> retreat from the challenge posed by the actual world after Galileo want to direct the Christian community into the confines of a sacred grotto, an enclosed, religiously defined world that is brought completely under the control of scripture and tradition; and they want to turn the ordained clergy into antiquities dealers.[25]

Dietrich Bonhoeffer, in a summary of Christianity's failure, wrote

> Men have banished divinity from their midst; they have relegated it to a sanctuary; the walls of a temple are the limits of its view; beyond these walls it does not exist. Madman that you are, destroy these enclosures which obstruct your horizon; liberate God; see him where he actually is or else say that he does not exist at all.[26]

Robert Funk also talks of the disconnect between Sunday and the rest of the week.

> The Sunday morning experience is a journey into another realm, alien and at odds with the work-a-day world. The plausibility of the Sunday experience is growing weaker and weaker. Little or nothing of that experience can be carried over to Monday morning! . . . The churches have been forced to intensify the Sunday experience in order to develop the thrust required to escape the gravitational pull of the dominant reality. It will get harder and take more energy to effect the escape as time goes by. And the churches will increasingly become private domains isolated from the dominant reality.[27]

Chapman Cohen, president of the National Secular Society in England, an association of free thinkers, describes religion's dilemma another way:

> We have reached the stage where genuine religion finds it increasingly hard to live honestly, and altogether lacks the courage to die with dignity. Anything will do, so long as it is given the name of God. It is still a term which exerts a hypnotic power over the unthinking, and it is by the support of the unthinking that established religion today hopes to carry on.[28]

Despite the role of religion, as portrayed in "The Grand Inquisitor," and despite the mutually damaging symbiosis between priest and religious peasant, change has been taking place, and the process continues as Europeans, in particular, have more and more come to set their own religious and, much more importantly, spiritual courses. The Great Western Transformation has steadily eroded religious traditions. A later major factor contributing to change was the aftermath of World

War II. The social and geographic upheaval it caused unmoored people from traditional sources of authority in family, church, and community. These sources were weakened further by the modern knowledge explosion. The dramatic increase in college education, particularly in America, gave many more people the equivalent educational training of their priests, as some felt entitled to make their own decisions about religious beliefs and spiritual activities. The changes stemming from the Second Vatican Council (1962-1965) also led many Catholics to question the authority of church leaders. People "began to question the authority of authority itself, and its narrative of divine origins."[29] The speed of change accelerated as the twentieth century progressed. By its end the traditional belief in God had rapidly declined. Even Christian theologians were beginning to abandon theism as Feuerbach's concept of God being a symbolic term referring to man's highest values and aspirations came to greater acceptance. As a result of the philosophical critique of theism, some parts of Christianity have been finding new ways of speaking about God. Since the time of Marx, the Christian religion has tended to become more "this worldly" and humanistic in its emphases. Milan Machovec, a late twentieth century Marxist writes, "Twentieth-century theologians have worked out new and more dynamic models for thinking about God so that often we Marxists no longer know whether we are still atheists or not in this regard."[30]

The effect of these changes in perspective is to be seen in the huge drop in church attendance and related religiosity. Newspaper headlines trumpet these trends: "Where Nothing is Sacred," "A Nation of Faith and Religious Illiterates," "A Faith Vacuum Haunts Europe."

Millions of pilgrims gathered in Rome in 2004 to attend the funeral of Pope John Paul II. Only a few miles from St. Peter's Square a soaring Baroque-style church echoed with emptiness. Twenty people were attending the noon Mass in a side chapel, while an 84-year-old priest sat alone near a confessional booth awaiting penitents who didn't come. On average, he hears just 10 confessions a day. "They don't come to say their sins, but only their troubles," he said.

The response to the death of John Paul II stands in stark contrast to how European Catholics now view the Church. His successor, Pope Benedict XVI, has been treated with short shrift in the academic circles of Rome itself. In 2008 he was scheduled to speak at La Sapienza University, an institution founded 700 years earlier by Pope Boniface VIII. More than 60 professors signed a letter protesting the Pope's appearance, seeing it as an affront to people of science and the "secular" nature of the institution. The issue was seen as going beyond Galileo. It was the church's current position on stem cell research, evolution, and genetic engineering which indicated that attitudes had not changed. The pope would have been welcome to speak had he been willing to allow opportunity for discussion and response. The Vatican announced that "it was considered opportune" to scrap the event.[31]

The Vatican has more to fret about than rejection of its antiquated scientific views. The fast spreading rights to abortion, acceptance of gay marriages, and rising divorce rates are proving to be unstoppable. Nowhere is divorce becoming more common than in three of the continent's most Roman Catholic countries, viz. Spain, Italy, and Portugal. For the decade starting in 1995, divorces rose 59 percent in Spain, 62 percent in Italy, and 89 percent in Portugal. A contributing factor is the lack of programs that assist the family in comparison with Northern Europe. The latter has realized the benefit of stable families and thus provides resources that help them when in crisis. In the Alpine principality of Liechtenstein, which is 75 percent Catholic, 81 percent of voters defied the archbishop in voting for abortion rights in the first trimester.

These challenges to Church authority are accompanied by a decline in church attendance. A recent survey found that 88 percent of Italians still considered themselves to be Catholic believers in God. Only 33 percent, however, said they attended mass every Sunday. In Spain, where Generalissimo Franco held the Catholic Church front and center during his dictatorship, a generation after his death saw only 30 percent now attending mass.

A similar pattern holds true throughout Europe, in both Catholic and Protestant communities. In Germany, for example, devotion is ebbing and church attendance has been dropping steadily for years. It is predicted that 50 percent of the churches will be closed or the buildings converted to other uses. The Lutheran Church, which has cut its clergy by about one-third since 1990, has sold or rented a number of its properties to immigrant groups, who often take a renewed interest in religion in their strange new countries. It is the one thing that is familiar to them and thus comforting. Churches have been adapted as restaurants, coffee houses, clubs, apartments, and music halls. A recent meeting of mainline Protestant churches held in Wittenberg, the home of the Reformation, predicted that by 2030 membership would drop by one-third from the present 25.6 million. In addition, income from the church tax, collected from all church members and which keeps thousands from joining, would be halved from the current $5.4 billion.

The Vatican is also experiencing a major shortfall in funding, no doubt partly due to the worldwide economic crisis. It suffered a $22 million deficit in 2008. Vatican Radio, the official voice of the Roman Catholic Church, has begun airing advertisements for the first time in its nearly 80-year history. The revenue thus generated was expected to be modest at best.[32]

A similar story of ever-shrinking interest in religion holds true for Eastern Europe. This may not be surprising as religion was condemned in this area once it came under Soviet influence and control. On average, less than half of professed church members attend services once a month or more. Estonia and the Czech Republic have the lowest proportion who claim allegiance to organized religion. In 1991, 4.5 million of the latter country's 10 million people claimed to be church members. A census held a decade later showed the number had plunged more than 25 percent to 3.3 million.[33]

It would not be surprising to learn that France has even lower church attendance figures because of its long-standing feud with Catholicism. Only 12 percent of the population attend mass weekly. France, however, is outdone by Sweden, which is considered to be the least religious country in the world.

Statistics for the United Kingdom tell a similar story where only one in five claim to attend church regularly. Prior to 1960 most marriages in England and Wales took place in a church: by the late 1990s only 40 percent were so doing. Fewer than a fifth of children baptized are now confirmed, about half of the figure for the period from 1900 to 1960. For the Church of Scotland, the decline has been even steeper.

Ireland, which, together with Poland, has been the staunchest of Catholic strongholds, has undergone the most dramatic change. In the 1970s more than 90 percent of Irish Catholics claimed to attend mass on a weekly basis. By 2005 only 44 percent did so. When Pope John Paul II visited Limerick in 1980, he preached against contraception, abortion, and divorce. A constitutional amendment granting a right to divorce was passed in 1995, having been roundly defeated nine years earlier. Contraception has also been legalized and accepted. Becoming a priest was at one time the most honored profession. Many were sent to other countries to serve as the Irish church could not absorb them all. There were only 26 new seminary students in 2004, compared to 500 in earlier years. The critic Fintan O'Toole has called Ireland a "post-Catholic country."[34]

The other great Catholic area is Latin America. The Atlantic Ocean has not held back the forces of change. They are, however, different. People are switching allegiance to the charismatic format, especially of the Protestant variety. A Brazilian Cardinal asked in 2005, "How long will Latin America remain a Catholic continent?" Brazil's Catholic community shrank from 83 percent of the population in 1991 to 57 percent in 2005. There is now one Catholic priest for every two Protestant ministers.

There has been a decline in faithful Catholics throughout the Americas, with the exception of Mexico and El Salvador. According to the Center for Applied Research in the Apostate less than half of all Catholics now attend once a week. In the United States only 32 percent attended mass regularly in 2004, down from 52 percent four years earlier. One in three adults who were raised as Catholics is no longer in the church. Roughly 10 percent of Americans are former Catholics. A study of Hispanic Churches in American Public Life shows Latinos moving in both directions: 3.2 million left the church while 700,000 converted to Catholicism or returned to the faith. The latter figure reflects the tendency for emigrants to seek out that which is familiar to them. About 68 percent of Latinos identify themselves as Roman Catholics. That makes up one-third of all United States Catholics - a proportion that is certain to rise.

The drastic decline of participation in Catholic life in America is even more pronounced in its institutions. For the last four decades the shriveling numbers of Roman Catholic sisters and nuns has prompted the Vatican to initiate a comprehensive study of the more than 400 women's religious orders. Between 1965 and 2000, the number of sisters declined by 94,600 from an earlier total of 173,865. The average age at the end of the twentieth century was between 65 and 70.[35] Enrollment in parochial schools began to decline at the same time: from more than 5 million students in almost 13,000 schools to 2.5 million in 1990. In the last decade 1,400 schools have closed while the number of students declined by 460,000.[36]

A question that begs to be asked is this: if a charismatic world-traveling pope, who enchanted millions and made personal evangelism a mark of his pontificate, could not stanch the hemorrhaging of Catholics in Europe and the Americas, how can his successor, Pope Benedict XVI be more effective?

It is not just the Catholic Church in America that has suffered loss. Most of the decline in Protestantism has been in the mainline churches. Judaism has shrunk as well. The number of Conservative Jewish synagogues has declined from 850 to 770 over the last 40 years. Part of this loss, in both America and Europe, is attributable to the decline in birthrates. But even so, the U.S.A., in comparison with Europe, is a very religious country. Over 80 percent of Americans claim that God is very important to them, and 70 percent would be willing to die for God or their beliefs. Participation in religious activities does not quite match these figures: the latest survey (2009) found that 45 percent of respondents considered themselves religious with 30 percent saying that they attend services at least once a week. That, however, leaves 70 percent who participate sporadically in organized religion or not at all.

A greater proportion of Americans (40 percent according to a 1987 Gallup Poll) believe that human beings were created by God in the last 10,000 years than in other Western countries. Only 15 percent in Iceland and 13 percent in Britain cling to similar beliefs. Even in Turkey a predominantly Muslim country, only 27 percent reject evolution.

The far less religious Europeans know much more *about* religion than Americans do. Religious education is the rule there, and it starts in the elementary grades. Because of the never-ending fight about separation between church and state in America, religion is seldom objectively taught as a subject. Europeans can name the Seven Deadly Sins and the Five Pillars of Islam, but according to a 1997 poll, only one out of three U.S. citizens is able to name the four Gospels and 12 percent think that Noah's wife was Joan of Arc.

A newspaper article, written at the end of the twentieth century, stated that Americans' dissatisfaction with traditional religion began in the 1960s when early photos of Earth were transmitted from space. It was then that the idea that one God might be better than another lost its primacy and people began to think that all religions are vital organs on the planet.[37] Membership in mainline Protestant denominations peaked around 1965. Even though Christian denominations have added 22 million members since 1990, the proportion of the Christian population shrank from 86 percent to 76 percent.

Religious dissatisfaction is reflected in more than one way, one being the loosening of church loyalties. According to a Pew Report, 44 percent of adults in recent years have switched religious affiliations or abandoned ties to a specific religion. Pollster George Barna, who works for Christian ministries, estimates that 20 million Christians have largely forsaken their local church in favor of discussion groups with friends, Bible study with colleagues, or spiritual questing online.

The number of Americans who claim to have no religious affiliation has more than doubled in a decade. In a 2009 survey, 27 percent of respondents said that they didn't practice any kind of religion. More than 27 million adults, nearly one in seven, reject all religious labels. This makes up 16 percent of the U.S. population. Only Catholics (24 percent) and Baptists (17 percent) outnumber them. Twelve percent of the population don't believe in an afterlife, seven percent aren't sure about the existence of God, and 5 percent are atheists. The latter tend to be more educated and affluent than Christians. Most of those who claim no religious identification are to be found on the West Coast and in New England. The latter, where Puritans and others sought religious freedom, has surpassed the former with 22 percent of residents identifying with no religion compared to the West's 20 percent.[38] Americans under 35 years of age are the ones most likely to have no religious affiliation.

A study that supports this trend is called "Spirituality in Higher Education: A National Study of College Students' Search for Meaning and Purpose." Out of the 112,000 entering freshmen surveyed at 236 universities and colleges, 80 percent of the students expressed interest in spirituality. Less than half of these said they considered it necessary to find ways to nurture their spiritual growth. Seventy-nine percent said they believed in God, but only 40 percent considered it "essential" or "very important" to follow religious teaching in everyday life. Seventy-six percent of students said that they are searching for meaning or purpose in life. Less than half said they feel secure in their current religious and spiritual views.

A similar study conducted by the University of California at Los Angeles' Higher Education Research Institute surveyed 14,000 college students as freshmen in 2004. They were then interviewed three years later in the spring of their junior year. It was found that they had grown in spirituality and related areas. This, however, did not translate to more regular attendance at religious services. The percentage of those who attended services regularly as freshmen (43.7 percent) had fallen to 25.4 percent by the end of their junior year.

Christian young people in America who go on to attend college find themselves to be in a similar state of flux. Of the almost 300,000 (85 percent) who chose to attend a non-Christian college, 53 percent will no longer identify themselves as born-again or will not have attended any religious services in the prior 12 months by the time that they graduate. The lion's share of this decline occurs in the freshman year.

Christian leaders and mission boards take comfort in the knowledge that Christianity is growing and flourishing in the third world. Eighty-two percent of West Africans, for example, attend church services at least once a week. As the Great Western Transformation spreads around the globe, one can only expect that the decline of Christianity, and religion in general, will follow a similar pattern to that which has taken place in Europe. It will, however, take place sooner and quicker due to the exponential growth in dissemination of knowledge. The collapse of Communism serves as a precursor to this trend.

If a grim legacy of religion, viz. that of violent coercion by its practitioners of people of a different persuasion, has been reduced, it is in spite of rather than because of religious influence. The first leader of a multi-ethnic state to insist on and enforce religious tolerance was Genghis Khan. Later it would be secular Western governments that would bring it to pass in their spheres of influence and control. An early example is that of Napoleon, who placed the pope under house arrest and brought the Spanish Inquisition to an end. These actions did not have a sobering effect on the Protestants who were delirious in the hope that these actions would be the death knell of the Catholic Church.

The positive effect of the Enlightenment was evidenced in the colonizing activities of the West. The earliest colonies were established in the Americas before the Age of Reason. The Spaniards, in particular, and the earliest English settlers rode roughshod over the spiritual practices of the indigenous populations, with the Spanish often resorting to the sword to make converts of the natives. By the nineteenth century, when all of Africa became colonized, religious tolerance became the order of the day, both in the now secular mother countries as well as in the colonies.

The Great Western Transformation would also have effects that would be anything but beneficial due to the debunking of myth and the concomitant rise in fundamentalism and absolutism.

15

SYMBOLS AND SYMBIOSIS

It is by means of symbols that *homo sapiens* has been able to come to an understanding of himself, the world at large, and his place in it. We are symbol-making and symbol-embracing creatures.

Symbols fall into two categories--those that have been consciously created, and those that arise from the unconscious. Armstrong notes that "Symbolism is the divine spark distinguishing the poorest specimen of true man from the most perfectly adapted animal.[1]

The role and power of symbolism is perfectly illustrated in the transformation of seven-year-old Helen Keller from a deaf, dumb, and blind creature to a human possessed of and by symbols. As she recalled the experience:

> Someone was drawing water (at the well-house) and my teacher placed my hand under the spout. As the cool stream gushed over my hand, she spelled into the other the word water, first slowly, then rapidly. Suddenly I felt a misty consciousness as of something forgotten . . . and somehow the mystery of language was revealed to me. I knew then that w-a-t-e-r meant the wonderful cool something that was flowing over my hand. That living word awakened my soul, gave it light, hope, joy, set it

> free. . . . Everything had a name, and each name gave
> birth to a new thought. As we returned to the house,
> every object which I touched seemed to quiver with life.
> That was because I saw everything with the strange new
> sight that had come to me.[2]

Symbolism "is a level of reality that is beyond both the material and mental levels of our existence."[3]

Symbols are not synonymous with signs. Carl G. Jung, who became a leading authority on symbols, described a sign as being "always less than the concept it represents, while a symbol always stands for something more than its obvious and immediate meaning. . . . [It] hints at something as yet unknown."[4] Jung pointed out that symbols appear not only in dreams, but in all kinds of psychic manifestations such as thoughts, feelings, symbolic acts and situations.[5]

The Introduction to *Man and his Symbols,* a book conceived and edited by Jung, states, "An examination of Man and his Symbols is in effect an examination of man's relation to his own unconscious" - the source of his symbols.[6] The study of symbols revealed that similar types occur in ethnic groups scattered all over the globe. Jung coined the term archetype in recognition of these recurring symbols. A prime example is found in creation myths. Myths, according to Jung, are symbols that have not been invented consciously.[7]

Myths also came from the unconscious to aid our ancestors to live with the many other unknowns, one being what happens after death. As Armstrong explains, "myths enable us to draw on the full resources of our humanity in order to live with the unacceptable."[8] If the world had a dramatic beginning, and all myths portray it as such, it would likely have a dramatic ending as well. And here again, "mythical thinking and practice helped people to face the prospect of extinction and nothingness, and to come through it with a degree of acceptance."[9]

Such myths are called apocalyptic. The Gospels have Jesus making such statements, and the last book of the New Testament is given wholly over to apocalyptic language. Revelation is also referred to as the Apocalypse. It, too, is myth.

The Age of Reason had a huge negative impact on the role of myth, but the foundation for such a trend was laid some 1,300 years earlier. It could be called the Constantine Curse. The Council of Nicea (325 CE), at Constantine's bidding, began defining for the first time that which would be "kosher" in Christianity. The Trinity, or Godhead, among other concepts, would come to be defined once and for all time. The foundation was laid for Mythos to be changed into Logos. The doctrine of the Trinity was not immediately absolutized, but the process was set in motion causing it to become fixed religious dogma by the eleventh century with the development of Scholasticism. This movement, among other things, sought to resolve what was seen as conflicts between faith and reason. Another way in which it contributed to the concreting of Christianity was to seek to establish proofs for the existence of God.

The Trinity did continue to be myth after Nicea. As mentioned in Chapter 9, Gregory, Bishop of Nyssa (335-395), explained that "Father, Son and Spirit were not objective, ontological facts, but simply 'terms that we use' to express the way in which the 'unnameable and unspeakable' divine nature adapts itself to the limitations of our human mind."[10] Sir Isaac Newton (1642-1727) would later go to great pains to purge Christianity of such doctrines as the Trinity, which were anathema to him.

The Enlightenment destroyed three illusions that humankind had entertained. Copernicus and Galileo destroyed the belief that man and Earth occupied the central place in the universe. Darwin in turn showed that humans were not unique in living nature. Man's possibly greatest illusion--that of being master of one's thoughts and actions-

-was destroyed by Freud, who produced the clinical evidence that supported the concept of the unconscious. It is now understood to be a limitless storehouse of past thoughts and experiences, together with primal instincts and other forces. Furthermore, our subconscious remains active, continually influencing our conscious life, such as the hidden motivation behind our feelings, thoughts, and actions.[11] Hence the need for, and role of, myth in our lives.

Armstrong reminds us that "fearful and destructive unreason has always been part of the human experience, and still is."[12] A powerful mythology is thus needed to explain people's unconscious fears. Mention has already been made of the box office success of movies about mythical heroes. Another theme that is similarly guaranteed to make money is that of horror movies. People are drawn to such stories as a moth to a flame. More than one such movie, made at a low five-figure cost has reaped earnings in the millions. The "fearful and destructive unreason" within us makes this kind of story irresistible. Such movies have long been preceded by fairy tales, most of which have an element of fear and dread. The looming threat of dragons and monsters is common to such stories. Annual celebrations held around the beginning of November, centered on death, are enthusiastically entered into by both children and adults. The principle aim of such activities is to scare and shock one another.

The sea change that the development of consciousness in the second millennium BCE wrought inevitably impacted mythos as well. It continued, however, to play a vital role in helping humans to understand that they are more than their material circumstances. The Enlightenment, on the other hand, encouraged the jettisoning of spiritual concepts, seeing them as superstitions of former ages. People would now be able to be guided and influenced by facts as opposed to myths. For example, Francis Bacon (1561-1626), the father of modern science, argued for a thorough reevaluation of myths. The role and contribution of creation stories would diminish, if not fall away. The scientists and technicians became caught up in logos as opposed to being inspired by mythos. "This meant that intuitive, mythical modes of thought would be neglected in favor of the more pragmatic, logical spirit of scientific reality."[13] People wanted to believe that their traditions were in harmony with this new scientific age, but treating myths as being literally true made such desires even more impossible.

Joseph Campbell listed four functions that mythology serves, viz. mystical, cosmological, social, and psychological. The second function, cosmological, has been most radically changed. Each new advance in knowledge caused old cosmologies to lose their hold as they were replaced by new ones. In order to be effective, myths need to be brought up to date. The leading claims of both Testaments in the Bible were founded on a cosmological image from the bicameral era, which was already out of date when the Scriptures were redacted and collated in the last centuries BCE and the early centuries CE.[14] It could be seen as ironic that, because of Logos, we have come to have an infinitely greater appreciation of the wonder and magnitude of our universe than anything stated in the Bible.

The discounting or misuse of myth, as opposed to adapting it to new knowledge, was further aided by the spread of literacy and individual access to the Scriptures. The mythical/mystical mode of liturgical recitation was gradually replaced by silent reading in isolation. The Bible became a source for information like any other book. Genesis, for example, came to be seen as historical fact. This in turn led to "bad science and bad religion."[15]

The concretizing of symbols has been far more than a matter of semantics. More than one student of symbols has warned about the potential for this practice to cause harm as opposed to providing help.

M.-L. von Franz, in his contribution to *Man and his Symbols* pointed out that symbols produced by the unconscious have a healing or destructive impact.[16] Von Bertalanffy believed that symbolism is a two-edged sword that can cut both for and against us.

> Symbolic systems may become more potent than man, their creator. Then symbolic entities--status, religion, party, nation, what-have-you--may govern man and human behavior more strongly than biological reality. This is the basis of the most sublime achievements of man. But it is also the cause of all the follies of human history. Thermonuclear bombs are not only the ultimate weapon but the ultimate of symbolisms run wild in technology and politics.[17]

Symbiosis refers to the intimate relationship between two dissimilar organisms. This association can be either beneficial or harmful. The turning of mythos into logos would cause the symbiotic relationship between myth and coping with life to be turned upside down. A symbol is invaluable as it helps one to understand and/or come to terms with the unknown and the profound. When a myth is treated as an absolute truth, its role and function are changed for the worse. At the very least the symbol loses all semantic value - it then has no meaning at all.

But, especially where monotheists are concerned, worse can, and does, take place. Such practitioners of religion came to view their scriptures as the final revelation from their particular god, and myths were now viewed as literal truths from the mouth of the Divine. In so doing, people took a major step back to the bicameral mindset when one and all unthinkingly embraced all that they heard from the gods. Symbiosis as a negative has resulted. Countless ugly and harmful things have been done because a myth has been abused by treating it as a literal fact.

In the last chapter of *A Short History of Myth,* Karen Armstrong has drawn attention to some of the damage done by discounting myth in the Age of Reason. This practice caused people to rationalize their fears into "fact." As a result, unreason was strongly displayed in the new Christian movements that attempted to translate the ideals of the Enlightenment into a religious form. Shakers literally shook at their meetings, and Quakers were so-called because they used to tremble and howl at their gatherings. The Puritans, too, were not without traumatic conversion experiences that at times resulted in depressive states and even suicide. A similar pattern was in evidence in the First Great Awakening in New England (1734-1740). The greatest excesses, however, became known as the Witch Craze. As already mentioned it was a collective fantasy where people believed that "witches" had sex with devils and flew through the air to attend satanic orgies. Hundreds of thousands of women, as well as men and children, were put to death.

Carl Jung would later warn of the danger of carrying reason too far:

> Modern man does not understand how much his 'rationalism' (which has destroyed his capacity to respond to numinous symbols and ideas) has put him at the mercy of the psychic 'underworld.' He has freed himself from 'superstition' (or so he believes), but in the process he has lost his spiritual values to a positively dangerous degree. His moral and spiritual tradition has disintegrated, and he is now paying the price for this break-up in world-wide disorientation and dissociation. . . . (He has) stripped all things of their mystery and numinosity; nothing is holy any longer.[18]

Not only was religion affected by the decline of myth--all aspects of life were negatively impacted. The degeneration of mythos into logos did not invalidate mythical concepts and vehicles, nor did they become objective truths. The mutation that appears to have taken place was the transmogrification of society, making it, at its worst, grotesque, as it lost its humanity/divinity. At best the absence of myth makes one an automaton--a robot, and at worst, a monster.

The denunciation of *mythos* seemed to be complete by the end of the nineteenth century. The British biologist Thomas H. Huxley (1825-1895) believed that people had to choose between mythology and rational science. "Reason alone was truthful and the myths of religion truthless."[19] Truth only applied to that which could be demonstrated and proved. No vital role was seen or appreciated for the arts. Modern scientists had indeed made myth incredible. When Nietzsche proclaimed in 1882 that God was dead, he was right in more ways than he meant. "Without myth, cult, ritual and ethical living, the sense of the sacred dies."[20] Armstrong has powerfully portrayed the ramifications of this death:

> By making 'God' a wholly notional truth, reached by the critical intellect alone, modern men and women had killed it for themselves. The Madman in Nietzsche's parable in *The Gay Science* believed that God's death had torn humanity from its roots. 'Is there still an above or below?' he asked. 'Do we not stray, as though through an infinite nothingness?'[21]
>
> Mythical thinking and practice had helped people to face the prospect of extinction, and to come through it with a degree of acceptance. Without this discipline, it has been difficult for many to avoid despair. The twentieth century presented us with one nihilistic icon after another, and many of the extravagant hopes of modernity and the Enlightenment were shown to be false.

The sinking of the *Titanic* in 1912 showed the frailty of technology; the First World War revealed that science, our friend, could also be applied with lethal effect to weaponry; Auschwitz, the Gulag and Bosnia spelled out what could happen when all sense of sacredness is lost. We learned that a rational education did not redeem humanity from barbarism, and that a concentration camp could exist in the same vicinity as a great university. The explosion of the first atomic bombs over Hiroshima and Nagasaki laid bare the germ of nihilistic self-destruction at the heart of modern culture; and the attack on the World Trade Center on 11 September 2001 showed that the benefits of modernity--technology, ease of travel and global communications - could be made instruments of terror.[22]

In similar vein Jung pointed out that

Our intellect has created a new world that dominates nature, and has populated it with monstrous machines. . . . In spite of our proud domination of nature, we are still her victims, for we have not even learned to control our own nature. Slowly, but it appears, inevitably, we are courting disaster. . . . Our present lives are dominated by the goddess Reason, who is our greatest and most tragic illusion. By the aid of reason, so we assure ourselves, we have 'conquered nature.'[23]

Logos has been anything but a complete triumph. The dark epiphanies of the twentieth century have made clear "that modern anxiety is not simply the result of self-indulgent neuroses.[24] Without a viable mythology we cannot, for example, resolve the anxieties connected with the unknown afterlife. The rejection of myth can appear to be noble and brave, "but purely linear, logical and historical modes of thought have debarred many of us from therapies and devices that have enabled [people] to draw on the full resources of their humanity in order to live with the unacceptable."

We may be more sophisticated in material ways,

> but we have not advanced spiritually beyond the Axial
> Age: because of our suppression of *mythos* we may even
> have regressed. We still long to 'get beyond' our imme-
> diate circumstances, and to enter a 'full time,' a more
> intense, fulfilling existence. We try to enter this dimen-
> sion by means of art, rock music, drugs or by entering
> the larger-than-life perspective of film. We still seek he-
> roes. Elvis Presley and Princess Diana were both made
> into instant mythical beings, even objects of religious
> cult.[25]

The cult of celebrity has become pervasive. People are now famous for being famous. They are often "stars" of pseudo-reality shows that are astonishing for their utter vacuity. What is even more dismaying is that these shows are made viable by the equally vacuous populace that watches them. Instead of seeking and following their own bliss, they follow after these "icons," giving pavlovian whoops and cheers whenever they appear in public--echoes of the bicameral mind.

> The myth of the hero was not intended to provide us with
> icons to admire, but was designed to tap into the vein
> of heroism within ourselves. Myth must lead to imita-
> tion or participation, not passive contemplation. We no
> longer know how to manage our mythical lives in a way
> that is spiritually challenging and transformative.[26]

Myth is not made false by a nineteenth century fallacy, nor does it represent an inferior mode of thought. "We are myth-making creatures and, during the twentieth century, we saw some very destructive modern myths which have ended in massacre and genocide."[27] Again these myths were disastrous because they came to be seen as being "facts." The Nazis with their Aryan theories provide probably the most horrendous example. The Japanese, too, saw themselves as a superior race. Myths like these "have failed because they do not meet the criteria of the Axial Age. They have not been infused with the spirit of compassion and respect for the sacredness of life.

> These destructive mythologies have been narrowly racial, ethnic, denominational and egotistic, an attempt to exalt the self by demonizing the other. Any such myth has failed modernity, which has created a global village in which all human beings now find themselves in the same predicament.

> We cannot counter these bad myths with reason alone, because undiluted *logos* cannot deal with such deep-rooted, unexorcised fears, desires and neuroses. That is the role of an ethically and spiritually informed mythology.[28]

In his 1922 landmark poem "The Wasteland," T. S. Eliot depicted the spiritual disintegration of Western culture. The wasteland is a place where people, who had lost the mythical underpinning of their culture, live inauthentic lives, blindly following the norms of their society without the conviction that comes from deeper understanding. By means of allusions to the worldwide mythologies of the past, "Eliot laid bare the sterility of contemporary life: its alienation, ennui, nihilism, superstition, egotism, and despair."[29]

A further painful effect of misuse of symbolic language can be found in the militant character of Christian fundamentalism. The apocalyptic passages, taken literally, provide justification for warfare to be the pathway to survival and victory. It has been easy for extremists to find passages that seem to give a seal of divine approval to hatred.

An innovation that developed in the nineteenth century among Protestant extremists was the claim that they read the Scriptures in the same way that early Christians did. This was carrying the factualization of myth a step further in order to reinforce their absolutist beliefs.

One effect of this calcification of conviction was a lack of toleration for any other belief systems. With the development of Scholasticism, the first appearance of fundamentalism, the Roman Catholic Church had long been convinced of its supreme and complete understanding of what is required for survival before and after death. Hence the missionary zeal that was part of their conquests and colonizations. The Protestant absolutist mindset, resulting from the Enlightenment, caused evangelical missionary zeal to mushroom from a few hundred workers in 1814 to 22,000 a century later.

The Enlightenment also led to a scientific study of history, which, when applied to the Bible, undermined the support for key Christian beliefs. This did not faze the fundamentalists--if Christian doctrine was "no longer demonstrably true *de facto*, it was made true *de jure*--defined and enforced as *law*."[30] Barzun believes that fundamentalists, rather than being anti-intellectual, "over-intellectualize, like all literalists; they interpret a text as a judge does a statute."[31]

Fundamentalism came to affect all three monotheistic religions. Until the establishment of modern Israel, Judaism was preoccupied with survival. The construction of settlements on the West Bank and in Gaza was fueled by claims based on literal application of Hebrew myth - that this land was deeded to them by Yahweh. The ugly scenes of young Israelis attempting to prevent the evacuation of Gaza-based settlements was the result.

The Roman Catholic accumulation of absolutist positions went beyond the work of the scholastics. One reaction to the Enlightenment was for the popes to claim that they spoke "ex cathedra"--with divine authority. The Vatican Council of 1870 made a decree that held the pope to be infallible in matters of faith and morals. Protestant fundamentalism, ironically, has mainly developed in America, which is, in theory, religiously neutral. Its culture and politics, however, have increasingly come under pressure from conservative Christianity. Today a person holding to the beliefs and convictions of Thomas Jefferson could never be voted in as president.

Islam itself started to circle the wagons long before the eighteenth century. Until the close of the twelfth century, Islam had a tradition of independent thinking known as *ijtihad*. It was a concept of creative thinking and at one time 135 schools of thought flourished. Córdoba, when Spain was Muslim, had 70 libraries. A major factor in the decline of ijtihad was the rise of dissident denominations which declared their own governments.

For 800 years now, three equations have informed mainstream Islamic practice. First, unity equals uniformity. In order to be strong, members of the worldwide Muslim community must think alike. Second, debate equals division. Diversity of interpretation is no longer a tribute to God's majesty. It is a hammer blow to the unity that Muslims must exhibit to those intent on dividing them. Third, division equals heresy. Soon after the gates of ijtihad closed, innovation came to be defined as a crime by dint of being *fitna*--that which divides.[32]

In more and more Muslim countries, cultural practices are perceived to be threatened by the infiltration of Western "evils." These cultural activities are thus now proclaimed to be the definition of Islam. A cultural change is therefore an attack on Islam. Islamic fundamentalism has become a form of cultural ideology taken to the extreme. Love of country comes to be equated with love of Allah, and to attack these "evils," either in a military venture or by subterfuge by becoming a human bomb, is to take a pure path to martyrdom. "Islam as a religion of compassion and of tolerance is being over-ridden by cultural ultimatums that have become the tools of political ideology."[33]

It is even more threatening to the leaders of Islam when Muslims themselves step outside of their ever narrowing parameters. The writer Salman Rushdie has been hounded for the last 20 years for daring to write the fanciful novel *The Satanic Verses*, seen as a blasphemy of Muhammad. The fulminations against him were revived recently when he was knighted by Queen Elizabeth II. Iran has shuddered in similar fashion because of recent statements made by Abdulkarim Soroush, its once leading public intellectual. He was chosen by Ayatollah Khomeni to "Islamicize" Iran's universities--a key part of its Islamic revolution. Soroush now looks at the Qur'an in a manner that resembles that of the nineteenth century German scholars who sought to understand the Bible in its original context. He now sees the Qur'an as being the words of Muhammad, he being no parrot, as opposed to Allah, seeing the former as the receiver *and* the producer of what was a "prophetic experience." Soroush also supports the separation of mosque and state, making an argument for religious pluralism.[34]

The columnist Maureen Dowd has vividly portrayed the damage that fundamentalism does to religion:

> Instead of addressing itself to the angels of our nature, religion seems to be inspiring the demons in our nature. . . . Religion should inculcate sympathy, patience, compassion, understanding, forgiveness, a love of peace. Instead, the name of God is used to justify vices that are the opposite of these virtues.
>
> It is not news that religion has its ugly tribalist and bellicose sides. What is news is that those sides are

having a field day. Just when we wish to flee to religion
for sanctuary, we find ourselves fleeing *from* religion for
sanctuary.[35]

Rabbi Arthur Hertzberg, a prominent figure in twentieth century
American Conservative Jewry said, "The greatest scourge in humanity
is not a pirate or a highway robber [but rather] the uncompromising
defender of the faith--any faith." Not long after September 11, somebody
scribbled on a wall in Washington: "Dear God, save us from the people
who believe in you."

Not only do those who are clearly identified as the enemy come
under fire, but differences within a religious group can lead to attack
and even death.

> The smallest divergence from the absolute is grave error
> and wickedness. From there it is a short step to declaring
> war on the misbelievers. When faith is both intellec-
> tual and visceral, the overwhelming justification is that
> heresy imperils other souls. If the erring sheep will not
> recant, he or she becomes a source of error in others.[36]

There are many painful examples of this reality in history. The
burning of heretics was not practiced just to drastically curtail their
influence but to save them from themselves. There was of course biblical
justification for the idea. "He himself will be saved, but only as one
escaping through the flames" (I Corinthians 3:15).

Perpetrators of such deeds are either blind followers of the system
or they have been able to smother all doubts about their beliefs and
convictions. A lack of the influence of myth leaves no room for
ambivalence and doubt, which in turn leads to the drastic treatment
of those who demonstrate uncertainty or openness. The confusion of
cultural pluralism, a fact of modern times, has only enhanced the need
to seal one's mind.

Donald Braxton speaks to this dynamic. Human beings evolved with the capacity to deceive themselves when it is deemed necessary. It is part of our psychological makeup. When doubt comes at too high a price, we become capable of self-deception by pushing countervailing evidence to the side, thus making possible a subjective sense of certainty. We all seek to not only survive but flourish, and thus the tendency to process knowledge accordingly. If information is received which challenges our most valued beliefs, we have evolved the capacity to resist the validity of non-acceptable information.[37] Similarly, Rollo May believes that dogmatism, which is synonymous with fundamentalism, is "a symptom of the fact that the person really doubts in his unconscious the truth he espouses so strongly."[38]

Because of the existence of these doubts, we tend to move in circles that prop up our worldview. Supporting communities are essential to reinforcing our key beliefs. In the more charismatic churches, people are encouraged from the pulpit to say "Amen!" and "Praise the Lord!" when their identifying positions are mentioned. The religious leader's beliefs need to be shored up as much as anyone else's. The joke about the preacher who wrote in the margin of his sermon notes "point weak--shout loud!" speaks to this pervasive pattern. Nietzsche aptly observed that "convictions are more dangerous enemies of truth than lies."[39]

The dictators of both left- and right-wing persuasion fear the slightest dissent because it reminds the totalitarian of his own doubts, and so he must move to crush it. Political correctness, a quality that comes primarily from the academic realm, as well as from the left side of the political spectrum, is another attempt to squash all doubt. Professors have even lost their positions for not marching in lock-step with the faculty at large.

The most pathetic, but also the most dangerous, are those who attempt to fulfill their own eschatological beliefs. This is peculiar to those of the religious right. The certainty about how the world will end is often undergirded by looking back into history through their distorted lenses. One rabid promoter of the Christian right-wing view, John Hagee, made the flabbergasting statement that Hitler was a tool used by God to bring the Jews back to Israel, an essential prerequisite of Hagee's take on the "last days." There are some among the religious right

> who are working hard to 'hasten the inevitable,' not merely anticipating the End Days with joy in their hearts, but taking political action to bring about the conditions they think are the prerequisites for that occasion. And these people are not funny at all. They are dangerous: they put their allegiance to their creed ahead of their commitment to democracy, to peace, to [earthly] justice--and to truth. If push comes to shove, some of them are prepared to lie and even to kill, to do whatever it takes to help bring what they consider celestial justice to those they consider the sinners.[40]

Not only are their doubts about their beliefs palpable, they even doubt the attributes of God, particularly his omnipotence. God is seen to need a nudge, if not a push, in the "right" direction in order to be sure that he will do their bidding.

The reality is that the modern world has not been delivered from the mystery of the ultimate. We may have many new possibilities and resources but are anything but free from danger. We have come to appreciate anew the place for symbols in our lives and that we need them as much as we ever did. There is, however, an important difference in our post-Enlightenment age.

As Carl Jung has stated it, "In former times men did not reflect upon their symbols. They lived them and were unconsciously animated by their meaning."[41]

> Today we do reflect on our symbols. We recognize the symbolic character of such words as 'spirit,' 'God,' 'soul.' We even know something of the way in which the symbols come to birth within the human psyche. The fact that they have a natural origin rather than a supernatural one does not in itself mean that we can dispense with symbols and myths.[42]

The discounting of myth caused the term to be mainly used in a derogatory way. A "myth" came, at best, to be a meaningless story of limited entertainment value and, at worst, a deliberately misleading deception. The dismissal of myth, however, was never entirely successful. Its historical positive value was beginning to be recognized anew by the end of the eighteenth century. The Romantic movement played a significant role in the revival of myth as it made a case for the work of "mind and heart." The poetry for which Romanticism is noted is the soul and essence of mythos.

The founder of modern Old Testament study, J. G. Eichorn (1752-1827), pointed out that the myths of the ancient world were not simply fairy-stories or falsehoods but constitute instead an ancient form of philosophy--expressing the thoughts and history of a people in a form amenable to the senses. David Strauss (1808-1874) developed what he called the mythical principle:

> The result, however surprising, of a general examination of the Biblical history, is that the Hebrew and Christian religions, like all others, have their *mythi*. And this result is confirmed if we consider the inherent nature of religion, what essentially belongs to it, and therefore must be common to all religions. . . . If religion is defined as

the perception of truth . . . invested with imagery, it is easy to see . . . that in the proper religious sphere [the mythical element] must necessarily exist.[43]

Søren Kierkegaard, a contemporary of David Strauss, was a Romantic thinker who insisted that religion demanded a commitment that could not be justified by any logical process - that it called for a "leap of faith." A century later Martin Buber (1878-1965), would refer to myth as "man's creative answer to the unconditioned," and "an eternal function of the soul."

It has been writers like Eliot and artists like Pablo Picasso, rather than religious leaders who have attempted to reacquaint us with the mythological wisdom of the past. After the bombing of Guernica, the Basque capital, on a market day at the height of the Spanish Civil War, Picasso created a painting depicting the event. A modern secular crucifixion is displayed. And like "The Wasteland," it is both a prophetic statement and a rallying cry against the inhumanity of our brave new world.[44]

James Joyce, in *Ulysses,* and others, like Salmon Rushdie, have turned to mythology to combine the realistic with the inexplicable in exploring the modern dilemma. Others, like George Orwell in *Nineteen Eighty-Four,* have looked into the future. Like great myths of the past, his book has entered popular consciousness.

> There is nothing new in the godless mythologies of contemporary novels, which grapple with many of the same intractable and illusive problems of the human condition as the ancient myths, and make us realize that - whatever the status of the gods - human beings are more than their material circumstances and that all have sacred, numinous value.[45]

In Europe, in particular, it is not myth that has become irrelevant but rather religion per se, which is no longer the principle vehicle for spirituality. The degree to which Christianity has become marginalized was demonstrated in the draft of the preamble of a proposed European Union constitution which said that Europe was nourished by "Hellenic and Roman civilizations" and "the philosophical current of the Enlightenment" but did not specifically mention Christianity. A revised draft referred only to Europe's "cultural, religious and humanist inheritance." Pope John Paul II appealed in vain for formal recognition of the Continent's Christian roots.

In Europe at large there is a steadily diminishing belief in the underlying truthfulness of Christianity - its power and integrity have dissipated. What is taking its place?

16

Religion in the New Millennium

At the beginning of the new millennium Episcopal Bishop Mark Dwyer made the observation that the Church has a big rummage sale every five hundred years or so and that we are in the midst of such a sale now. In the rummage sale of the Protestant Reformation the Roman Catholic Church lost hegemony, and in the current one it is Protestantism that has lost hegemony.[1]

Thomas Berry described the problem in starker terms at the end of the twentieth century, saying that we are in trouble because we are between stories. The old story sustained us for a

> long time--it shaped our emotional attitudes, it provided
> us with life's purpose; it energized our actions, it conse-
> crated suffering, it guided education. We awoke in the
> morning and knew who we were. We could answer the
> questions of our children. Everything was taken care of
> because the story was there. Now the old story is not
> functioning. And we have not yet learned a new one.[2]

It is well beyond debate that The Great Western Transformation, which began in the sixteenth century and is still in progress, has inaugurated a wholly different world. Most of it is now based on technology and capital investment instead of upon a surplus of agriculture. The modern and post-modern eras have shattered old sanctities and radically altered human life in ways that are only beginning to be appreciated.

The emergence of a different world, not to mention worldview, is reflected in the gravestone epitaphs of England's churchyards. The dominant theme in the seventeenth century was the last judgment and resurrection of the dead. In the eighteenth century the virtues of the deceased were extolled in the hope that they would be in good standing when they met their maker. This theme was enlarged on in the nineteenth century as the social standing and the greatness of the achievements of the deceased were listed. And in the twentieth century explicit talk about life after death disappears from tombstones. What has been taking place is not the secularization of religion but rather the sacralization of life.

Furthermore, authoritarian government, both civil and religious, has been seriously challenged. *No* beliefs, including those arrived at by the use of reason, can now be imposed unwillingly on others. The age of imposed dogma is over, in theory if not yet in practice. The worldview consisting of a sacred heaven and a fallen earth has been replaced by a view which emphasizes the world's infinitely complex, and yet essential, unity.

In one area of human experience after another what was once believed to be supernatural has come to be seen as belonging to the natural world; what was thought to be of divine origin has been found to be of human origin; what was treated as absolute has come to be seen as relative. Even the established morés of society have not been immune from questioning. Long established standards of both personal and social morality are undergoing change. Instead of seeing themselves as subservient to God as law maker, people are coming to see themselves as the law makers as they move from heteronomy to autonomy.

These accumulating changes have caused people to become prone to nostalgia and a sense of loss. The old story seemed to provide security and comfort. Because of this we are tempted (like Lot's wife in the Hebrew Scriptures) to look back and mourn for that which is no more. We cannot, however, "go back, in spite of our nostalgia for the past and the siren voices that pretend we can choose to live there again if we want to. The past is gone from us, with all its pain and joy, with all its goodness and badness."[3]

The transforming change, occurring in the space of a thousand years, an exceedingly brief period of time, that overlapped the last two millennia BCE, saw humankind move from bicamerality to consciousness. In the bicameral era one and all were subject to auditory hallucinations that came from one's mind and that controlled what one did.

With the origin of consciousness one could now perceive what to do by and for oneself. It was a new era as the stage was set for the Axial Age, brought about by the Axial Sages, as they articulated that which people were now waiting for and wanting to hear.

The now-conscious human being still longed to hear from the gods--the bicameral auditory hallucinations--and with it the potential to come under the thrall of those who claim a divine role for themselves. Humankind in general still longs to hear from the gods. And it's not just under the banner of some sect or religious group that blind and total commitment takes place. It's not just the David Koreshes, the Jim Joneses, and the Sun Myung Moons who are blindly followed. There have always been those political leaders who obtain absolute control and come to be seen as gods by their countrymen. Kim Il-sung, followed by his son, Kim Jong Il, claimed and received absolute allegiance. North Korea was utterly bereft when Kim Il-sung died. Self-help gurus, too, can demand and receive total commitment from their clients. James Ray has been able to command $10,000 from each client who attends his five-day Spiritual Warrior retreats. On one held in October of 2009 (in all probability the last one) and attended by 50 clients, a makeshift sweat lodge was used on the last evening. It was two hours of being under increasing stress, ending with three people being dead, and a further eighteen suffering burns, dehydration, respiratory arrest, or kidney failure. One assistant observed that Ray seemed to be indifferent to the disastrous consequences.

The potential to abandon all for some "god" is always there. It is a pervasive part of the human condition. Intelligence, education, and culture have not proved themselves to be preventative factors. Highly intelligent women, for example, with feminist sympathies, will fervently embrace Islam, including the inferior status that it dictates for them.

The various religions, especially the monotheistic ones, that emerged as vehicles to aid in one's spiritual journey, have far more often than not, in varying degree, returned their followers to a bicameral mindset. It has become worse than a prison because no physical restraints are needed--although groups, such as Mormons and Scientologists, can apply great pressure to those who may wish to leave. For the most part, religion has diminished our humanity. Dostoevsky's parable of The Grand Inquisitor painfully portrays this achievement.

Joseph Campbell lamented that the supernatural had been presented as something over and above the natural:

> In the Middle Ages this was the idea that finally turned the world into something of a wasteland, a land where people are living inauthentic lives, never doing a thing they truly wanted to because the supernatural laws required them to live as directed by their clergy. In a wasteland people are fulfilling purposes that are not properly theirs but have been put upon them as inescapable laws.[4]

In similar vein, James Joyce in *A Portrait of an Artist* has his hero say, "When the soul of a man is born in this country there are nets flung at it to hold it back in flight. You talk to me of nationality, language, religion. I shall try to fly by these nets.[5] The wielders of these nets are variations of the bicameral gods who seek to ensnare the seekers of freedom and haul them back into being blind followers of the gods.

Albert Einstein saw the bicameral mindset when he visited the Wailing Wall in Jerusalem in 1923: "Where dull-witted clansmen of our tribe were praying aloud, their faces turned to the wall, their bodies swaying to and fro. A pathetic sight of men with a past but without a future."[6]

Even now, as we have entered the new millennium, religion continues to be fixated on the past. It doesn't even begin to know how to engage with the present as it continues to be heteronomous in an autonomous age. Religion remains sealed off in its ivory towers, failing miserably to engage with the real world as it continues to hold so many under its control.

Freud also saw religion as failing to be aware of human development. He regarded the perpetuation of traditional religious beliefs in the modern world as a dangerous illusion, leading people into a false sense of security. Such beliefs bore 'the stamp of the times in which they originated, the ignorant childhood days of the human race.' To continue to hold such beliefs, at a time when the human race is reaching adulthood, is to be compared with the neurosis of an adult who avoids facing the harsh realities of life by regressing to a childhood state of mind.[7] Freud also put it another way, seeing belief in God as an expression of yearning for the all-powerful father who will take care of us.[8]

Carl Jung framed the problem as follows in 1961:

> Man today is painfully aware of the fact that neither
> his great religions nor his various philosophies seem to

> provide him with those powerful animating ideas that
> would give him the security he needs in face of the pres-
> ent condition of the world.[9]

Jung saw religion as being a defense *against* the experience of God.

The mystery that is the unknown, and to which one is drawn (the process that makes homo sapiens a meaning-seeking creature), has been reduced by religion to a set of dogmas and ideas, and it is this reduction that short-circuits the transcendent experience.[10]

One of the Sages, Gautama Buddha, sought to prepare people to resist the seductive and controlling powers of authority figures by teaching, "If you meet the Buddha on the road, kill him." This was a metaphorical admonishment for people to think for themselves. The Buddha didn't want to be seen as the truth or to show the truth but rather to show the way to the truth. James Joyce recognized the same need. In *Ulysses* his hero, while tapping his brow, muses: "In here it is I must kill the priest and king."[11] For the vast majority of people the most common controller is the ubiquitous priest.

One needs to bear in mind that all of the various religions, promoted and enforced by priests, have been humanly created, as opposed to having a divine source. This is also true for all philosophies and concepts such as gods and the heavenly world. The term "god" is itself a symbolic word which originated in ancient mythology and represents a personification of man's highest ideals and values. And, at its best, being religious is the making of our response to these ultimate issues. It is being connected to something far greater than one's self as we try to make sense of what we experience in wonder and awe. And yet it isn't about "God" but rather human communities gathered together in search of truth and the meeting of needs. It is being a part of rather than apart from.

Campbell describes religion as being "a kind of second womb. It's designed to bring this extremely complicated thing, which is a human being, to maturity, which means to be self-motivating, self-acting."[12] Religion, at its best, is a self-chosen tool of personal growth. As the philosopher Richard Rorty put it, what religion speaks to is our need to make sense of ourselves to ourselves--a matter of one's private or inner life, as opposed to one's public life.[13]

Religion has evolved as humanity has learned and grown. Don Cupitt has described its evolution:

> The whole of humanity nowadays takes part in a single
> global conversation, within which a major religious shift
> is taking place. Roughly, we are changing over from a
> very long-termist, otherworldly, and mediated religion
> of eternal salvation in another world beyond death to a
> very short-termist, this-worldly, and immediate religion
> of ethical commitment to this life here and now.[14]

Because of this Cupitt says that religion today must become autonomous--a creative human activity, a way of adapting ourselves to life. One must in every sense *own* one's own life.[15] This will lead to diversity on a grand scale.

No one can claim his/her life without claiming and exercising his/her freedom. Freedom is of profound importance as it goes to the "core" of being human. As Rollo May puts it, "Freedom and being human are identical."[16] They are inseparable. A diminishment of one's freedom is also a diminishment of one's humanity.

Evidence of freedom being the object of extreme devotion is that it is considered to be more precious than life itself. Multitudes have unhesitatingly risked and sacrificed their lives in its cause. Freedom is an inalienable right.

Erich Fromm has pointed out that freedom must first be exercised in its negative sense of "freedom from" before its positive sense of "freedom to" can take place. One has to first be freed from instinctual

311

determination of one's actions, a uniquely human attribute.[17] Human beings can, and have, resisted instincts and drives, such as reproduction, that have been essential to survival. Of even more vital importance is freedom from the calls of our bicameral roots by resisting a blind following of some or other authority figure. In a more contemporary context, freedom includes rejection of the absolute demands and limitations of religious dogma.

Freedom has played a central role in the lives of mystics, who are noted for their rejection of such dogma. It is to be seen in the intensive exercise of their own freedom in achieving their inspirations. In arguing that God does not constrain the will, Meister Eckhart (1260-1327) said, "Rather, he sets it free so that it may *choose* him, that is to say, freedom." Similarly, Jakob Böhme (1575-1624), an uneducated cobbler, believed that "will--freedom--is the principle of all things . . . (and that) freedom is deeper than and prior to all nature. . . . (He) made freedom the first foundation of being . . . deeper and more primary than all being, deeper and more primary than God himself.[18]

The philosopher Dame Iris Murdock indicated the seat of one's freedom when she said there is "one freedom only that matters, of the mind."[19] Because of this fact, it is possible to live without physical liberty and yet be free. When Aung San Suu Kyi was released from what turned out to be her first period of house arrest, she was asked what it felt like to be free. She immediately replied, "They did not set me free; I was already free." A person can live without liberty, but not without freedom.[20]

A San Quentin prisoner wrote:

Though we're wrapped in chains
the jailor is not free.

A prisoner can be freer than his guards, for this is not a freedom of security but of the mind, of discovery. The same prisoner wrote, "The discovery of my thoughts gives me joy. For until they find a way to take

312

my thoughts away, I am free." Knowledge is freedom, and is the source of hope, even in the most hopeless places.[21]

Freedom, which is integral to being human, isn't limited to a state of mind. "There is no authentic inner freedom that does not, sooner or later, also affect and change human history."[22] Bobbie Kirkhart, when being interviewed about the association known as Atheists United, described it as being a free thought community, adding, "I don't think there's any higher moral force than the thoughtful, informed, individual human conscience.[23]

Joan Chittister has described this moral force in revolutionary terms:

> The revolutions that count come silently, come first in the heart, come with the force of steel, because they come with no force at all. Revolutions of this magnitude do not overturn a system and then shape it. They reshape thought, and then the system overturns without the firing of a single cannon. Revolutions such as this dismantle walls people thought would never fall because no wall, whatever its size, can contain a people whose minds have long ago scaled and vaulted and surmounted it.[24]

Our recent history is replete with stunning "revolutionaries" such as Martin Luther King, Jr., Aleksandr Solzhenitsyn, Nelson Mandela, and Aung San Suu Kyi.

Freedom is foundational to so much more. The capacity to experience awe and wonder, to imagine and write poetry, to conceive of scientific theories and great works of art, presupposes freedom."[25]

And yet to exercise freedom is to also experience certain tensions, one being that of evil. To deny evil is also to deny freedom because its exercise requires that choices be made, and the possibility of making the wrong choices comes into play. And some of them can be catastrophic. But to relinquish the capacity to make choices is to surrender that which is integral to one's humanity.

"The ultimate error is to refuse to look evil in the face. This denial of evil--and freedom along with it--is the most destructive approach of all."[26] It can, and does, lead to becoming a camp follower of people like Sun Myung Moon, who will, among other things, choose your marriage partner for you. Or even worse, commit spiritual suicide by seeking a haven with a David Koresh or a Jim Jones, where people surrendered their freedom in the hopes of evading the evils of life, only to end up demonstrating the final evil in their own mass suicides.

Another tension that is linked with freedom is that of anxiety. As Kierkegaard stated it, "Anxiety is the dizziness of freedom." In similar vein, James Truslow Adams said, "Eternal anxiety is the lot of the freeman."[27] "Anxiety is potentially present whenever we are free; freedom is oriented towards anxiety and anxiety toward freedom."[28]

Dostoevsky's Grand Inquisitor starkly states,

> Nothing has ever been more insupportable for a man and a human society than freedom. . . . Man is tormented by no greater anxiety than to find someone quickly to whom he can hand over that gift of freedom with which the ill-fated creature is born. . . . Man prefers peace and even death to freedom of choice in good and evil.[29]

Freedom is a burden because it brings anxiety in its wake.

"Every human being experiences this anxiety when he or she exercises the freedom to move into the no-man's land of possibility. We can escape the anxiety only by not venturing--that is by surrendering our freedom."[30] There is no effort required to surrender one's freedom. All that is needed is to passively yield to fate. A Persian named Hafiz once said, "'Tis written on the gate of Heaven, 'Woe unto him who suffers himself to be betrayed by Fate!'"[31] As Emerson observed, "The one serious and formidable thing in nature is a will. Society is servile from want of will, and therefore the world wants saviors and religions."[32]

Surrendering totally to a seemingly superior or supreme being is in our human DNA. It is what people did before the emergence of consciousness. This practice has survived and thrived, especially in the monotheistic religions. Jews, for the longest time, would not even pronounce the name of Yahweh. Muslims, especially those who are unhesitatingly prepared to blow themselves up in supposed devotion to Allah, say "May Allah be praised!" when some "martyr" succeeds in ending the lives of others. Christians, in countless hymns, proclaim that they are nothing and that God is everything. People willingly make themselves prisoners in their own stockades in order to escape anxiety. They reject freedom, the essence of which is accepting responsibility for one's own life.

It goes without saying that freedom demands that people think for themselves, and that thinking for oneself will inevitably lead to questions and doubts. Descartes, the pioneer philosopher noted for saying, "I think, therefore I am," also exclaimed, "Doubt!", a word that has reverberated ever more loudly through the last four centuries. One of Blaise Pascal's statements says, "Man is obviously made for thinking. Therein lies all his dignity and his merit; and his whole duty is to think as he ought."[33]

The questions and doubts that arise from thinking will inevitably put one at odds with others. And as Emerson pointed out, "Society does not like to have any breath of question blown on the existing order. . . . The wise skeptic is a bad citizen. . . . He says, "There are doubts.""[34] Thomas A. Harris, M.D., in his widely read book *I'm OK - You're OK,* goes to the heart of the need for each generation to think for itself:

315

It takes only one generation for a good thing to become a bad thing, for an inference about experience to become dogma. Dogma is the enemy of truth and the enemy of persons. Dogma says, "Do not think! Be less than a person." The ideas enshrined in dogma may include good and wise ideas, but dogma is bad in itself because it is accepted as good without examination.[35]

Other prominent voices have expressed similar sentiments. Thomas Paine: "It is necessary to the happiness of man that he be mentally faithful to himself. Infidelity does not consist in believing or disbelieving; it consists in professing to believe what he does not believe."[36] Emerson: "People wish to be settled; only as far as they are unsettled is there any hope for them."[37] "The spiritualist finds himself driven to express his faith by a series of skepticisms."[38] Bertrand Russell: "Our questions keep us human." Clarence Darrow: "I have always felt that doubt was the beginning of wisdom, and the fear of God was the end of wisdom."[39]

It is not unusual for conservative Bible colleges and seminaries to urge their students not to questions Christian faith and beliefs. A woman participating in a Jewish-Christian alumni discussion group caused heads to turn when she said, "I was converted when I began to question." Campbell stressed that all of us "are competent to know the mind of God. There is no special revelation to any people."[40] "Anybody from any quarter can speak truth because his mind is not cut off from the truth."[41]

Emerson believed strongly in this concept as well. He also warned of the danger of thinking that any question has been definitively answered: "Who shall forbid a wise skepticism, seeing that there is no practical question on which anything more than an approximate solution can be heard."[42] "The learned person is someone who is aware of his ignorance" is a Socratic maxim from the Axial Age.[43] Pascal counseled that "Reason's last step is the recognition that there are an infinite number of things which are beyond it. It is merely feeble if it does not go so far as to realize that."[44] John Allen Paulos used seven words to state the same facts: "Uncertainty is the only certainty there is."[45] A Sanskrit verse (also found in the Chinese *Tao-te Ching*) says: "He who thinks he knows, doesn't know. He who knows that he doesn't know, knows. For in this concept, to know is not to know and not to know is to know."[46]

John Donne said it in verse:

> The farther our faith reaches, the more doubt it encompasses,
> as far from the highest hills there are the fullest vistas
> Doubt wisely, in a strange way
> To stand inquiring right is not to stray;
> To sleep or run wrong is.
> On a huge hill,
> Craggy and steep,
> Truth stands, and he that will
> Reach her, about must and about must go;
> And what the hill's suddenness resists, win so.

John Donne, "Satire III"[47]

The higher one climbs, the broader the vistas become. The nearer one gets to comprehending the true nature of our existence, the more skeptical one becomes about being able to express that understanding. As one enters into "the cloud of unknowing," one's doubts and uncertainties are sharpened rather than muffled. "To believe greatly, it's necessary to doubt greatly."[48]

An encouraging sign of the times appeared in an article in the *Los Angeles Times* (November 10, 2005) with the heading "Doubt Is Their Co-Pilot." It describes a new faith called Universism, whose sole dogma is uncertainty.

The Bible begins with two complementary creation myths. In the Garden of Eden, God points out one thing that is forbidden to man, knowing full well that he would eat the forbidden fruit. As Campbell expresses it, "It is by doing that that man becomes the initiator of his own life. Life really began with that act of disobedience."[49] The concept of being your own source of volition (the central essence of consciousness), runs through the various versions of the myth of the Holy Grail. King Arthur's knights had to each make their own path in the quest for the grail. "The grail has been shown to us of the individual quest, the individual life adventured in the realization of one's own inborn potential."[50]

Geering, in summing up the Axial Age and its Sages, said that their

> paths were widely divergent in their conviction and dogma but common to all of them is man's reaching out beyond himself by growing aware of himself within the whole of Being and the fact that he can tread these paths only as an individual on his own.[51]

Europe realized by the thirteenth century that every individual is unique and every life adventure equally unique.[52]

Emerson echoed the Sages' aspirations. His life project was to encourage people to discern and unlock their own potential. He believed that this called for intuition, choice, and action--a self-trusting process that was a radical departure from the then prevailing Calvinism. Emerson believed, above all, in the moral authority of the individual intellect and conscience, believing that one and all could choose to pursue the paths that make us most ourselves:

> Liberation of the will from the sheaths and clogs of organization which he has outgrown, is the end and aim of this world.

There is a divine Providence in the world, which will not
save us but through our own cooperation.[53]

Emerson was convinced that one and all could intuit truth for
themselves. We need to bear in mind that "the *truth* is not something
which has been brought to finality at an ecclesiastical summit meeting or
bound in a black book."[54] Neither is it possible to formulate a statement
that will capture truth for all and for all time. Cupitt points out that

> Truth is free: you don't have to bow down to anyone for
> it. Truth is common property. . . . We should give up all
> ideas of revelation and all ideas of traditional authority,
> and instead look for truth in the midst of common life
> and in the voices of ordinary people. We don't have to
> search for truth: it is already here among us.[55]

Long, long ago the Vedas said, "Truth is one, the sages call it by many
names.[56]

The finding of truth for oneself involves a crucial dynamic, that is,
moving from heteronomy--"deference to or dependence upon external
authorities . . . in religious or spiritual matters"--to autonomy, that is,
where the authority is "located in the individual who embraces beliefs
and practices, not because they have been prescribed by some external
source (heteronomously), but because they are 'intrinsically valuable.'"[57]
What matters is whether a saying or concept, regardless of its origin

> resonates with the mind, heart, and spirit of the reader.
> In other words autonomy demands that ideas and utter-
> ances be inherently compelling, regardless of the source.
> . . . Under the principle of autonomy, authority derives
> its sanction from the individual, and might be better
> characterized as *authenticity*. . . . Authenticity (auton-
> omy) always trumps authority (heteronomy).[58]

Among the many benefits, being autonomous makes one a better citizen. As Rabbi Abraham Joshua Heschel put it, "The grand premise of religion is that man is able to surpass himself."[59] One is enabled to fulfill the role of the mythical hero as one works out one's life for oneself. As Campbell defined it, "The courage to face the trials and to bring a whole new body of possibilities into the field of interpreted experience for other people to experience--that is the hero's deed.[60]

Nietzsche's "Übermensch" provides another description of the autonomous person. When he proclaimed, "God is dead and we have killed him," Nietzsche was saying that any meaning of life in the sense of a supernatural purpose was gone. The Übermensch is the one who gives himself meaning by raising himself above all the other animals and the all-too-human.[61] The Übermensch is the one who has overcome the HUMAN (mensch) in himself. He does not hope for life in another world (for which there is no need to exert oneself unduly) but instead he

> says Yes to life in spite of the absence of any ultimate
> meaning to history or to human existence. Any signifi-
> cance people come to recognize in life must be found in
> the present, for only the present truly exists.[62]

It is this planet on which we expend our lives that is of sole importance, and it behooves us well to participate in its preservation. Becoming responsible for oneself includes being responsible for the Earth. As Robert Funk states it, "We have reached the end of the homocentric and the beginning of the ecocentric age."[63]

Geering has made plain our options:

> What we choose to make of ourselves and of our world
> is over to us. We are walking a tightrope. Humankind
> can bring about its own ruin and even destroy this
> planet. . . . Humans now have to live without the divine
> and other supernatural props thought to exist in the

past. . . . (We) are now required to play the role we once
attributed to an external deity.[64]

Rabbi Jonathan Romain has put human action in religious terms: "The
heretic is not the person who believes the wrong thing, but does the
wrong thing."[65]

Edward O. Wilson, a recipient of many of the world's leading prizes
in science and conservation, believes that stewardship is an intensely felt
value common to humans and that it

> appears to arise from emotions programmed in the very
> genes of human social behavior. Because all organisms
> have descended from a common ancestor, it is correct
> to say that the biosphere began to think when human-
> ity was born. If the rest of life is the body, we are the
> mind.[66]

The second of the biblical creation myths recognizes our oneness with
the earth: "The Lord God formed man from the dust of the ground."
(Genesis 2:7) We are of the earth. Campbell enlarges on this concept:

> If we think of ourselves as coming out of the earth,
> rather than having been thrown in here from some-
> where else, (we) are the earth, we are the consciousness
> of the earth. These are the eyes of the earth. And this is
> the voice of the earth.[67]

John A. Wheeler, the most imaginative explicator of 20th century
physics, coining and explaining such terms as "black hole," was the
source of many probing questions: "How come the universe? How come
us? How come anything?" He went on to conclude that the answer lies
in the observers. "That's us," he said. Wheeler's central vision was

> the picture that the whole of this existence will some
> day have its single, central principle spring to life, that
> will be so natural we will say to ourselves: 'How can it

have been otherwise? And how could we have been so stupid all these years not to have seen it?' (Obituary)

Ludwig von Bertalanffy described the human being as "the ultimate expression of organized complexity . . . with uniquely emergent qualities of creativity.[68] Man's creativity is primarily expressed in art, which is seen as being our highest expression of spirituality. As Armstrong describes its role, "In art, liberated from the constraints of reason and logic, we conceive and combine new forms that enrich our lives."[69]

James Joyce spoke of the "radiance" that shines through all things, and Campbell claimed that the artist is the one who has learned to recognize and render this radiance through the created object--to make one say "aha!"[70] As Cupitt explains it,

> The point about art is that it gives us an understanding
> that is neither metaphysical nor scientific: it presents
> us with a powerful compressed image of the whole, of
> which it and we are a part.[71]

Artists are able to be inspired by the "strange ancient furniture of the unconscious mind," universally evocative images and ideas which in turn "make us aware of the old kinship with all life and being."[72] Their "ears are open to the song of the universe."[73] Artists have in fact always been with us, the mythmakers of earlier days being their forerunners. Campbell saw mythology as "the homeland of the muses, the inspirers of art," and artists in turn as having the vital task of keeping myth alive.[74] Both myth and art "express in momentous symbols the core of reality."[75]

Armstrong reminds us that to experience art is to be challenged and changed by it:

> Any powerful work of art invades our being and changes
> it forever. British critic George Steiner claims that art,

like certain kinds of religions and metaphysical experience, is the most '"ingressive," transformative summons
available to human experiencing.' It is an intrusive, in-
vasive indiscretion that 'queries the last privacies of our
existence'; an Annunciation that 'breaks into the small
house of our cautionary being,' so that 'it is no longer
habitable in quite the same way as before. It is a transcendent encounter that tells us, in effect: "change your
life."'[76]

The positive effects of art have been proved through research.
Sociologist Robert Wuthnow, in a national survey, found that people
with greater exposure to the arts were more interested in spiritual growth,
devoted more time to it, and more regularly engaged in such spiritual
activities as prayer and meditation. This relationship held true when
controlled for factors such as age, gender, and level of education.[77]

Emerson saw poets as being "liberating gods." Their benefits have
long been recognized. The order of ancient British bards had as its
title

'Those who are free throughout the world.' They are free
and they make free. . . . We love the poet, the inventor,
who in any form, whether in an ode or in an action, or
in looks and behavior, has yielded us a new thought. He
unlocks our chains and admits us to a new scene.[78]

Artists are often known for their bohemian lifestyles.

This freedom from inhibiting norms and beliefs does not only apply
to artists per se, but to scientists as well, who came to regard imagination
as being more important than knowledge. One well-known example is
that of Albert Einstein. He alone was willing to discard the notion of
absolute time, a sacred tenet since Isaac Newton had declared that time
ticked along "without relation to anything external."

The Polish astrophysicist Bohdan Paczynski had novel ideas often at odds with the conventional wisdom of his peers. More often that not he was proved to be correct, and his insights opened many new areas of research. A citation given by the American Astronomical Society read, "His research has been distinguished by its creativity and breadth."

These benefits were obviously recognized by Albert Camus when he stated, "The aim of art, the aim of life, can only be to increase the sum of freedom and responsibility to be found in every person and the world."[79]

Religion, more often than not, not only has not appreciated the benefits of art, but, at times, has sought to nullify it. Artists have often been treated by religions in a similar way to that of mystics. Nietzsche drew attention to this trend. He referred to the zealous practitioners of religion as "the good and just," adding, "their spirit is imprisoned in their good conscience."

> "Whom do they hate most?" 'The *creator* they hate most. He breaks the tablets and old values. He is a breaker, they call him lawbreaker. For the good are unable to create; they are always the beginning of the end: they crucify him who writes new values on new tablets.[80]

The creator not only creates objects of art, he "writes new values on new tablets." The Constantine Curse was that he forced the Church to freeze the Christian tradition by embedding it in a creed, thus making it "merely repeatable." This led in turn to the dark ages. It took the Great Western Transformation to break the Church's stranglehold on European life.

> The Jesus tradition in its original form was metaphorical and non-literal and therefore not simply transmissible as words. Mere repetition of metaphors is deadening.

> Living traditions have to be restated, retranslated, and
> reinterpreted in new and different contexts. Only in
> that way do they remain alive and thriving.[81]

Referring to an artist as being a creator is an apt use of the term. The human being reaches the peak of his potential when he is creating. She is partaking in a divine activity. "God" becomes humanized and man becomes divine. As Campbell expresses it, "the artist interprets the divinity in nature."[82]

In a religious context things are coming full circle. Tertullian, one of the earliest Christian theologians, claimed at the beginning of the third century CE that it was a fundamental human right, a privilege of nature that every man should worship according to his own convictions (*Ad Scapulam,* 202). There is abundant evidence that the world at large, at a rapidly increasing rate, is now exercising this right.

In mid-twentieth century, Paul Tillich observed, "We are in the midst of a world-revolution affecting every segment of human existence forcing upon us a new interpretation of life and of the world."[83] In the area of religious activity, this revolution can be seen in the exponential growth of new vehicles that contribute to our spiritual journeys.

In *A New History of Christianity* (1996), Vivian Green, Rector and Religious Historian at Oxford University, predicted that in this current century beliefs in such concepts as heaven and hell would no longer be relevant to many people. As if on cue a group of Vatican theological advisors has recommended to the Pope the elimination of the concept of limbo (where baptized babies are supposed to languish). In 1999 Pope John Paul II said that rather than being a fiery torture chamber, hell was a more docile place. On an earlier occasion he said that heaven is a state of mind. It can only be a matter of time before purgatory is destined for oblivion.

It is not just the church leaders who are making and sanctioning these changes. The congregants themselves are often taking the initiative. In a newspaper article entitled "The Do-It-Yourself Doctrine," Charlotte Allen has complained about "Christianity Lite."

> It's the assertion--no, the insistence--that you can be a Christian in good standing though you reject all or significant parts of the brand of Christianity to which you formally adhere. Even Jesus Christ--and who he was--is negotiable, not to mention traditional teachings on sex, abortion and divorce. Who's to tell you what to think and do as a Christian--or to judge you wanting. It's heresy nowadays to accuse someone of heresy. . . . That's having your Christian cake and eating it, too. The phenomenon--a pervasive anti-authoritarianism, a readiness to accommodate religious teaching to prevailing secular mores and an insistence that individuals have a right to carve out their own relationship with the Christian tradition--exists.[84]

It is not just Christianity that is mutating with Darwinian restlessness. Islam, for example, does not just consist of the Shia-Sunni divide. There is also Sufism, the mystical side of Islam; concerned with a personal, experiential approach to Allah. It exists throughout the Muslim world, most significantly in Pakistan, and its millions of followers generally embrace Islam as a spiritual experience rather than a social or political one. The Taliban have been able to attract a few hundred to witness beheadings in Pakistan's tribal areas. More than three hundred thousand Sufis showed up to honor Lal Shahbaz Qalandar, one of four early thirteenth century founders of Sufism.[85] There are another twenty million members of various splinter Muslim groups around the world.

Buddhism consists of more than two hundred distinct bodies, many of which don't see eye-to-eye at all. Hinduism was profoundly reshaped into major strands in the nineteenth century as it came under strong Western and Christian influence. So many new religious groups have come into being in Japan since World War II that local religious scholars have been forced to distinguish between "new religions" and "new, new religions."

A recent edition of the World Christian Encyclopedia suggests that by 2050 there may be more than a billion people affiliated with Pentecostalism and other charismatic movements. It reports that there are now 9,900 distinct and separate religions in the world and that two or three new ones appear every day. Almost all of these new religious movements fail, a typical lifespan being less than a decade.[86]

The Generation X, which followed the Baby Boomers, are in the vanguard of the new religious movements. They tend to be well-educated, relatively affluent, and born into an established religious order; but they understand truth as being less fixed and more pluralistic than do their parents. This explains why they are more experimental about religion. They tend to be drawn to these new movements primarily for social rather than theological reasons. Most soon leave of their own free will.[87]

Even evangelical Christians are widening their fields of interest and concern. They no longer want to be defined by gay marriage and abortion. They are talking instead about global warming and affordable housing. The National Association of Evangelicals is urging its members to fight poverty as well as pornography, to protect the environment and promote good government.[88]

A "Theology after Google" forum took place in March 2010. It talked about Church 2.0 vs. Church 1.0. The latter is all about creeds and doctrines--top-down, whereas Church 2.0 is like a wiki-theology--

bottom-up. Everyone is seen as being capable of learning and providing feedback. This transition is being compared with that brought about by Gutenberg's printing press in the fifteenth century, which led to the Protestant Reformation. A forum speaker said that in this new world, "You can be a free agent. You could start your own church, go to a little faith community down the street. You could be a megachurch. You could be a Methodist today, an Anglican tomorrow--it's your choice."[89]

This is happening more and more as people test various religious teachings against the truth in their own hearts. A recent survey involving 35,000 participants revealed that almost half had switched religions.[90] Many others "mix and match" religions, blending Christianity with Eastern and New Age beliefs. Another poll of 4,013 adults found that a third regularly or occasionally attended religious services at more than one location--and 24 percent of the public overall was worshipping outside their faith. Three in 10 Protestants and 20 percent of Roman Catholics said they sometimes attended services representing other faiths. Over a lifetime, more Americans will try out different religions than will stay true to one faith.[91]

Blending or braiding the beliefs of different spiritual traditions has become so rampant in America that the Dalai Lama has called it the spiritual supermarket, the melding of Judaism with Buddhism, for example, has become so commonplace that marketers who sell spiritual books, etc., have a name for it: "Jew-Bu." It is also spelled "Jubu." No one knows for certain how many there are, but by some estimates, at least 30 percent of all newcomers to Buddhism are Jewish.

Some draw on more than two religions. "I literally feel like I am at a buffet," said one woman who finds solace in the practice of three religions, viz. Christianity, Judaism, and Buddhism. A theologian observed that younger people live with ambivalence. "It's not *either or* but *both and*."[92]

For the traditional denominations, this cross-pollination presents an excruciating dilemma. If they bend the rules to accommodate the hybrids, they risk watering down their identities. But if they stick to the straight and narrow, they define themselves out of existence--a growing possibility.

Membership is growing in organized religions that take a broad view of God. Unitarian Universalists increased their numbers by 25 percent over the last 15 years of the last century. Two religious movements rooted in nineteenth century transcendentalism, Unity and Science of Mind, have exploded. The number of Unity churches grew from 400 to 1,000 in 15 years.[93]

Membership is also growing in two other religious vehicles that are in total contrast to each other, viz. house churches and megachurches. A megachurch is defined as having at least 2,000 attendees. (The average is over 4,100. By contrast most American churches attract 500 or fewer on Sundays.) It averages 20 full-time paid ministerial staff persons, 22 full-time paid program staff persons, and as many as 300 volunteer workers who give 5 hours or more a week to the church. Protestantism has more than 1,350 such entities, more than double the number of a decade earlier.[94]

Texas and California are each home to more than 190 megachurches. Most of the Golden State's establishments are to be found between Los Angeles and San Diego. Students of this phenomenon call it the Southern California Bible belt.

Worship services usually feature a variety of means of communication, such as video, dance, and mime, which add visual and emotional impact. Church attendance becomes a more comfortable, positive experience, bound by fewer rules and obligations than traditional churches. Not a few are charismatic in tone, thus encouraging individual expressions of worship. Parishioners are organized into small groups where people can share experiences. Some churches appeal to niche interests such as dog lovers, rock climbers, skateboarders, four-wheel drive enthusiasts, people with eating disorders, etc. Members are also encouraged to get involved in the world outside of the church.

Because the leaders of megachurches are usually strong personalities, the danger is always there of congregants being in thrall to them at the expense of their own autonomy.

There are also religious gatherings that totally break the mold. Mosaic is a multiethnic congregation that has its main Sunday service in a nightclub in downtown Los Angeles. It includes live bands, drama, dance, and artists working at easels during worship. Many of its members are artists and like to perform for fellow attendees.[95] There is in Albuquerque the Church of Beethoven. It is primarily served by members of the New Mexico Symphony Orchestra. It has none of the usual elements of a church service and features such activities as poetry, visual art, and other types of music. The first meeting place was an abandoned gas station off old Route 66. When the group outgrew that building, it moved to a renovated warehouse in downtown Albuquerque. About 100 or so attend. The founder pointed out that most regulars are not religious but are "simply people looking to be uplifted on a Sunday morning."[96]

Students of religious activities refer to such groups as the Emerging Church. In the emerging movement, small is beautiful and creativity in worship is key. They vary widely in membership and practices, shun hierarchy, emphasize outreach to the poor, and worship creatively. Church can be spending an afternoon at a park. Their tithe will be to buy buckets of chicken to share with the down and out and engage them in conversation. A mostly white group will worship at an African-American church or visit a Buddhist gathering. Such no-name churches are small, have a collaborative approach, and creativity. There is no "in group," everyone being a leader in his own right.[97]

The increasing prominence of megachurches has tended to cause an unawareness of another countervailing trend. As Patricia Williams has pointed out, "There has been a change in consciousness about religion from public and social to private and individual."[98] Religious practices are becoming increasingly personal in the Western world, resulting not only in a fragmentation of religious beliefs and well established traditions, but people are increasingly doing their own thing. George Barna, an analyst of religious trends, predicts that by the year 2025 the market share of conventional churches will shrink by 50 percent.[99]

The main vehicle that is serving this transition is the house church, also referred to as the underground church, the organic church, the simple church, the church without walls. This trend is partly fueled by a pushback against megachurches, which are characterized by their marketing, head-counting, and high-power programming. Said one who had made the transition, "It's about authenticity. Church services have succeeded at being characterized by excellence, but one of the consequences of that excellence is artificiality and the feeling that everything is produced and that it is a show." Another one said, "What is exciting about doing small-group house-church is just the chance to be real."[100]

A survey conducted in 2006 found that 9 percent of U.S. adults attend house churches weekly, a tenfold increase in a decade. Roughly 70 million Americans have experienced a home service, with about 20 million attending either full-time or occasionally. John Zogby, a leading pollster, projects that number to grow even more dramatically in the years ahead.[101]

As mentioned earlier in this chapter, things have come full circle with respect to the conduct of worship. This is how Christianity began--meeting in homes. The Amish always have. Both detractors and proponents say that going to church in a home has the potential of forever changing the way people worship. Barna predicts that we are at "the initiation point of a transformational shift.[102]

Appendix E contains a list of fourteen hallmarks of healthy emerging Communities of Faith.

The central fundamental change that is fueling this revolution is that people now feel entitled to make choices about things that used to be within the exclusive purview of the priestly class. No one is now being seen to have the right to tell anyone how to practice his or her faith, or indeed what that faith should consist of. Individual belief now increasingly governs religious affiliations and practices. And just as important, participants in house churches are articulating their own faith instead of leaving it to the professional clergy to explain. "When others interpret religion for us, our experience is narrowed. We become consumers rather than participants in the creative process.[103]

The last three hallmarks of healthy emerging Communities of Faith are: 12: Will make no distinction between "clergy" and "laity." 13: The role of those currently considered clergy will be that of midwife, assisting in the birth of this emerging community of faith. 14: This role will require courage and a willingness to forsake status.[104]

Five hundred years ago Martin Luther made the seminal statement, "Every man is a priest." He later reinforced this concept by adding the principle he called Christian liberty: "A Christian man is a perfectly free lord, subject to none." The Lutheran Church soon became as hierarchical as the Catholics, but the Pietism reform movement that began in the seventeenth century revived Luther's principle. It believed in a spiritual priesthood, thus all Christians had been consecrated kings and priests. Both men and women could speak. A preacher-centered Church is not part of the Pietist vision. Philipp Jakob Spener (1635-1703) gave greater definition to Pietism, believing that Christians were not hirelings but priests, sources of regeneration and hope. He is recognized as the forerunner of the small group movement.[105]

The Society of Friends, also known as Quakers, began in the seventeenth century in England and represents the extreme left wing of the English Puritan movement. Its founder was George Fox, who stressed the immediacy of Christ's teachings and guidance, with the consequent irrelevance of special buildings or ordained ministers, and the application of Christ's teachings to the whole of life. Quakers are especially known for their efforts on behalf of social reform.

Baptist Churches also first emerged in England in the seventeenth century during the Puritan reform movement. "The priesthood of all believers" has long been a central tenet, and to varying degrees it has been put into effect.

The Plymouth Brethren community of Christians began in Plymouth, England in 1831. They have become a worldwide variety of associations, all of them recognizing no order of clergy or ministers as distinct from the laity.

The Roman Catholic Church and its kissing cousins, the Anglicans and Episcopalians, have continued to symbolize their adherents as being spiritual serfs. Their role during the service is to be that of an inert mass of meat. When the elements of the mass are served, they become beggars as they submissively receive the elements from the priest, being considered unworthy to even touch the wafer and the wine.

Unitarian Universalists are generally more enlightened, having, for example, highly praiseworthy beliefs expressed in the statements, "Priesthood and prophesying for all members," and, "Each person should be authoritative about, and responsible for, his own spiritual journey." These, however, are "customs more honored in the breach than the observance" (*Hamlet*, Act I, Scene IV). For example, when a new minister is installed, in a grand ceremony, a legal contract is drawn up giving him/her sole and absolute say over the pulpit. The congregants have no choice but to assume the fetal position in that setting. Their role, as in most churches, is to provide the dull background foil to the stage on which the priest struts his stuff.

Starting in 1998 Zogby has conducted a survey based on one simple question: "Which of four different statements about the American dream represents your goal in life?"

A. It means material success.

B. It is achieved through spiritual fulfillment.

C. Material success is more likely to be attained by my children.

D. The American dream, whether material or spiritual, cannot be achieved by most middle-class Americans.

Those who choose A are classified as Traditional Materialists, and those who choose B are Secular Spiritualists. An almost identical proportion (36 percent) choose A or B.

More than a third of the population believe that spiritual fulfillment is paramount. Zogby believes that the potential growth curve of Secular Spiritualists is "off the charts--the stealth force in American society." They are establishing a new set of expectations of what our humanity is all about.[106] The upheavals of the last century have also evoked a resurgence of interest in spirituality in all religious spheres.

This growing desire for spiritual fulfillment is another way of saying that we seek meaning--the thesis of Chapter 1. Paul Tillich suggested that to live spiritually is to live in the presence of meaning.[107] Campbell believed that the seeking for a meaning for life was in fact the seeking of "an experience of being alive, so that our life experiences on the purely physical plane will have resonances within our innermost being and reality, so that we actually feel the rapture of being alive."[108] This concords with the view of Telhard de Chardin, who believed that "we are not physical creatures having a spiritual experience, we are spiritual creatures having a physical experience."[109] Long ago the Hindu rishis claimed that we are souls with bodies rather than bodies with souls.[110]

A recent survey conducted by *Parade* magazine found that Americans are now separating spirituality from religion. Twenty-four percent put themselves in a whole new category: "Spiritual but not religious."[111] Spirituality is now being seen as being much more important than religion, the latter being only one of many ways available to us to make sense of our lives. In fact, more often than not, religion has contributed to a loss of meaning and spirituality. Its original function was to be a vehicle to aid in our spiritual journeys. At its worst, religion has been a bleak desert that drains its followers of spiritual vitality.

Religion, Christianity in particular, has made a separation between matter and spirit. Campbell lamented that this

> has really castrated nature. The European mind and
> life has been, as it were, emasculated by this separation.
> The true spirituality, which would have come from the
> union of matter and spirit, has been killed.[112]

Religion instead continues to urge its followers to believe in concepts that are no longer believable. And a faith that has lost its credibility has lost its meaning. To insist that one cling to such traditions is to deprive people of spiritual life.[113]

Campbell tells of a social philosopher from New York attending an international conference on religion in Japan, who said to a Shinto priest, "We've been now to a good many ceremonies and have seen quite a few of your shrines. But I don't get your ideology. I don't get your theology." The priest paused as though in deep thought and then slowly shook his head. "I think we don't have ideology, we don't have theology. We dance."[114]

Religion serves no useful purpose at all if it doesn't move beyond cold, hard concepts, if it does not take us to a place where we otherwise would not go.

> [I]n the permanent religious sanctuaries--the temples and cathedrals--where an atmosphere of holiness hangs in the air, the logic of cold, hard fact must not be allowed to intrude and spoil the spell. The gentile, the 'spoilsport,' the positivist who cannot or will not play, must be kept aloof. Hence the guardian figures that stand at either side of the entrances to holy places: lions, bulls, or fearsome warriors with uplifted weapons. They are there to keep out the 'spoilsports,' the advocates of Aristotelian logic, for whom *A* can never be *B*; for whom the actor is never to be lost in the part; for whom the mask, the image, the consecrated host or tree or animal, cannot become God, but only a reference. Such heavy thinkers are to remain without. For the whole purpose of entering a sanctuary or participating in a festival is that one should be overtaken by the state known in India as "the other mind" (Sanskrit, *anya-manas:* absent mindedness, possession by a spirit), where one is "beside oneself," spellbound: set apart from one's logic of self-possession and overpowered by the force of a logic of indissociation, wherein *A* is *B,* and *C* also is *B*.[115]

Until recently science too has contributed to a loss of meaning and spirituality. Scientific endeavor has tended to become disconnected from historical and local context, "an activity carried out in a void--a story that has lost its meaning, its purpose, and its ability to touch and inform."[116] Frank Schaeffer has provided an example: "Maybe science explains the 'how' of the brain but not the 'why,' in the same way that a chemical analysis of the pigments used by van Gogh only explains what a painting is made of, not why we like it, much less what it is."[117] Or as Einstein explained upon being asked, "Do you believe that absolutely everything can be explained scientifically?" replied, "Yes, it would be possible but it would make no sense. It would be description without meaning--as if you described a Beethoven symphony as a variation in wave pressure."[118]

From earliest times the mystery of life has been beyond all human conception. But science is now breaking through into the mystery dimension. It has pushed itself into the sphere that myth addresses. Science has come to the edge, the interface between what can be known and what is never to be discovered because it is mystery that transcends all human research.[119] We need and use myth as we look for "a way of experiencing the world that will open to us the transcendent (the unknown and unknowable) that informs it."[120] We thus speak of the divine, that which holds us in an attitude of awe and wonder, which, as Armstrong says, is "the essence of worship."[121] Campbell says, "An intense experience of mystery is what one has to regard as the ultimate religious experience."[122]

We do not seek for, nor can we experience, a constant high. As Emerson explains it,

> Our faith comes in moments; our vice is habitual. Yet there is a depth in those brief moments which constrains us to ascribe more reality to them than to all other experiences.[123]

Human beings have a need that encompasses all others, including the physical and social, "an aspect of human life that is so mysterious it is often disregarded or denied. . . . We need spiritual connection; we need to understand where we belong."[124]

> 'Spirituality,' as we conceive it, is the apprehension of the sacred, the holy, the divine. In our modern world we see matter and spirit as antithetical, but our myths reveal a different understanding. They describe a world permeated by spirit, where matter and spirit are simply different aspects of the totality: together they constitute 'being.'[125]

In similar fashion Campbell says that true spirituality comes from the union of matter and spirit.

> Spiritual life is the bouquet, the perfume, the flowering and fulfillment of a human life, not a supernatural virtue imposed upon it. And so the impulses of nature are what give authenticity to life, not the rules coming from a supernatural authority.[126] Thomas Mann talked about mankind being the noblest work because it joins nature and spirit.[127]

As science is breaking through into the mystery dimension, it is merging with spirituality. Appendix F contains excerpts from Mani Bhaumik's book *Code Name God*. Dr. Bhaumik, the co-inventor of the excimer laser (that made LASIK corrective eye surgery possible), is a world-class physicist who has sought to integrate the findings of science, religion, and the spiritual quest.

Amy Hassinger uses a set of Russian nesting dolls as a metaphor for the universe. We humans are nested within the divine whole, and God is not outside of creation, God is an integral part of it--in fact, *is* it.

> In this metaphor, we humans are nested within the divine whole. We are not plunked here by a maker separate from us. Nor is our existence a meaningless

evolutionary fluke. The basic elements that make up our bodies--carbon, calcium, iron--were forged inside supernovas, dying stars, and are billions of years old. We are, in fact, made of stardust. We are intimately related to the universe. As an early-twentieth-century British biologist put it, 'we are the universe becoming conscious of itself.' . . . We humans (are) the consciousness of the universe.[128]

Because humans have this role, we have, from the beginning, searched the skies, and now spend ever vaster sums to learn more about our universe. There was huge excitement in recent years when a rock found in Antarctica, determined to have come from Mars, revealed signs of once existing primitive life. On the earthly level the most visited public places are zoological gardens. The appreciation of, and desire to preserve, all forms of life on our planet are growing exponentially. Many centuries ago the mystic Meister Eckhart (1260-1327) said that "the human spirit . . . can never be satisfied with what light it has but storms the firmament and scales the heavens to discover the spirit by which the heavens are driven in revolutions and by which everything on the earth grows and flourishes."[129]

The truth that the West has brought to the understanding of life and humanity's place and role in it is that each one of us, each human being, is a unique creature. There is no such thing as an ordinary mortal. The Knights of the Round Table each had to make his own individual search for the Holy Grail. If each of us is ever to make any contribution to the world, it will have to come out of the individual fulfillment of our own potential. In so doing we will each become a Hero.

Sanskrit, which Campbell calls the great spiritual language of the world, has three terms that represent the brink, the jumping-off place to the ocean of transcendence. "Sat"--being, "chit"--consciousness, and "ananda"--bliss or rapture. It is the latter that enhances one's state of being and consciousness. Campbell's mantra was, "Follow your bliss." Everybody has his own possibility of rapture in the experiences of life. He simply has to recognize it and then cultivate it. Campbell believed that, "If you do follow your bliss you put yourself on a kind of track that has been there all the while, waiting for you."[130]

In the preface to the first edition of *Leaves of Grass* (1855) Walt Whitman wrote these prophetic lines: "There will soon be no more priests, their work is done. A superior breed will take their place. A new order shall arise and they shall be the priests of men. And every man shall be his own priest."

NOTES

CHAPTER 1: THE EMERGENCE OF A MEANING-SEEKING CREATURE

1. "The Great Human Migration," Guy Gugliotta, *Smithsonian,* July 2008, p. 59-60.
2. Ibid., pp. 59-60.
3. *The Sacred Balance,* David Suzuki, p. 9.
4. "The Great Human Migration," Guy Gugliotta, *Smithsonian,* July 2008, p. 63.
5. As related in *Dark Star Safari,* Paul Theroux, pp. 398-403.
6. *The Sacred Balance,* David Suzuki, pp. 10-12.
7. *A Short History of Myth,* Karen Armstrong, p. 27.
8. *The Power of Myth,* Joseph Campbell and Bill Moyers, p. 62.
9. "The God Gene: How Faith Is Hardwired into Our Genes," Dean H. Hamer, *Los Angeles Times,* Friday, December 17, 2004.
10. *The Essential Tillich,* edited by F. Forrester Church, p. 41.
11. Ibid., pp. 41-42.
12. *Uncommon Sense,* Mark Davidson, pp. 135-136.
13. "Is Christianity Going Anywhere?" Part I, Lloyd Geering, *The Fourth R,* March-April 2004, pp. 7-8.
14. "Spiral Dynamics, Evolution and History," Patricia A. Williams, *The Fourth R,* November-Decemter 2006, p. 17.
15. *The Origin of Consciousness in the Breakdown of the Bicameral Mind,* Julian Jaynes, pp. 135-136.)

16. "Is Christianity Going Anywhere?" Part I, Lloyd Geering, *The Fourth R,* March-April 2004, p. 8.

17. "The Great Human Migration," Guy Gugliotta, *Smithsonian,* July 2008, pp. 57-58.

18. *Code Name God,* Mani Bhaumik, p. 181.

19. *A Short History of Myth,* Karen Armstrong, p. 17.

20. Ibid., p. 84.

21. *The Soviet Archipelago,* Aleksandr Solzhenitsyn, pp. 611-612.

CHAPTER 2: MYTH

1. "Some Meanings of Myth," Harry Levin, *Myth and Mythmaking,* edited by Henry A. Murray, p. 105.

2. *The Power of Myth,* Joseph Campbell and Bill Moyer, p. 59.

3. *A Short History of Myth,* Karen Armstrong, p. 3.

4. *The Intellectual Adventure of Ancient Man,* H. Frankfort, p. 7, as quoted in *Myths, Dreams and Religion,* p. 51.

5. *The Old Testament against Its Environment,* G. Ernest Wright, p. 19; Ibid., p. 51.

6. "The Meaning of Mythology," *Vetus Testamentum,* ix, p. 3; Ibid., p. 51.

7. *A Short History of Myth,* Karen Armstrong, p. 7.

8. *The Power of Myth,* Joseph Campbell and Bill Moyers, p. 21.

9. *A Short History of Myth,* Karen Armstrong, p. 11.

10. "The Historical Development of Mythology," Joseph Campbell, *Myth and Mythmaking,* edited by Henry A. Murray, p. 20.

11. *A Short History of Myth,* Karen Armstrong, pp. 37, 39, 32.

12. "*Mythological* Themes in Creative Literature and Art," *Myths, Dreams and Religion,* Joseph Campbell, p. 143.

13. *The Power of Myth,* Joseph Campbell and Bill Moyers, pp. 138, 141.

14. *A Short History* of *Myth,* Karen Armstrong, p. 11.

15. *The Power of Myth,* Joseph Campbell and Bill Moyers, p. 72.

16. Ibid., p. 81.

17. Ibid., p. 71.

18. *A Short History of Myth,* Karen Armstrong, p. 40.

19. Ibid., pp. 28-29.

20. Ibid., pp. 24, 27.

21. *The Power of Myth,* Joseph Campbell and Bill Moyers, pp. 72, 73, xvi, xvii.

22. Ibid., pp. 79, 80.

23. *A Short History of Myth,* Karen Armstrong, p. 32.

24. *The Power of Myth,* Joseph Campbell and Bill Moyers, p. xvii.

25. Ibid., p. 21.

26. *Counter Culture through the Ages,* Ken Goffman, p. 21.

27. "The Historical Development of Mythology," Joseph Campbell, *Myth and Mythmaking,* edited by Henry A. Murray, pp. 21, 19.

28. Ibid., p. 19.

29. *A Short History of Myth,* Karen Armstrong, pp. 65-66.

30. Ibid., pp. 70, 71, 42.

31. "Recurrent Themes in Myth and Mythmaking," Clyde Kluckhohn, *Myth and Mythmaking,* edited by Henry A. Murray, p. 48.

32. Lecture #2, *The Old Testament,* Part I, *The Great Courses,* Amy-Jill Levine.

33. Ibid.

34. "The Yearning for Paradise in a Primitive Tradition," Mircea Eliade, *Myth and Mythmaking,* edited by Henry A. Murray, p. 61.

35. "Recurrent Themes in Myth and Mythmaking," Clyde

Kluckhohn, *Myth and Mythmaking*, edited by Henry A. Murray, p. 52.

36. Lecture #3, *The Old Testament*, Part I, *The Great Courses*, Amy-Jill Levine.

37. *A Short History of Myth*, Karen Armstrong, p. 22.

38. *A Short History of Myth*, Karen Armstrong, p. 62; "Recurrent Themes in Myths and Mythmaking," Clyde Kluckhohn, *Myth and Mythmaking*, edited by Henry A. Murray, p. 50.

39. Lecture #3, *The Old Testament*, Part I, *The Great Courses*, Amy-Jill Levine.

40. *The Hero with a Thousand Faces*, Joseph Campbell, Preface.

41. As quoted in Ibid., Preface.

42. Ibid, p. 315.

43. Ibid., pp. 315-316.

44. "Recurrent Themes in Myth and Mythmaking," Clyde Kluckhohn, *Myth and Mythmaking*, edited by Henry A. Murray, pp. 56-57.

45. *The Hero with a Thousand Faces*, Joseph Campbell, pp. 30, 319-356.

46. "Myths and Dreams in Christian Scriptures," Amos N. Wilder, *Myth and Mythmaking*, edited by Henry A. Murray.

47. "Mythological Themes in Creative Literature and Art," Joseph Campbell, *Myths, Dreams and Religion*, edited by Joseph Campbell, pp. 153-157.

48. Ibid., p. 155.

49. Ibid., p. 159.

50. *A Short History of Myth*, Karen Armstrong, pp. 31-32.

51. *The Hero with a Thousand Faces*, Joseph Campbell, p. 3.

52. Ibid., p. 382.

53. "Myths and Dreams in Hebrew Scripture," John F. Priest, *Myths and Dreams in Religion,* edited by Joseph Campbell, p. 51.

54. "Mother Nature, God, and Modern Religion," Charles W. Hedrick, *The Fourth R,* September-October 2008, p. 18.

CHAPTER 3: THE SOURCE FOR THE CONCEPT OF GOD – THE BICAMERAL MIND

1. As quoted in *The Origin of Consciousness in the Breakdown of the Bicameral Mind,* Julian Jaynes, p. 164.

2. *A Short History of Myth,* Karen Armstrong, pp. 60-61.

3. As quoted in *Freethinkers,* Susan Jacoby, pp. 134-135.

4. *A Short History of Myth,* Karen Armstrong, p. 67.

5. Ibid., p. 68.

6. "Western Mythology: Its Dissolution and Transformation," Alan W. Watts; *Myths, Dreams, and Religion,* edited by Joseph Campbell, pp. 11-13.

7. *The Power of Myth,* Joseph Campbell and Bill Moyers, pp.169-170.

CHAPTER 4: THE ORIGIN OF CONSCIOUSNESS

1. Confessions, 9: 7; 10: 26, 65, as quoted in *The Origin of Consciousness in the Breakdown of the Bicameral Mind,* Julian Jaynes, p. 2.

2. *Philosophie der Mythologie,* Friedrich Schelling, as quoted in "Myth, Dream and Imagination," by Stanley Romaine Hopper in *Myth, Dreams and Religion,* edited by Joseph Campbell, p. 111.

3. Republic, 4, 427B.

4. *A Short History of Myth,* Karen Armstrong, p. 77.

CHAPTER 5: VESTIGES OF THE BICAMERAL MIND

1. As quoted in *The Origin of Consciousness in the Breakdown of the Bicameral Mind,* Julian Jaynes, p. 335.
2. *Los Angeles Times,* September 5, 2006.
3. *Los Angeles Times,* February 16, 2009.
4. *A History of the End of the World,* Jonathan Kirsch, pp. 165-166.
5. *The Selfish Gene,* Richard Dawkins, p. 12.
6. *Breaking the Spell,* Daniel C. Dennett, p. 131.
7. *A Portrait of the Artist as a Young Man,* James Joyce, p. 133.
8. *The Portable Nietzsche,* edited and translated by Walter Kaufmann, p. 579.
9. *From Dawn to Decadence,* Jacques Barzun, p. 26.
10. *The Portable Emerson,* edited by Carl Bode, p. 32.
11. *So Help Me God,* Forest Church, p. 227.
12. *Freethinkers,* Susan Jacoby, p. 165.
13. *The Great Questions of Life,* Don Cupitt, p. 59.

CHAPTER 6: THE AXIAL AGE

1. *A Short History of Myth,* Karen Armstrong, pp. 63-64.
2. *The Power of Myth,* Joseph Campbell and Bill Moyers, pp. 123-124, 136, 66.)
3. Ibid. p. 58.
4. *The Portable Emerson,* edited by Mark van Doren, p. 140.
5. *The Power of Myth,* Joseph Campbell and Bill Moyers, p. 127.
6. As quoted in *Christian Faith at the Crossroads,* Lloyd Geering, p. 15.
7. *The Origin and Goal of History,* Karl Jaspers, pp. 1, 2 as quoted in *Christian Faith at the Crossroads,* Lloyd Geering, pp. 15, 21.
8. *Los Angeles Times,* Monday, March 20, 2006, Swati Pandey.

9. *A Short History of Myth,* Karen Armstrong, p. 88.

10. *The Power of Myth,* Joseph Campbell and Bill Moyers, p. 58.

11. *A Short History of Myth,* Karen Armstrong, pp. 83, 90.

12. "Is Christianity Going Anywhere?" Lloyd Geering, *The Fourth R,* March-April 2004, p. 10.

13. *The Power of Myth,* Joseph Campbell and Bill Moyers, p. 62.

14. *A Short History of Myth,* Karen Armstrong, p. 97.

15. *Axial Sages,* Karen Armstrong, p. 29.

16. As quoted in *Counterculture through the Ages,* Ken Gofferman, p. 52.

17. Ibid., p. 52.

18. *Los Angeles Times,* April 1, 2006, Interview with Karen Armstrong, conducted by Louis Sahagun.

19. *Uncommon Sense,* Mark Davidson, pp. 95, 96.

20. "Compassion's Fruit" *AARP,* March/April 2005, p. 63; *A Short History of Myth,* Karen Armstrong, p. 81, 100, 89, 90; *The Axial Sages,* Karen Armstrong, pp. 29-31.

21. "The Historical Development of Mythology," by Joseph Campbell, p. 20; *Myth and Mythmaking,* Henry A. Murray, editor.

22. Ibid., p. 24.

23. Ibid., pp. 24-25.

24. Ibid., p. 24.

25. Ibid., p. 25.

26. Ibid., p. 25.

27. *A Short History of Myth,* Karen Armstrong, pp. 93-95.

28. Ibid., pp. 97-102.

CHAPTER 7: THE RISE OF RELIGION

1. *Guns, Germs and Steel,* Jared Diamond, p. 278.

2. *Breaking the Spell,* Daniel C. Dennett, p. 4.

3. *Christian Faith at the Crossroads,* Lloyd Geering, p. 25.

4. *Hinduism,* K. M. Sen, p. 90.

5. *Constantine's Sword,* James Carroll, p. 26.

6. *A Short History of Myth,* Karen Armstrong, p. 102.

CHAPTER 8: CHRISTIAN EUROPE

1. *The Axial Age,* Karen Armstrong, p. 26.

2. *The Fourth R,* July-August 2006, Arthur Dewey, editorial.

3. *Constantine's Sword,* James Carroll, p. 50.

4. Ibid., p. 171.

5. Ibid., p. 189.

6. *The Alphabet Versus the Goddess,* Leonard Schlain, p. 250.

7. "The Present Paradise," *UU World* Vol. XXII, No. 2, Rita N. Brock and Rebecca A. Parker, pp. 27-31.

8. Ibid., p. 28.

9. Ibid., pp. 30-31.

10. *How the Irish Saved Civilization,* Thomas Cahill, p. 181.

11. Ibid., p. 124.

12. Ibid., p. 151.

13. Ibid., p. 194.

14. *The Power of Myth,* Joseph Campbell and Bill Moyers, p. 200.

15. Ibid., p. 192.

16. Ibid. pp. 196, 198, 187.

CHAPTER 9: MYSTICISM AND MYTH IN RELIGION

1. *A Short History of Myth,* Karen Armstrong, p. 109.

2. *The Rise of Consciousness in the Breakdown of the Bicameral Mind,* Julian Jaynes, p. 318.

3. *The Power of Myth,* Joseph Campbell and Bill Moyers, p. 61.

4. *A Short History of Myth,* Karen Armstrong, pp. 129-130.

5. *The Power of Myth,* Joseph Campbell and Bill Moyers, p. 59.

6. *A Short History of Myth,* Karen Armstrong, p. 105.

7. Ibid., p. 105.

8. Ibid., pp. 106-107.

9. Ibid., pp. 107-108.

10. *Jesus Christ and Mythology,* Rudolf Bultmann, p. 15.

11. *A Short History of Myth,* Karen Armstrong, p. 126.

12. Ibid., pp. 112-113.

13. Ibid., pp. 111-112.

14. Ibid., pp. 108-109.

15. Ibid., pp. 114-115.

16. Ibid., pp. 117-118.

17. Ibid., pp. 104-118, 128.

CHAPTER 10: THE BEST LAID PLANS

1. *From Dawn to Decadence,* Jacques Barzun, p. 180.

2. *The Power of Myth,* Joseph Campbell and Bill Moyers, p. 56.

3. Ibid. p. 141.

4. Ibid., p. 56.

5. "The Historical Development of Mythology," by Joseph Campbell; *Myth and Mythmaking,* edited by Henry A. Murray, p. 43.

6. *The Axial Age,* Karen Armstrong, pp. 23, 23.

7. *The Portable Nietzsche,* edited and translated by Walter Kaufmann, p. 92.

8. *The Axial Sages,* Karen Armstrong, p. 23.

9. *The Portable Nietzsche,* p. 598.

10. *The Power of Myth,* Joseph Campbell and Bill Moyers, pp. 99, 100.

11. *So Help Me God,* Forest Church, p. 227.

12. *Freethinkers,* Susan Jacoby, p. 18.

13. *The Brothers Karamazov,* Fyodor Dostoevsky, p. 232.

14. *The Alphabet Versus the Goddess,* Leonard Shlain, p. 245.

15. Ibid., p. 300.

16. Holy War: *The Crusades and Their Impact on Today's World,* Karen Armstrong, p. 393, as quoted in *The Grand Inquisitor's Manual,* Jonathan Kirsch, p. 45.

17. *Europe's Inner Demons: An Inquiry Inspired by the Great Witch-Hunt,* Norman Cohn, p. 8, as quoted in Ibid. p.59.

18. Ibid., pp. 5, 8, 9, 57-59, 87, 95-96, 101, 203-204.

19. Ibid., pp. 153-154.

20. Ibid., p. 154.

21. *The Alphabet Versus the Goddess,* Leonard Shlain, p. 364.

22. Ibid., pp. 272-273.

23. *The Grand Inquisitor's Manual,* Jonathan Kirsch, pp. 84, 169, 195, 202.

24. *The Alphabet Versus the Goddess,* Leonard Shlain, p. 348.

25. *The Grand Inquisitor's Manual,* Jonathan Kirsch, pp. 159-160.

26. Ibid., p. 241.

27. As quoted in *The Grand Inquisitor's Manual,* Jonathan Kirsch, p. 210.

28. "The Eve of Destruction," Karen Armstrong, *The Guardian,* January 1, 2004.

CHAPTER 11: RENAISSANCE AND REFORM

1. *Ghengis Khan and the Making of the Modern World,* Jack Weatherford, p. 237.

2. Ibid., p. 239.

3. *Out of the Flames,* Lawrence and Nancy Goldstone, p. 129.

4. *From Dawn to Decadence,* Jacques Barzun, p. 61.

5. *Leonardo da Vinci,* Charles Nicholl, p. 3.

6. Ibid., p. 3.

7. Ibid., p. 7.

8. *From Dawn to Decadence,* Jacques Barzun, p. 44.

9. Ibid., p. 64.

10. Ibid., p. 11.

11. Ibid., p. 12.

12. *The Portable Nietzsche,* edited and translated by Walter Kaufmann, p. 653.

13. *From Dawn to Decadence,* Jacques Barzun, p. 52.

14. *The Alphabet Versus the Goddess,* Leonard Shlain, p. 350.

15. *The Alphabet Versus the Goddess,* p. 333.

16. Ibid., p. 334.

17. *The Story of Civilization,* Volume 6, Will Durant, p. 490, as quoted by Shlain, p. 336.

18. As quoted in *From Dawn to Decadence,* Jacques Barzun, p.24.

19. *Reforming Christianity,* Don Cupitt, p. 52.

CHAPTER 12:

1. *Breaking the Spell,* D. C. Dennett, p. 369.

2. *The Origin of Consciousness in the Breakdown of the Bicameral Mind,* Julian Jaynes, p. 437.

3. As quoted in Robert Lee Hotz's review of *The God Delusion* by Richard Dawkins.

4. Ibid.

5. *The Origin of Consciousness in the Breakdown of the Bicameral Mind,* Julian Jaynes, p. 434.

6. *The Age of Reason,* Book II, Thomas Paine, p. 124.

7. *The Origin of Consciousness in the Breakdown of the Bicameral Mind,* Julian Jaynes, p. 475

8. *The Portable Nietszche,* edited by Walter Kaufmann, p. 629.

9. *Christian Faith at the Crossroads,* Lloyd Geering, p. 176.

10. "At Home in the Universe" by Stuart Kauffman, as quoted in *The Once and Future Faith,* p. 13.

11. *The Great Questions of Life,* Don Cupitt, p. 50.

12. *The Sacred Balance,* David Suzuki, p. 13.

13. Ibid., p. 13.

14. *The Origin of Consciousness in the Breakdown of the Bicameral Mind,* Julian Jaynes, pp. 437, 438.

15. *A Christianity for Tomorrow,* Arthur Spong, p. 77.

16. As quoted by Sara Lippincott in her review of *Physics of the Impossible,* Michio Kaku.

17. "Illuminating Black Boxes," Patricia Williams, *The Fourth R,* Vol. 19, No. 1, pp. 5, 6.

18. *Christian Faith at the Crossorads,* Lloyd Geering, pp. 130, 131.

19. Ibid., pp. 15, 136.

20. Ibid., p. 143.

21. *The End of Conventional Christianity,* W. H. van de Pol, p. 94, as quoted in *Christianity at the Crossroads,* Lloyd Geering, p. 143.

22. *History of Psychology,* H. Misiak, p. 378, as quoted in *Christian Faith at the Crossroads,* Lloyd Geering, pp. 146, 147.

23. Ibid., p. 158.

24. Sermon entitled "What is religion? What is Spirituality?" delivered at Neighborhood Church, Pasadena, California on October 9, 2005.

25. *The Masks of God: Occidental Mythology,* Joseph Campbell, pp. 519-521.

26. *Myths, Dreams and Religion,* edited by Joseph Campbell, "Mythological Themes in Creative Literature and Art," Joseph Campbell, p. 153.

27. As quoted in *Breaking the Spell,* D. C. Dennet, p. 67.

28. *The Power of Myth,* Joseph Campbell and Bill Moyers, p. 29.

29. *Maimonedes,* Joel L. Kraemer, pp. 366, 368.

30. *Myths, Dreams and Religion,* edited by Joseph Campbell, "Myth, Dream, and the Vocation of Contemporary Philosophy," Richard A. Underwood, pp. 241-245.

31. *Christian Faith at the Crossroads,* Lloyd Geering, pp. 52, 53.

32. Ibid., p.54.

33. "Put Your Trust in Doubt," Gregory Rodriguez, *Los Angeles Times,* Monday, August 10, 2009.

34. *The Meditations and Selections from the Principles of René Descartes,* p. 130, as quoted in *The Alphabet Versus the Goddess,* Leonard Shlain, p. 375.

35. *From Dawn to Decadence,* Jacques Barzun, p. 378.

36. "Poem upon the Lisbon Disaster," Anthony Heckt, as quoted in *From Dawn to Decadence,* p. 378.

37. *The Philosophy of the Enlightenment,* Cassirer, p. 163; Ibid., p. 53.

38. *From Dawn to Decadence,* Jacques Barzun, p. 466.

39. *The Sacred Balance,* David Suzuki, p. 203.

40. *From Dawn to Decadence,* Jacques Barzun, p. 469.

41. *Lectures on the Essence of Religion,* p. 15, as quoted in *Christian Faith at the Crossroads,* Lloyd Geering, p. 87.

42. *Principles of the Philosophy of the Future,* pp. 47, 48, as quoted in Ibid., p. 89.

43. Ibid., pp. 90, 91.

44. Ibid., pp. 83, 84.

45. As quoted in "That Need for Opium," Gregory Rodriguez, *Los Angeles Times,* Monday, October 6, 2008.

46. *Christian Faith at the Crossroads,* Lloyd Geering, p. 113.

47. Introduction to the translation of *Thus Spake Zorathustra,* p. 18, as quoted in Ibid., p. 211.

48. As quoted in *Martin Buber, the Life of Dialogue,* p. 34, Maurice S. Friedman, Ibid., p. 211.

49. *Beyond Good and Evil,* Friedrich Nietzsche, p. 78, Ibid., 219.

50. *From Dawn to Decadence,* Jacques Barzun, p. 670.

51. *Christian Faith at the Crossroads,* Lloyd Geering, p. 221.

52. *Maimonides,* Joel L. Kraemer, p. 378.

53. "Our Humanist Legacy: Seventy Years of Religious Humanism," William F. Schulz, *UU World,* November/December 2003.

CHAPTER 13: RELIGION AND ETHICS

1. *The Alphabet versus the Goddess,* Leonard Shlain, pp. 157-158.

2. *Basic Writings of Nietzsche,* interpreted by Walter Kaufmann, p. 275.

3. *Myths, Dreams and Religion,* edited by Joseph Campbell, "Mythological Themes in Creative Literature and Art," Joseph Campbell, p. 144.

4. "Morality," Nathaniel Frank, *Los Angeles Times,* March 15, 2007.

5. *Ethics in a World of Strangers,* Kwame Anthony Appiah, p. 5.

6. "The Evolution of Good and Evil," Patricia Williams, *The Fourth R,* January-February, 2005, pp. 3-8.

7. *The Future of Life,* Edward O. Wilson, p. 151.

8. *Godless Morality,* Richard Holloway, p. 71.

9. As reported by Rabbi Marvin Hier in the *Los Angeles Times,* May 11, 2009.

10. *Redemption–The Last Battle of the Civil War* (Nicholas Lemann), Charles Rapplenge, *Los Angeles Times,* September 17, 2006.

11. *The Fourth R,* March-April, 2004.

12. *Godless Morality,* Richard Holloway, p. 8.

13. *The Power of Myth,* Joseph Campbell and Bill Moyers, p. 65.

14. Ibid., p. 13.

15. *Godless Morality,* Richard Holloway, pp. 30, 31, 33.

16. *Future of Life,* Edward O. Wilson, p. 157.

17. *Myths, Dreams and Religion,* edited by Joseph Campbell, "Mythological Themes in Creative Literature and Art," Joseph Campbell, p. 146.

18. "Resisting the Urge," David P. Barash, *Los Angeles Times,* Wednesday, May 10, 2006.

19. *Thus Spake Zarathustra,* Friedrich Nietzsche, p. 26.

20. Ibid., p. 616; *From Dawn to Decadence,* Jacques Barzun.

CHAPTER 14: RELIGION AND THE NEW REALITY

1. *The Power of Myth,* Joseph Campbell and Bill Moyers, p. 24.

2. *Out of the Flames,* Lawrence and Nancy Goldstone, p. 231.

3. Idem., p. 232.

4. *So Help Me God,* Forrest Church, pp. 237-240.

5. Ibid., pp. 443, 444.

6. *Freethinkers,* Susan Jacoby, p. 173.

7. *The Brothers Karamazov,* Fyodor Dostoevsky, p. 229.

8. Ibid., p. 229.

9. Ibid., p. 231.

10. Ibid., p. 232.

11. Ibid., p. 232.

12. Ibid., p. 235.

13. *Godless Morality,* Richard Holloway, p. 11.

14. *The Origin of Consciousness in the Breakdown of the Bicameral Mind,* Julian Jaynes, p. 439.

15. Ibid., p. 439.

16. *Reforming Christianity,* Don Cupitt, p. 52.

17. As quoted in *Freethinkers,* Susan Jacoby, pp. 30, 31.

18. *Los Angeles Times,* Saturday, July 21, 2007.

19. *The Antichrist,* Friedrich Nietzsche, p. 47.

20. *Los Angeles Times,* August 7, 2010.

21. *Dawn to Destiny,* Jacques Barzun, p. 35.

22. Ibid., p. 239.

23. Ibid., p. 247.

24. *Christian Faith at the Crossorads,* Lloyd Geering, p. 157.

25. "Traditions and Faith in a New Era," Roy W. Harris; 4th R, Vol. 17, #1, p. 5.

26. Quoted in *The Philosophy of the Enlightenment,* p. 166, as quoted in *Christianity at the Crossroads,* p. 52.

27. "The Sunday Morning Experience and the Monday Morning Reality Check," The Fourth R, November-December 2003, pp. 15, 16.

28. *Einstein and Religion,* Max Jammer, pp. 49, 50.

29. *Godless Morality,* Richard Holloway, p. 154.

30. As quoted in *Christian Faith at the Crossroads,* Lloyd Geering, p. 111.

31. Reported in the *Los Angeles Times,* January 16, 2008.

32. As reported in the *Los Angeles Times,* July 26, 2009.

33. *Los Angeles Times,* September 28, 2009.

34. *Los Angeles Times,* July 20, 2009.

35. *Los Angeles Times,* January 30, 2009.

36. *Los Angeles Times,* April 27, 2009.

37. "The Age of Divinity," Rabbi Schachter-Shalomi, *Wall Street Journal,* February 10, 1999.

38. *Los Angeles Times,* March 16, 2009.

CHAPTER 15: SYMBOLS AND SYMBIOSIS

1. *Uncommon Sense,* Mark Davidson, p. 137.

2. *The Story of My Life,* Helen Keller, as quoted in *Uncommon Sense,* Mark Davidson, pp. 137, 138.

3. Ibid., p. 139.

4. *Man and his Symbols,* Carl Jung, p. 55.

5. Ibid., p. 55.

6. Ibid., John Freeman, p. 12.

7. Ibid., p. 89.

8. *A Short History of Myth,* Karen Armstrong, p. 134.

9. Ibid., p. 132.

10. Ibid., p. 126.

11. *Christianity at the Crossroads,* Lloyd Geering, p. 146-148.

12. *A Short History of Myth,* Karen Armstrong, p. 129.

13. Ibid., p. 120.

14. "Mythological Themes in Creative Literature and Art," Joseph Campbell, *Myths, Dreams, and Religion,* edited by Joseph Campbell, p. 145.

15. *A Short History of Myth,* Karen Armstrong, p. 126.

16. "The Process of Individuation," M.-L. von Franz, *Man and his Symbols,* Carl G. Jung, editor, p. 160.

17. *Uncommon Sense,* Mark Davidson, p. 139.

18. *Man and his Symbols,* Carl Jung, p. 94.

19. *A Short History of Myth,* Karen Armstrong, p. 132.

20. Ibid., p. 132.

21. Ibid., p. 132.

22. Ibid., pp. 132-137.

23. *Man and his Symbols,* Carl G. Jung, p. 101.

24. *A Short History of Myth,* Karen Armstrong, p. 134.

25. Ibid., p. 134, 135.

26. Ibid., p. 135.

27. Ibid., p. 136.

28. Ibid., p. 136.

29. Ibid., p. 138.

30. *The Great Questions of life,* Don Cupitt, p. 26.

31. *From Dawn to Decadence,* Jacques Barzun, p. 272.

32. "Islam - a Forgotten Facet," Irshad Manji, *Los Angeles Times,* also *Times of London.*

33. "Where is Fundamentalism Leading Us?" David Galston, *The Fourth R,* May-June, 2003, p. 18.

34. "Who Wrote the Koran?," Mhammad Ayatollahi Tabaar, *New York Times Magazine,* December 7, 2008, p. 24.

35. *New York Times,* April 7, 2002.

36. *From Dawn to Decadence,* Jacques Barzun, p. 271.

37. "Certainty and Self-Deception in Fundamentalists," Donald M. Braxton, *The Fourth R,* September-October 2006, pp. 14-16.

38. *Freedom and Destiny,* Rollo May, p. 201.

39. Aphorism No. 483, *Human, All-Too-Human,* Friedrich Nietzsche.

40. *Breaking the Spell,* Daniel C. Dennett, p. 338.

41. *Man and His Symbols,* Carl Jung, p. 69, as quoted in *Christian Faith at the Crossroads,* Lloyd Geering, pp. 156-157.

42. Ibid., p. 157.

43. *The Life of Jesus Critically Examined*, by David Strauss, p. 80, as quoted in *Christian Faith at the Crossroads,* Lloyd Geering, p. 77.

44. *A Short History of Myth,* Karen Armstrong, p. 139.

45. Ibid., p. 142.

CHAPTER 16: RELIGION IN THE NEW MILLENNIUM

1. *The Fourth R,* July-August 2006, p. 11.
2. As quoted in *The Power of Myth,* Joseph Campbell and Bill Moyers, p. 139.
3. *Godless Morality,* Richard Holloway, p. 156.
4. *The Power of Myth,* Joseph Campbell and Bill Moyers, pp. 98-99.
5. As quoted in *Myths, Dreams and Religion,* Joseph Campbell editor, "Mythological Themes in Creative Literature, and Art," Joseph Campbell, p. 168.
6. *The New Quotable Einstein,* edited by Alice Calaprice, p. 129.
7. *Christian Faith at the Crossroads,* Lloyd Geering, p. 153.
8. *Freedom and Destiny,* Rollo May, p. 23.
9. *Man and His Symbols,* Carl G. Jung, p. 101.
10. *The Power of Myth,* Joseph Campbell and Bill Moyers, p. 209.
11. *Ulysses,* James Joyce, p. 552; as quoted in *Myths, Dreams and Religion,* edited by Joseph Campbell, p. 172.
12. *The Power of Myth,* Joseph Campbell and Bill Moyers, p. 56.
13. "A Fine Mess - The Realist/Anti-Realist Dispute," John kelly, *The Fourth R,* January-February 2009, p. 13.
14. *The Great Questions of Life,* Don Cupitt, pp. 3, 4.
15. Ibid., p. 12.
16. *Freedom and Destiny,* Rollo May, p. 8.
17. *Escape from Freedom,* Erich Fromm, p. 5.
18. As quoted in *Freedom and Destiny,* Rollo May, p. 223.
19. As quoted in *Freedom and Destiny,* Rollo May, p. 202.
20. Ibid., p. 56.
21. Ibid., pp. 56, 57.

22. Ibid, p. 57.

23. *Los Angeles Times*, December 12, 2009.

24. As quoted in "Integrity on Trial," Andrew Furlong, *Sea of Faith*, May 2002, p. 7.

25. *Freedom and Destiny*, Rollo May, p. 54.

26. Ibid., p. 227.

27. As quoted in *Freedom and Destiny*, Rollo May, p. 185.

28. Ibid., p. 185.

29. *The Brothers Karamazov*, Fyodor Dostoevsky, pp. 233, 235.

30. *Freedom and Destiny*, Rollo May, p. 191.

31. As quoted in *The Portable Emerson*, edited by Carl Bode, p. 362.

32. Ibid., p. 362.

33. *Les Pensees*, No. 620.

34. *The Portable Emerson*, edited by Mark Van Doren, pp. 503-504.

35. *I'm OK - You're OK*, Thomas A. Harris, M.D., p. 260.

36. *Common Sense*, Thomas Paine, p. 114.

37. *The Portable Emerson*, edited by Carl Bode, p. 239.

38. *The Portable Emerson*, edited by Mark Van Doren, p. 510.

39. As quoted in *Freethinkers*, Susan Jacoby, p. 247.

40. *The Power of Myth*, Joseph Campbell and Bill Moyers, p. 29.

41. Ibid., p. 28.

42. *The Portable Emerson*, Mark Van Doren, p. 494.

43. As quoted in *Uncommon Sense*, Mark Davidson, p. 212.

44. *Les Pensees*, No. 188.

45. *Los Angeles Times*, March 4, 2008.

46. *The Power of Myth*, Joseph Campbell and Bill Moyers, p. 55.

47. As quoted in *The End of Christendom*, Malcolm Muggeridge, p. 5.

48. Ibid., p. 27.

49. *The Power of Myth,* Joseph Campbell and Bill Moyers, p. 51.

50. *Myths, Dreams and Religion,* edited by Joseph Campbell; "Mythological Themes in Creative Literature and Art," Joseph Campbell, p. 147.

51. *Christian Faith at the Crossroads,* Lloyd Geering, pp. 21-22.

52. *Myths, Dreams and Religion,* edited by Joseph Campbell; "Mythological Themes in Creative Literature and Art," Joseph Campbell, p. 146.

53. *The Portable Emerson,* edited by Carl Bode, pp. 366, 557.

54. *I'm OK - You're OK,* Thomas A. Harris, M.D., p. 265.

55. *The Great Questions of Life,* Don Cupitt, pp. 15, 16.

56. As quoted in *The Hero with a Thousand Faces,* Joseph Campbell, pp. 389-390.

57. "Putting the Historical Jesus in His Place, Alan Laughlin, *The Fourth R,* January-February 2006, p. 17.

58. Ibid., p. 17.

59. As quoted in *Constantine's Sword,* James Carroll, p. 48.

60. *The Power of Myth,* Joseph Campbell and Bill Moyers, p. 41.

61. *The Portable Nietzsche,* edited by Walter Kaufmann. The editor's notes on *Thus Spake Zarathustra,* p. 115.

62. *Christian Faith at the Crossroads,* Lloyd Geering, pp. 221-222.

63. Commencement address at Butler University, May 2005.

64. *Christian Faith at the Crossroads,* Lloyd Geering, p. 222.

65. "God, Belief and Action," Dr. Jonathan Romain, *The Guardian,* September 18, 2004.

66. *The Future of Life,* Edward O. Wilson, p. 132.

67. *The Power of Myth,* Joseph Campbell and Bill Moyers, p. 32.

68. *Uncommon Sense,* Mark Davidson, p. 36.

69. *A Short History of Myth,* Karen Armstrong, p. 9.

70. *The Power of Myth,* Joseph Campbell and Bill Moyers, p. 107, 162.

71. *The Great Questions of Life,* Don Cupitt, p. 42.

72. "Myth, Dream and Contemporary Philosophy," Richard A. Underwood; *Myths, Dreams and Religion,* edited by Joseph Campbell, p. 249.

73. *The Power of Myth,* Joseph Campbell and Bill Moyers, p. 85.

74. Ibid., pp. 55, 85.

75. *Uncommon Sense,* Mark Davidson, pp. 217-218.

76. *A Short History of Myth,* Karen Armstrong, p. 48.

77. *Los Angeles Times,* January 22, 2005.

78. *The Portable Emerson,* edited by Carl Bode, pp. 258-259.

79. As quoted in *Freedom and Destiny,* Rollo May, p. 64.

80. *The Portable Nietzsche,* edited by Walter Kaufmann, pp. 374-375.

81. "The Sunday Morning Experience," Robert W. Funk, *The Fourth R,* November-December 2003, p. 17.

82. *The Power of Myth,* Joseph Campbell and Bill Moyers, p. 89.

83. *The Protestant Era,* Paul Tillich, p. 150, as quoted in *Christian Faith at the Crossroads,* Lloyd Geering, p. 2.

84. *Los Angeles Times,* May 30, 2004.

85. "Faith and Ecstacy," Nicholas Schmidle, *Smithsonian,* December 2008, pp. 38, 39.

86. "Oh Gods," Toby Lester, Atlantic Monthly, February 2002.

87. "Religious Progressives, the Next Generation," Diane Watson, *Los Angeles Times,* February 5, 2006.

88. *Los Angeles Times,* January 31, 2006.

89. *Los Angeles Times,* March 15, 2010.

90. *Los Angeles Times,* March 4, 2008.

91. *Los Angeles Times,* December 10, 2009.

92. *Los Angeles Times,* December 27, 2003.

93. *Wall Street Journal,* February 10, 1999.

94. *The Way We Will Be,* John Zogby, pp. 204-205.

95. *Los Angeles Times,* January 22, 2005.

96. *Los Angeles Times,* December 27, 2009.

97. *Los Angeles Times,* August 14, 2004.

98. "Spiral Dynamics, Evolution and History," Patricia Williams, *The Fourth R,* November-December 2006, p. 17.

99. "Seeking the living word - in their living rooms," David Haldane, *Los Angeles Times,* July 23, 2007.

100. *The Way We'll Be,* John Zogby, pp. 204-205.

101. Ibid., p. 206.

102. *Los Angeles Times,* February 5, 2006.

103. "The Fellowship Movement," Holly Ulbrich, *UU World,* p. 41.

104. "Hallmarks of Healthy Emerging Communities of Faith," John Shuck.

105. "Pietism: Reborn in Order to Renew," C. John Weborg, *Fuller Theology News and Notes,* pp. 11, 12.

106. *The Way We'll Be,* John Zogby, pp. 121-129.

107. As quoted in "Tradition and Faith in a New Era," Roy Hoover, *The Fourth R,* January-February 2004, p. 65; *The Religious Situation,* p. 35.

108. *The Power of Myth,* Joseph Campbell and Bill Moyers, p. 3.

109. As quoted in *Why Faith Matters,* David J. Wolpe.

110. *Code Name God,* Mani Bhaumik, p. 73.

111. *Parade,* October 4, 2009, p. 4.

112. *The Power of Myth,* Joseph Campbell and Bill Moyers, p. 197.

113. As quoted in "Tradition and Faith in a New Era," Roy Hoover, *The Fourth R,* January-February 2004, p. 6.

114. *The Power of Myth,* Joseph Campbell and Bill Moyers, p. xix.

115. "The Historical Development of Mythology," Joseph Campbell, *Myth and Mythmaking,* edited by Henry A. Murray.

116. *Sacred Balance,* David Suzuki, p. 10.

117. *Crazy for God,* Frank Schaeffer, p. 369.

118. *Sacred Balance,* David Suzuki, p. 19.

119. *The Power of Myth,* Joseph Campbell and Bill Moyers, p. 132.

120. Ibid., p. 53.

121. *A Short History of Myth,* Karen Armstrong, p. 19.

122. *The Power of Myth,* Joseph Campbell and Bill Moyers, p. 209.

123. *The Portable Emerson,* Carl Bode, editor, p. 209.

124. *The Sacred Balance,* David Suzuki, p. 184.

125. Ibid., p. 188.

126. *The Power of Myth,* Joseph Campbell and Bill Moyers, p. 197.

127. As quoted in Ibid., p. 197.

128. "Welcome to the Ecozoic Era," Amy Hassinger, *UU World,* Spring 2006, p. 28.

129. As quoted in *Freedom and Destiny,* Rollo May, pp. 222-223.

130. *The Power of Myth,* Joseph Campbell and Bill Moyers, pp. 120, 163.

APPENDIX A: Two Versions of The Flood
1. *Who Wrote the Bible?,* Richard E. Friedman, pp. 54-59.

APPENDIX C: The Four Rs
1. "The Evolution of Good and Evil," *The Fourth R,* January-February 2005, and "Inescapable Overlapping Magisteria:

Why Biblical Scholarship and Theology Need Science," Westar Institute Fall 2005 Seminar Papers.

APPENDIX D: The Four Rs
1. *Basic Writings of Nietzsche,* Friedrich Nietzsche, pp. 233-234.
2. "On the Genealogy of Morals," *Basic Writings of Nietzsche,* Friedrich Nietzsche, p. 488.

Appendix A

Two Versions of The Flood

Friedman's translation of Genesis 6:5 through 8:22 reveals two versions of The Flood that have been merged into one. They are shown here in two different types. A reading of each version from beginning to end clearly shows that there are two complete, continuous stories, each with its own vocabulary and concerns.

The Flood - Genesis 6:5 - 8:22

GENESIS 6:

5 And Yahweh saw that the evil of humans was great in the earth, and all the inclination of the thoughts of their heart was only evil all the day.

6 And Yahweh regretted that he had made humans in the earth, and he was grieved to his heart.

7 And Yahweh said, 'I shall wipe out the humans which I have created from the face of the earth, from human to beast to creeping thing to bird of the heavens, for I regret that I have made them.'

8 But Noah found favor in Yahweh's eyes.

9 These are the generations of Noah: Noah was a righteous man, perfect in his generations. Noah walked with God.

10 And Noah sired three sons: Shem, Ham, and Japheth.

11 And the earth was corrupted before God, and the earth was filled with violence.

12 And God saw the earth, and here it was corrupted, for all flesh had corrupted its way on the earth.

13 And God said to Noah, 'The end of all flesh has come before me, for the earth is filled with violence because of them, and here I am going to destroy them with the earth.

14 Make yourself an ark of gopher wood, make rooms with the ark, and pitch it outside and inside with pitch.

15 And this is how you shall make it: Three hundred cubits the length of the ark, fifty cubits its width, and thirty cubits its height.

16 You shall make a window for the ark, and you shall finish it to a cubit from the top, and you shall make an entrance to the ark in its side. You shall make lower, second, and third stories for it.

17 And here I am bringing the flood, water over the earth, to destroy all flesh in which is the breath of life from under the heavens. Everything which is on the land will die.

18 And I shall establish my covenant with you. And you shall come to the ark, you and your sons and your wife and you sons' wives with you.

19 And of all the living, of all flesh, you shall bring two to the ark to keep alive with you, they shall be male and female.

20 Of the birds according to their kind, and of the beasts according to their kind, and of all the creeping things of the earth according to their kind, two of each will come to you to keep alive.

21 And you, take for yourself of all food which will be eaten and gather it to you, and it will be for you and for them for food.'

22 And Noah did according to all that God commanded him--so he did.

GENESIS 7:

1 And Yahweh said to Noah, 'Come, you and all your household, to the ark, for I have seen you as righteous before me in this generation.

2 Of all the clean beasts, take yourself seven pairs, man and his woman; and of the beasts which are not clean, two, man and his woman.

3 Also of the birds of the heavens seven pairs, male and female, to keep alive seed on the face of the earth.

4 For in seven more days I shall rain on the earth forty days and forty nights, and I shall wipe out all the substance that I have made from upon the face of the earth.'

5 And Noah did according to all that Yahweh had commanded him.

6 **And Noah was six hundred years old, and the flood was on the earth.**

7 And Noah and his sons and his wife and his sons' wives with him came to the ark from before the waters of the flood.

8 **Of the clean beasts and of the beasts which were not clean, and of the birds and of all those which creep upon the earth,**

9 **Two of each came to Noah to the ark, male and female, as God had commanded Noah.**

10 And seven days later the waters of the flood were on the earth.

11 **In the six hundredth year of Noah's life, in the second month, in the seventeenth day of the month, on this day all the fountains of the great deep were broken up, and the windows of the heavens were opened.**

12 And there was rain on the earth, forty days and forty nights.

13 **In this very day, Noah and Shem, Ham, and Japheth, the sons of Noah, and Noah's wife and his sons' three wives with them came to the ark,**

14 **They and all the living things according to their kind, and all the beasts according to their kind, and all the creeping things that creep on the earth according to their kind, and all the birds according to their kind, and every winged bird.**

15 **And they came to Noah to the ark, two of each, of all flesh in which is the breath of life.**

16 **And those which came were male and female, some of all flesh came, as God had commanded him.** And Yahweh closed it for him.

17 And the flood was on the earth for forty days and forty nights, and the waters multiplied and raised the ark, and it was lifted from the earth.

18 And the waters grew strong and multiplied greatly on the earth, and the ark went on the surface of the waters.

19 And the waters grew very, very strong on the earth, and they covered all the high mountains that are under all the heavens.

20 Fifteen cubits above, the waters grew stronger, and they covered the mountains.

21 **And all flesh, those that creep on the earth, the birds, the beasts, and the wild animals, and all the swarming things that swarm on the earth, and all the humans expired.**

22 Everything that had the breathing spirit of life in its nostrils, everything that was on the dry ground, died.

23 And he wiped out all the substance that was on the face of

the earth, from human to beast, to creeping thing, and to bird of the heavens, and they were wiped out from the earth, and only Noah and those who were with him in the ark were left.

24 **And the waters grew strong on the earth a hundred fifty days.**

GENESIS 8:

1 **And God remembered Noah and all the living, and all the beasts that were with him in the ark, and God passed a wind over the earth, and the waters were decreased.**

2 **And the fountains of the deep and the windows of the heavens were shut,** and the rain was restrained from the heavens.

3 And the waters receded from the earth continually, **and the waters were abated at the end of a hundred fifty days.**

4 **And the ark rested, in the seventh month, in the seventeenth day of the month, on the mountains of Ararat.**

5 **And the waters continued receding until the tenth month; in the tenth month, on the first of the month, the tops of the mountains appeared.**

6 And it was at the end of forty days, and Noah opened the window of the ark which he had made.

7 **And he sent out a raven, and it went back and forth until the waters dried up from the earth.**

8 And he sent out a dove from him to see whether the waters had eased from the face of the earth.

9 And the dove did not find a resting place for its foot, and it returned to him to the ark, for waters were on the face of the earth, and he put out his hand and took it and brought it to him to the ark.

10 And he waited seven more days, and he again sent out a dove from the ark.

11 And the dove came to him at evening time, and there was an olive leaf torn off in its mouth, and Noah knew that the waters had eased from the earth.

12 And he waited seven more days, and he sent out a dove, and it did not return to him ever again.

13 **And it was in the six hundred and first year, in the first month, on the first of the month, the waters dried from the earth.** And Noah turned back the covering of the ark and looked, and here the face of the earth had dried.

14 **And in the second month, on the twenty-seventh day of the month, the earth dried up.**

15 **And God spoke to Noah, saying,**

16 **'Go out from the ark, you and your wife and your sons' wives with you.**

17 **All the living things that are with you, of all flesh, of the birds, and of the beasts, and of all the creeping things that creep on the earth, that go out with you, shall swarm in the earth and be fruitful and multiply in the earth.'**

18 **And Noah and his sons and his wife and his sons' wives went out.**

19 **All the living things, all the creeping things and all the birds, all that creep on the earth, by their families, they went out of the ark.**

20 And Noah built an altar to Yahweh, and he took some of each of the clean beasts and of each of the clean birds, and he offered sacrifices on the altar.

21 And Yahweh smelled the pleasant smell, and Yahweh said to his heart, 'I shall not again curse the ground on man's account,

for the inclination of the human heart is evil from their youth, and I shall not again strike all the living as I have done.

22 All the rest of the days of the earth, seed and harvest, and cold and heat, and summer and winter, and day and night shall not cease.'[1]

Appendix B

Passages from *Code Name God* by Mani Bhaumik

p. 90   The ecstatic feeling that comes through meditation has been described as "bubbling from the inside." It is the great divine calm that ensures when one has dimmed down the organs of sensory perception enough to feel connected to the ground of being and it is remarkably accessible. The software is pre-installed.

Various Religious Practices of Mysticism

p. 118   In *Buddhism* one must free oneself from desire and pursue "right consciousness" through meditation and an awareness of the "oneness" of all creation. India ultimately foreswore Buddhism on the grounds that its austere language made no room for a transcendent God. . . . Buddhism finds little dispute with modern science.

p. 119   *Taoism* might also be described as a spiritual analog of quantum physics. It urges alignment with a Way (the Tao) that flows ultimately from the unity of opposites (yin-yang) at the heart of nature. Taoism, in contrast to ethical monotheism, is as much a way of seeing as a way of being, for the Tao, the Way, is the very fabric of the universe, the "self so" order that underlies all.

Chinese philosophy anticipated the Big Bang theory by insisting that everything sprang from emptiness, or the void. Creation occurs from nothing.

Lama Anagarika Govinda in his *Foundations of Tibetan*

Mysticism: "The relationship of form and emptiness cannot be conceived of as a state of mutually exclusive opposites, but only as two aspects of the same reality that co-exist and are in continual cooperation."

p. 120 In the whimsically mind-teasing parlance of *Zen* "God is a no-thing," but that does not mean that God is nothing. It means that God is not a thing.

The central discipline of Zen is zazan (sitting meditation), which is practiced for hours at a time in the usually remote and sublimely peaceful monasteries. Again the emphasis is on relaxed attention, a "coherent consciousness" by which the mind is tuned into the presence of the infinite, eternal One, as if all other noises but the soft buzzing of the cosmic had ceased.

. . . Modern physics suggest that when we penetrate the subatomic levels of reality down through the very fabric of space, we will find that everything is interconnected. Long before David Bohm and Basil Hiley, Zen monks intuited this interconnectedness. Could it be that the connectedness lay in consciousness itself?

. . . Paradoxically (and the essence of both mysticism and quantum physics is paradox), what is perceived as empty can also be perceived as full, in the sense of an infinite potential. Zero . . . implies more than nothing.

p. 121 *The Gnostics*--their doctrine an ancient bridge between the East and West. A varied group of nominally Christian thinkers and mystics whose influence was most strongly felt in the first and second centuries CE. They identified the First Cause--the True God--as residing in the Pleroma (the Fullness) beyond space, time, and causation, while material reality is a kind of counterfeit, the creation of lesser gods. Branded as heretics for questioning the Catholic clergy's authority and for their belief that an immanent "God spark" remained even in fallen Man (thereby eliminating the need for redemption from Original Sin), the Gnostics moved underground and later fed the roots of both Protestantism and Theosophy.

Gnosticism shared much with the philosophy of Neo-Platonism, which postulated a higher dimensional realm of ideal forms whose source is the One and whose shadows are what we mistake for reality.

p. 122   Nothing in Jesus' teachings conflicts with the essential tenets or mystical foundations of the other world religions, which is one reason he is revered by them all. "The kingdom of heaven is within" is a perfectly cogent statement of fact, that we are all participants in the great concert of creation, that the macrocosm is the microcosm, and that we are connected to one another and to the source of all being--the 'I am that I am' of Exodus, the One of the Neo-Platonists. *Islamic* Creed, "There is no God but Allah" states the obvious: God is One.

p. 123   The common ground of all these great faiths is to be found in their essence: mystical insight. Insight, by its nature, is experiential. It cannot be effectively taught, or preached, or read about, except by way of analogy, allegory, or, most clumsily, dogma. . . . Whether one is a Christian quietist, a Jewish Kabbalist, a Muslim Sufi, a Hindu yogi, a Buddhist Tantrist, or a Zen master, when you get down to the level of religious epiphany, the experience is the same: *dissolution of ego boundaries, a merging of the observer and the observed, a union with the one source of all.* Contrary to the scientific bias that mysticism is a vague metaphysical thing, the mystical experience itself is a great clarity; otherwise, how could so many from such diverse backgrounds describe it in such similar terms?

The precepts of mysticism differ form those of modern physics mostly in language and methodology. Could it be that the common experience of the mystics has an analog in the "unbroken wholeness" of the quantum physicists?

THE FOUR RS

Patricia Williams, a philosopher of science and a philosophical theologian has described how ethics was part of the evolutionary process.[1]

She writes that by the 1970s, sociobiology offered an evolutionary explanation of animal social behavior based on genetics that was extrapolated to humanity. This has led to evolutionary psychology. Observers have learned that in creatures of a like species the amount of cooperation between them correlates with the degree to which they are related. The causes of cooperative behaviors among related organisms are called inclusive fitness and/or kin selection. This has been found in thousands of species. Cooperation with relatives and mutual sharing, or reciprocity, among nonrelatives, a common trait with human beings, forms the basis of evolutionary psychology. Four words, all beginning with R, capture the fundamentals of the evolution of our dispositions. They are resources, reproduction, relatives (from kin selection), and reciprocity.

1. **Resources:** All living organisms require and seek resources to survive, even unicellular organisms. They need food, suitable temperature, water, and shelter. They also seek to avoid harmful things. A working definition of "good" and "evil" that is neither philosophical nor theological needs to be assumed: those things that help organisms thrive are "good" and those that harm them are "evil."

In a very loose sense one could say that even unicellular organisms know good and evil. Those cells that did not seek the "good" and avoid the "evil" perished, and their kind became extinct. Natural selection retained only those cells able to distinguish resources from ruinous things. Knowing what is good and evil for oneself is fundamental to life.

2. **Reproduction:** Unicellular organisms (and some multi-cellular ones) reproduce asexually, but eventually sexual reproduction evolved. This necessitated another kind of seeking and avoidance, the quest for members of one's own species of the opposite sex and deterrence from pursuing the same sex or a different species. Life got more complicated--organisms grew smarter--those who habitually erred went extinct. For humans this means sexual reproduction and the pursuit of sex.

3. **Relatives:** The disposition to engage in behaviors that aid one's relatives to survive to reproduce and to avoid unrelated organisms. The evidence of the evolution of care of relatives is overwhelming. We give more to our own children than to the children of others. Copies of genes survive into the next generation and beyond. This is achieved by mating, and through close kin carrying copies of each other's genes, and surviving to reproduce more of these genes. This is the driving force in the formation of extended clans. Organisms that helped their kin had more copies that survived than those who did not, so genes for identifying kin, and helping them, proliferated. Organisms thus became smarter. Those that excelled at aiding kin became able to make finer discriminations. Helping one's relatives was "good" but mistakingly aiding non-kin was "evil"--there was no reward for such behavior.

4. **Reciprocity:** This has to do with the equal exchange of goods and services. Thus obtaining rewards for aiding non-kin also evolved. Highly intelligent organisms were needed as they had to remember who helped them, who they had helped, the help given, and the value of the help. This development of trade appeared almost from the dawn of humanity, and humans provide the highest examples of this R, but it exists in other species, and even across species, but in less complex forms. These activities meant seeing equal exchange as good and justice being valued.

Appendix D

Humanity's Relation to Ethics

In *Beyond Good and Evil*, Nietzsche describes early man as being pre-moral. "During so-called prehistoric times the value or disvalue of an action was derived from its consequences. The action itself was considered as little as its origin. . . . It was the retroactive force of success or failure that led men to think well or ill of an action. Let us call this the *pre-moral* period of mankind."[1] Nietzsche believed that over the last 10,000 years a change in outlook gradually developed to "where it is no longer the consequences but the origin of an action that one allows to decide its value." He believed that a "considerable refinement of vision and standards" brought about this change in values. He called this a *moral* era, "achieved only after long struggles and vacillations. . . . One came to agree that the value of an action lay in the value of the intention."

Nietzsche believed that society stood "at the threshold of a period" that was about to undergo a "fundamental shift in values, owing to another self-examination of man, another growth in profundity." He designated it as the beginning of the *extra-moral* era.

In the pre-moral early world, survival of the group, its continued existence, was the highest, if not the only, value. The continued existence of any one individual did not even figure in the group's thinking. He was viewed as a member of the whole, part of the group, and only in that context, of any worth. There was no place for self interest. Moral codes included injunctions against yielding to one's impulses. That which preserved the species was called good. Individualism was considered to be evil. Nietzsche says that these two opposing values of "good" and "evil" have been engaged in a fearful struggle on earth for thousands of years.[2]

Appendix E

Hallmarks of Healthy Emerging Communities of Faith
John Shuck

1. Honesty, candor, and religious literacy.
2. Will find inspiration from the sciences, humanities and other faith traditions.
3. An unfettered search for truth.
4. Will not be restricted by any canon including the Bible or creeds.
5. Reason alone will not be sufficient for the vitality of this community of faith.
6. Rituals, poetry, music and symbols that gather the community and give it focus will be necessary for its vitality.
7. Preaching, sacraments and worship will be optional.
8. Each community of faith must have autonomy in interpreting and using rituals and practices.
9. Decisions in the emerging community of faith will be made democratically, seeking consensus wherever possible.
10. May be independent of current church structures.
11. May exist within current church structure but cannot be burdened by them.
12. Will make no distinction between "clergy" and "laity."
13. The role of those currently considered clergy will be that of midwife, assisting in the birth of this emerging community of faith.
14. This role will require courage and a willingness to forsake status.

Appendix F

Excerpts from *Code Name God* by Mani Bhaumik

p. 28   A true science does not favor substance over spirit, but recognizes each in the other.

p. 74   Einstein: "Religion without science is blind and science without religion is lame."

p. 124   By far the greatest obstacle to reconciling science and spirituality has been the personification of God. . . . God is abstract and not a person or symbol that people might worship. . . .

Einstein remarked that science grew out of the refinement of our daily thinking. In its infancy science was a close cousin of philosophy. Newton's *Principia*--the first great scientific text is titled, *The Mathematical Principles of Natural Philosophy.* Ever since relative theory and quantum physics described a reality strikingly at odds with our perception, physics increasingly has become the province of mathematicians. This is because math furnishes the only vocabulary capable of precisely describing this reality.

p. 126   A clear-eyed appraisal of the warp and weft of physical reality reveals that woven throughout the universe is an abstract intelligence, which we may, without offense to either science or religion, be permitted to call divine.

Cosmology, which explores the evolution of the universe, has revealed such sublime order in the design of the physical world that it often seems to suggest the hand of a single architect. And indeed, the elegant symmetries and incredible precision of universal laws do argue for some kind of governing force, a higher code of reality.

p. 127   A good way to understand the material world is to think of it as consisting of three layers, like the layers of pigment on a painter's canvas, each seen through the others and all forming the impression of "one color."

The first layer of reality is the observable universe of material objects and natural phenomena with which we interact through our five primary senses.

p. 128   The second layer of reality requires a leap in imagination. It is characterized by a microscopic scale, at an unimaginably fast rate, a level that our senses are not equipped to perceive. Electron microscopes, particle accelerators and intricate mathematical constructs have to be used.

The atom, first perceived in the fifth century BCE, consists of a positively charged nucleus in which protons and neutrons (made up of tinier particles called quarks) are bound together, balanced by the negatively charged electrons surrounding it. All the matter that makes up our everyday world is composed of two kinds of fundamental particles--quarks and electrons. These are discrete packets of energy. The constituent parts of objects in our midst that appear to be as solid as the Rock of Gibraltar are in a constant state of flux. The engine of this flux is energy, and its top speed is the speed of light.

p. 129   These fundamental particles don't fall apart because they are confined to fields--known to us by way of the forces associated with them. A prime example--the gravitational field, which we can neither see nor touch.

Michael Faraday moved a magnet within a coil and produced electrical current. He perceived that magnetism, a nonmaterial entity, was inducing current in the coil, and the concept of a field was christened. Only in the mid-nineteenth century did James Clerk Maxwell see the close relation between electricity and magnetism, uniting them as electromagnetism.

p. 131   It took Albert Einstein to recognize that electromagnetism operated in empty space. He showed, furthermore, that space, time and field cannot exist separately; they are always magnificently intertwined in their existence. Gravity and electromagnetism are manifest fields, those whose influence is felt locally.

p. 132   The third layer of reality consists of unmanifest fields. They pervade all space and time, and are known as quantum fields. [A quantum is simply a small discrete unit in which a form of energy may express itself. A quantum of light, for example, is a photon.] The unmanifest field's interest is nonlocal, *in the sense that it is felt equally in all parts of the universe.*

P. 134   A most mysterious aspect of quantum physics is that elementary particles, such as electrons, are *absolutely* identical everywhere in the universe, no matter when or where they are created. A new branch of physics, known as quantum field theory, was the foundation for this revelation. Nobel laureate Frank Wilczek sums it up, "In quantum field theory, the primary elements of reality are not individual particles, but underlying fields. Thus, for example, all electrons are but excitations of an underlying field, naturally called the electron field, *which fills all space and time.*"

Things once thought of as solid and inert, in fact consist of the quantized "lumps of energy," called fundamental particles. Something "virtual" becomes something "real."

All of the known quantum fields are not, in any geometrical sense, locatable, yet they are everywhere.

p. 135 The notion that all fields fluctuate at the quantum level has now been validated, thus providing our strongest evidence of the actuality of the unmanifest quantum fields themselves. Empty space is not empty at all. It is a seething cauldron of quantum activity.

The unmanifest quantum fields interlace throughout the cosmos like multidimensional fabrics woven on a celestial loom, and strangest of all, each infinitesimal weave of the fabric contains, so to speak, the whole cloth. William Blake saw "a world in a grain of sand."

p. 136 In summary, there is no such thing as empty space, and the most crucial elements of one's existence are things that cannot be seen.

The fact that one speaks almost interchangeably about fields, on the one hand, and the force and matter they give rise to, on the other, is at the core of quantum field theory.

p. 137 The triumph of the quantum field theory in explaining all of the observed fundamental particles is a hallmark of twentieth century physics. Physicists have constructed what is known as the standard model of particle physics, which successfully categorizes the observed fundamental particles in a manner somewhat similar to the well-known periodic table of the elements.

The omnipresent quantum fields are yet a further step

into a phantom world. They remain stubbornly and definitely there permeating even the darkest sectors of space.

p. 146   All the fields in our universe are now believed to arise from a common source, which may be appropriately called the primary field. . . .

p. 147   Quantum physics suggests that the primary field, possessing the basic blueprint of all things physical, is encoded in the fabric of space . . . where it orchestrates the continuing symphony of our universe, having unfolded sequentially to create it.

p. 148   Could it be that nature repeats its pattern in the human genome? Our genome (DNA) possesses the blueprint of an entire human being. While miraculously putting together about a hundred trillion cells in the right proportion to create the various organs of the human body, the genome remains ever-present in each of those cells, administering different aspects of our biological existence. . . . This is now vividly illustrated in cloning, where, for instance, an entire sheep can be replicated from any adult sheep cell.

p. 150   It was the construction of the Mt. Wilson observatory above Los Angeles in the 1920s that made it possible for Edwin Hubble to discover that, not only was the universe not static, it was undergoing dynamic expansion. It took a couple of decades and the concerted efforts of several astronomers to put the issue on the table: if the future was taking the galaxies farther and farther apart, then it stood to reason that in the past they must have been closer together. So close, ultimately, that matter's compression (due to the effects of gravity) might result in what Einstein's equations predicted to be a singularity, a point where the laws of the universe would simply break down.

p. 151   The conditions immediately preceding this jaw-dropping event would have been hotter than any hell one can possibly imagine because that's what happens when matter is compressed. This fact of physics pointed to clues that eventually made the case for a cosmic explosion as the event that kicked off the explosion of the universe. Georges Lemaître, a Belgian priest, conceived the idea, and the astronomer Fred Hoyle, in jest, coined the term "Big Bang" to describe the explosion.

It was an explosion of space itself and not an explosion in any existing space. In the expanding universe today, it is space between galaxies that is expanding. There was no space before; it appeared along with the bang.

p. 158   Although some of the details of the inflation process remain unclear, cosmologists generally agree on the fact that something as enormously vast as our universe has emerged from an infinitessimally small nugget of space . . . .

p. 160-161   The universe's biography now accounts for everything in its nearly fourteen-billion-year history but for a very tiny fraction of a second after its moment of creation. . . . The sudden rush of inflation erased all the evidence. Until further evidence is found one can only turn metaphysical. At least for now physics has become almost indistinguishable from metaphysics.

p. 163   The philosophical question--suppose they gave a party and nobody came--could be framed another way: Suppose a universe was made and nobody was there to see it? Pondering riddles like this, scientists have lately warmed up to an idea they once considered unscientific.

The idea goes by the esoteric name of weak anthropic cosmological principle. Its essence is that if the initial conditions and the natural constants of our universe were not exactly what they are, there would be no one to observe it, much less to inquire into its origin. The principle's corollary is awe-inspiring; it suggests that the conditions were such at the moment of the creation of our universe to presage eventual emergence of intelligent life in it.

p. 164   The human mind's ability to understand the laws of nature has presented many eminent scientists with a mystery. Einstein, for example, said, "The most incomprehensible fact about nature is that it is comprehensible." Distinguished British mathematician Roger Penrose is also bemused by the fact that the universe has developed in obedience to laws that our consciousness seems designed to grasp. . . . The anthropic principle provides a means for reconciling these two miracles.

Stephen Hawking asserts that "the anthropic principle can be given a precise formulation, and it seems to be essential when dealing with the origin of the universe." Eminent physicist Freeman Dyson also finds that "the universe in some sense must have known that we were coming." This is about as close as a scientist will come to acknowledging that the party was given with the expectation that we would attend.

p. 165   The anthropic principle seems to offer a unique solution for the particular way our universe came to be. At its inception the entire universe was much smaller than an atom and, therefore subject to the laws of quantum physics. This means that the universe could have begun in many possible ways. The anthropic principle can be factored in, thus requiring that the evolution of intelligent beings be a necessary condition for the beginning of the universe. . . . John Wheeler concludes from his extensive studies of quantum mechanics that "it is incontrovertible that the observer is a participator in genesis." The observer. That's consciousness, and we are conscious agents, vehicles for manifestation of a potentiality that was there from the start.

p. 170 Penrose insists that "a scientific worldview which does not profoundly come to terms with the problem of conscious minds can have no serious pretension of completeness. Consciousness is part of our universe, so any physical theory which makes no proper place for it falls fundamentally short of providing a genuine description of the world. . . . Nobel physicist Eugene Wigner: "The principal argument is that thought process and consciousness are the primary concepts, that our knowledge of the external world is the content of our consciousness and that consciousness, therefore, cannot be denied." By his famous pronouncement "Cogito, ergo sum"--I think, therefore I am--even Descartes, who is recognized for the Cartesian divide between mind and matter, premised his arguments based on the primary reality of consciousness.

p. 171 Quantum physicists have demonstrated beyond any reasonable doubt that observer and observed are fundamentally connected; their relationship is interactive and participatory.

p. 175   Although its systematic study has only just begun, consciousness--in the opinion of some eminent scientists today--is an absolutely fundamental part of this universe and cannot be dismissed as airy metaphysics.

p. 176   The fundamental realities of the primary field (from which all the fields in our universe arose) and consciousness are inseparable aspects of the same underlying process. David Bohm has named this underlying process the implicate order. Basil Hiley suggests: "Mind and matter are but different projections from this deeper implicate order where such a division does not exist." He also emphasizes that "the implicate order is not some woolly metaphysical construction, it is a precise description of the underlying process," which is supported by credible mathematical analysis.

p. 177   The essence of the implicate order is the one source that enfolds both the primary field and consciousness. Based upon this thesis, it would be logical to infer that the one source of the world's great spiritual traditions is grounded in scientific reality.

It is a Vedic concept that all conscious beings are aspects of the same universal entity. Expressed in terms of our scientific worldview today, consciousness would be manifest when the individual brain's quantum state is in resonance with the cosmic potentiality of consciousness. We may humbly assert that we are all equipped to be tuners of the universal source of consciousness.

p. 179-180   For more than three hundred years, consciousness has been a refugee in the universe. Through much of ancient history and prehistory, man perceived himself as a part of nature, a nature that was fully animate and ensouled. Whether monotheistic or polytheistic, man felt his god/gods to be close at hand.

p. 181   Such panpsychism (literally, soul through all) was not limited to aboriginal or primitive cultures; it infused the classical civilizations of Greece and Rome, and it extended into the high Middle Ages thanks to Aristotle's continuing influence. . . . A profound shift began to occur shortly after the pivotal year of 1600, for when Cartesianism removed mind from matter, it also removed most traces of the genuinely sacred from the everyday world.

Since then we have tended to dismiss the ancient ways as superstition, swept away by the great mechanistic discoveries of Enlightenment science.

p. 183-184   It is arguable that after mind and matter had been put asunder consciousness needed time to integrate the new paradigms of individuality that took root in the Renaissance. The mind's software was updated, but now it is again obsolete.

The dilemma we face is that our science is racing far ahead of our sensibilities. We know that our science has revealed a new order, but we cannot see it. As a result most of us spend a good deal of time feeling vaguely out of phase, a condition that manifests itself as dis-ease. . . .

p. 185   Consciousness is clearly integrated with things like memory, attention, and language, all of which are presumed to have their location in the brain itself. But consciousness is not simply in our heads. It's everywhere we are, and it's everywhere we are not. . . . Consciousness, like events in the quantum world, isn't something you can point a stick at.

p. 186   Our brain's ability to actualize the potentiality of universal consciousness may make us, in a sense, the eyes and ears of God. In the words of Meister Eckhart: "The eye in which I see God is the same eye in which God sees me."

p. 187   Science now shows us that our consciousness plays an active role in determining our actions and bringing out specific manifestations of nature. We have also learned that we are part of something much larger, which we have referred to as one source. Perhaps our sense of morality stems from the realization that we are indeed part of something much larger than ourselves. Therefore, our actions should be appropriate to what is implicit in that knowledge. When we act from this realization, we bridge the Cartesian divide of mind from matter and the wound it caused is healed.

p. 196   As the notable science writer Charles Seife records in his book *Zero: The Biography of a Dangerous Idea,* zero has been an enigma to theologians, philosophers and mathematicians alike over the millennia.

Mathematicians have long recognized that zero is invariably connected to infinity. When we divide something by infinity, we get zero; when anything is divided by zero, we get infinity. Zero appears as a vanishing point between positive and negative infinities. In other words, once we include negative numbers, could zero as easily stand for the source of everything as the realm of nothing?

It was not until well into the Middle Ages that Europe began to hail zero as representing the creative potential of God (creation ex nihilo) rather than as a symbol of that ultimate nihilist, the devil. By the 1600s, zero finally obtained worldwide legitimacy at the crux of all higher mathematics. We have seen that the late visionary physicist David Bohm did not stop at zero. He conceived of something transcending zero and named it the implicate order, which consists of the concurrent existence of all potentialities in the multidimensional pre-space. As we have discussed earlier, he suggests material reality and consciousness are projections from this implicate order.

p. 197 Finally, there is Bohm's assertion that the implicate order enfolds the entire universe holographically, in that every part of itself echoes much of what we have said of the cosmic genome; like the human genome, every stitch of the universe contains the blueprint of the whole enchilada. It should be evident by now that you and I are part and parcel of this implicate order.

What are we really talking about here? What "immortal hand or eye," to quote Blake, could fashion such a marvelous symmetry, one in which we can truly "see a world in a grain of sand"? Since it is sensible to believe that something like Bohm's implicate order does exist and is the agent of the universal potentiality of consciousness, then we may at last have found a ship that will sail us beyond the Big Bang, a story that will tell us what happened before "Once upon a time." Though it may not close our detective's case with a verdict that is beyond all reasonable doubt, we may, perhaps, have seen a faint glimmering of the nature of God and of how the abundant majesty of the cosmos arises from an address numbered zero.

Transcending all theologies and denominations, humankind has had a conviction of a creator divinity, which, having brought the universe into existence, remains present throughout it, upholding the ongoing creation. People seem to have always accepted that the Creator will never be revealed to us empirically. Yet for eons we have deemed this divinity worthy of adoration and have directed ardent prayers to it, making it the vessel of our hope. Now, I believe for the first time in human history, we find remarkable support from science for the *one source* of religion. We have objective knowledge of an abstract entity that permeates the entire universe. Inseparable association of that universal entity with consciousness also appears credible.

p. 198   We have to keep in mind that science is always a work in progress. Centuries or even decades from now, new vistas are sure to open up in the scientific landscape. It may then provide a better answer to the "why" question. For now, it is amazing that science is meeting the core of religion and that the two are stimulating each other, as Einstein believed they always would.